IMAGES
of America

VESTAL

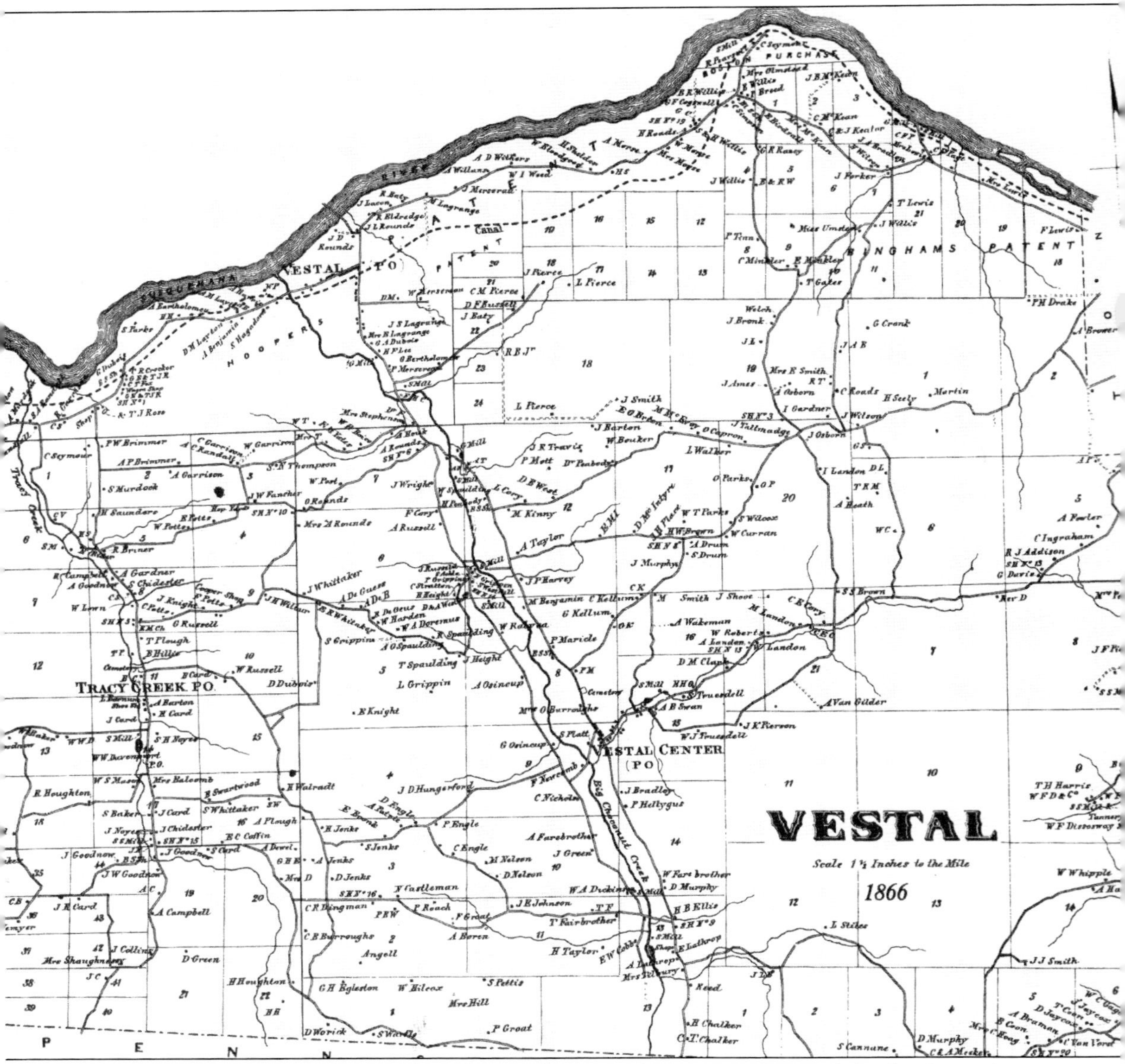

The town of Vestal is bordered on the west by Tioga County, on the north by the Susquehanna River, on the east by the town of Binghamton, and on the south by the commonwealth of Pennsylvania as shown in this 1866 map. The Chenango Canal extension identified by a dashed line running parallel to the river was dug but never completed.

On the cover: Built in 1881, the Vestal depot with its pagoda style served as a model for later stations built between Vestal and Buffalo. The Delaware, Lackawanna and Western Railroad station at Vestal was the transportation hub for freight, mail, and passengers until it closed in 1960. Used for a time as a warehouse, the deteriorated building was purchased by the town in 1971 and moved to its present location a year later. The town renovated the historic building for use as a museum under the stewardship of the Vestal Historical Society. (Author's collection.)

IMAGES
of America

VESTAL

Margaret Hadsell

ARCADIA
PUBLISHING

ISBN 978-0-7385-5773-1

Published by Arcadia Publishing
Charleston, South Carolina

Printed in the United States of America

Library of Congress Catalog Card Number: 2007936592

For all general information contact Arcadia Publishing at:
Telephone 843-853-2070
Fax 843-853-0044
E-mail sales@arcadiapublishing.com
For customer service and orders:
Toll-Free 1-888-313-2665

Visit us on the Internet at www.arcadiapublishing.com

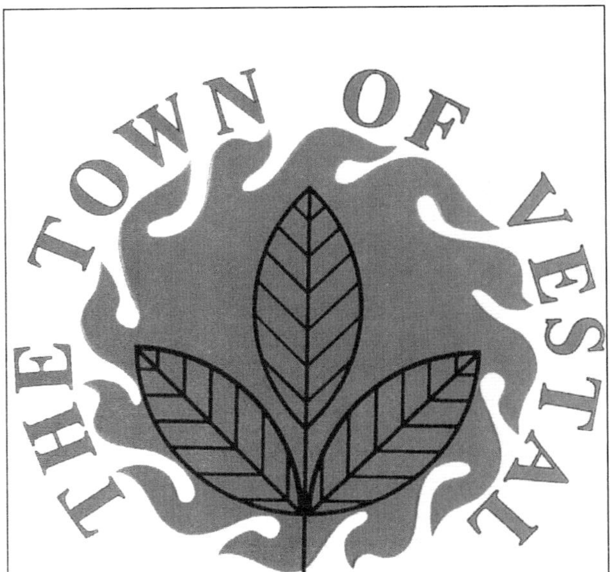

The town seal of Vestal exemplifies a tradition of united community effort for the common good. The circular motif signifies enduring public initiative. The sun, which actively depicts life and hope, symbolizes a continuing undercurrent of concern for a better community. The sprig in the center of the seal symbolizes both orderly new growth and adaptation to the environment of a changing world.

Contents

ACKNOWLEDGMENTS

The completion of this book would not have been possible without the contributions of many local residents who searched through their private photograph collections to provide this glimpse into Vestal's past. Thank you all for your interest, knowledge, and support.

I would also like to thank the many wonderful people who have stopped by my office to share their remembrances of days past and those who contributed information or took the time to record an oral history. In the words of Winnie Andrews, "When we lose pieces of our past, we also lose important pieces of our present and our future. The present and future are, in part, the result of our past. Let's not lose any more pieces."

Special thanks go to Virginia Wood and Janice Roosa at the Vestal Museum for allowing me to feature the previously unpublished Walter P. Gates glass plate negative collection as well as to the members of the Vestal Historical Society who opened their photograph collection for my use.

I am also grateful to Broome County historian Gerald Smith, the Broome County Historical Society, the Town of Binghamton Historical Society, Dr. Nina Versaggi of Binghamton University, and photographer Edward Aswad for allowing me to use key photographs from their collections.

INTRODUCTION

Amos Draper, considered the town's first settler, built a trading post near the mouth of the Choconut Creek in 1782, where he traded with Native Americans who lived at that location and at Willow Point. Their village, known as Chugnuts, was destroyed in August 1779 by the advancing armies of Gen. James Clinton and Gen. Enoch Poor. Native American artifacts have been found at Willow Point and in the Castle Gardens area of what is now Vestal.

At the beginning of the 19th century, fertile soil and an abundance of natural resources encouraged farming, fishing, and lumbering south of the Susquehanna River. Farms quickly proliferated along the riverbank and spread south over the gently rolling hills, while lumber mills took advantage of the waterpower on the Big Choconut and Tracy Creeks and their tributaries.

On January 22, 1823, the fledgling community, on the south side of the Susquehanna River, was established as the Town of Vestal.

By 1838, Vestal contained 2 gristmills, 15 sawmills, 1 fulling mill, 1 cotton mill, 1 distillery, 1 oilcloth factory, and 2 tanneries. Lumbering had declined substantially by 1875, and with the exception of a few sawmills, this industry had all but disappeared by 1900.

Clusters of farms, churches, stores, and mills evolved into five hamlets, three with their own post office: Ross Corners, which was settled by lumberman and storekeeper David Ross; Tracy Creek, the most prominent of the five hamlets, named for early settler Thomas Tracy; Vestal Center, which eclipsed Tracy Creek as the population grew along the north-south Choconut Creek Road, running from Pennsylvania north thorough Vestal; Willow Point, named for the willow trees that grew at that location along the river; and Twin Orchards, with its rich farmland where apple orchards flourished on both sides of the Vestal-Binghamton concrete highway. The "Five Corners" in what some called the hamlet or village of Vestal became the hub of activity as the lumbering business declined in Ross Corners and Tracy Creek.

John Boutch taught at the first school in 1793 when each one-room school was identified as a district. The 4 original districts serving 210 children in 1823 had increased to 18 districts serving 372 children by 1858. In 1936, 16 districts remained when they were consolidated into the Vestal Central School district.

The Broome County board of supervisors, composed of a supervisor representing each township and ward in the city of Binghamton, was the governing body. In 1868, at the request of the Town of Binghamton, the board of supervisors voted to assign a mile-wide strip of land on the eastern side of Vestal to the Town of Binghamton. The strip commenced at the Binghamton city line and extended south to the Pennsylvania border. The actual boundary change, which occurred in 1873, reassigned two schools, a cemetery, a tannery, and two mills along with farms and residences to the Town of Binghamton.

The original population of 784 increased rapidly, reaching 1681 by 1908. Farming, particularly dairy farming, continued, but lumbering began to decline. Flour mills, tanneries, and small factories composed Vestal's manufacturing base, producing overalls, cigars, safety pins, and paint.

At 9:45 p.m. on the evening of June 8, 1901, as train No. 61 was stopped at the Vestal depot taking on water, a wildcat train traveling at a high speed was unable to stop before crashing into the stopped train. The car immediately in front of the caboose on No. 61 held five tons of dynamite that exploded, killing five trainmen, hurling pieces of iron across the river, and breaking windows as far away as Binghamton. The explosion was reportedly heard 30 miles away. Residents of surrounding communities believed the four powder houses, located on Powderhouse Road, which stored black powder and dynamite, had exploded. Thousands traveled to the site to view the scene and collect a souvenir. Newspaper accounts state that the debris from both trains was cleared, the coal fires extinguished, and the destroyed tracks repaired 24 hours after the crash.

Disaster struck again in 1927, when a major portion of the business district at Vestal's Five Corners was destroyed by fire. That fire led to the establishment of the first municipal water supply.

Early settlers enjoyed the enriched soil that resulted from the Susquehanna River's spring floods, but when river flat farms were turned into subdivisions, the once beneficial floods destroyed homes. The particularly severe floods of 1936 and 1948 initiated the construction of protective floodwalls.

Subdivisions of modest homes replaced the herds of grazing cattle as Vestal became the bedroom community for employees of industrial giants Endicott-Johnson Shoe Company and IBM across the river. The Vestal Parkway grew from a two-lane road to a four-lane, divided, east-west highway along which businesses popped up almost overnight. Building permits reached all-time highs in the 1960s, making Vestal the fastest-growing community in the county.

When Endicott's Harpur College needed room for future expansion, it chose the Hazard Lewis dairy farm in Willow Point for its 347-acre campus. Harpur College grew to become the State University of New York at Binghamton and was recently renamed Binghamton University. Kopernik Space Education Center, the largest observatory on the East Coast, chose a hilltop in Vestal Center for its facility. Services, light industry, and retail malls located along the 5.5-mile Vestal Parkway play a major role in the economy of the town. Twenty public parks and the Rail Trail, occupying the former Delaware, Lackawanna and Western Railroad track bed, provide community spaces for many types of sports and recreation.

One

Prehistoric Vestal

Long before the earliest settlers arrived, small nomadic bands of Native Americans were hunting and fishing in the area recognized today as Vestal. Archaeological evidence of Native Americans has been found in Vestal along the Susquehanna River at Willow Point, near the mouth of the Choconut Creek, and in the Castle Gardens subdivision.

Using the newest dating technique of accelerator mass spectrometry (AMS), Dr. Nina Versaggi, director of the Public Archaeology Facility at Binghamton University, and Dr. Laurie Miroff dated nut fragments associated with projectile points in the Castle Gardens soil to the Late Archaic Period, 3000 to 2000 BC.

Native Americans from the Late Archaic Period, living in small groups, subsisted by hunting, fishing, and gathering seasonal foods. Artifacts and organic materials recovered from these sites provide archaeologists with information that can be used to interpret their prehistoric culture. Projectile points, broken pottery, burned bone, fire-cracked rock, and stone tools, or lithics, documented in the context of where they are found can reconstruct cultural activities. For example, the abundance of net sinkers and the 1960s research of the late Dr. Robert Funk from the New York State Museum suggests that this narrow spot in the Susquehanna River may have been a fish-processing site.

Archaeologists know that during the approximately 4,000 years before the Mersereaus, DuBois, Eldridges, Winans, LaGranges, Willis, and other early settlers arrived in Vestal, Native Americans from various cultural groups had grown crops in the rich soil, fished shad from the river, and hunted game in the forested hillsides.

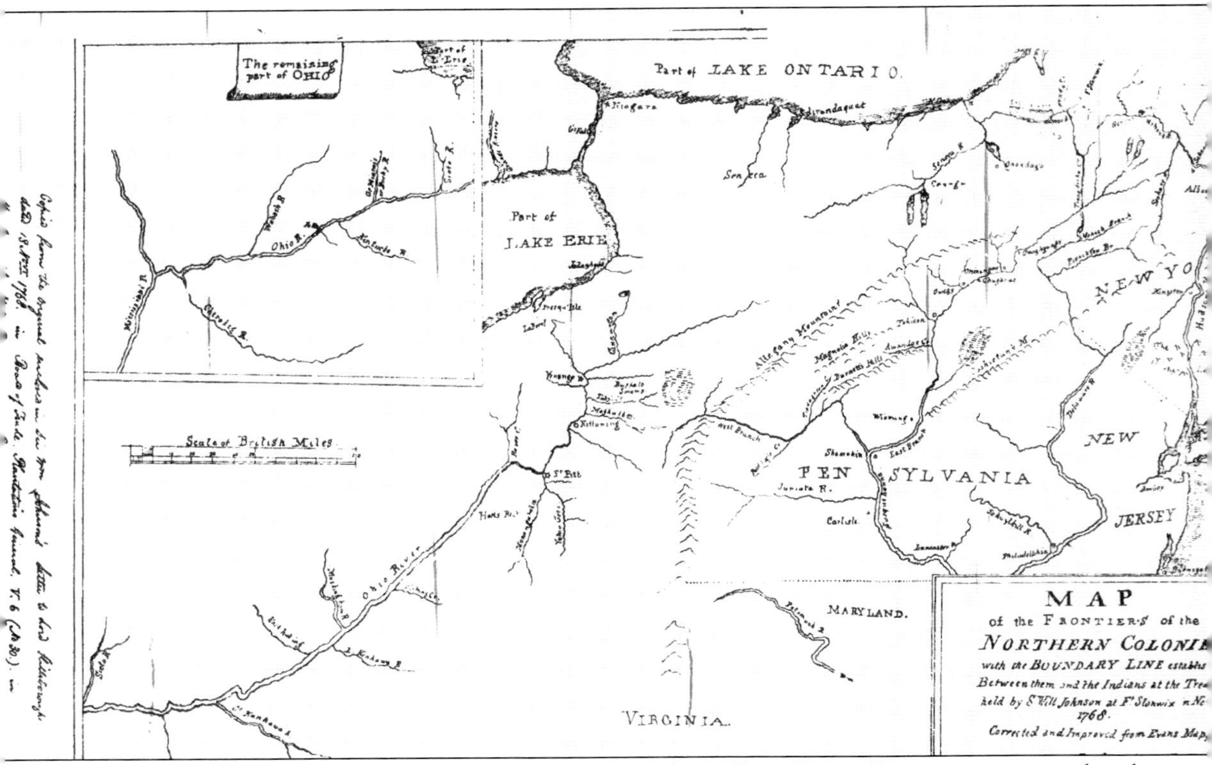

Guy Johnson prepared this map of the Six Nations for William Tryon, Esq., captain general and governor-in-chief of the province of New York in 1771. Chughnut is identified near the right of the map on the south side of the Susquehanna River in future Vestal.

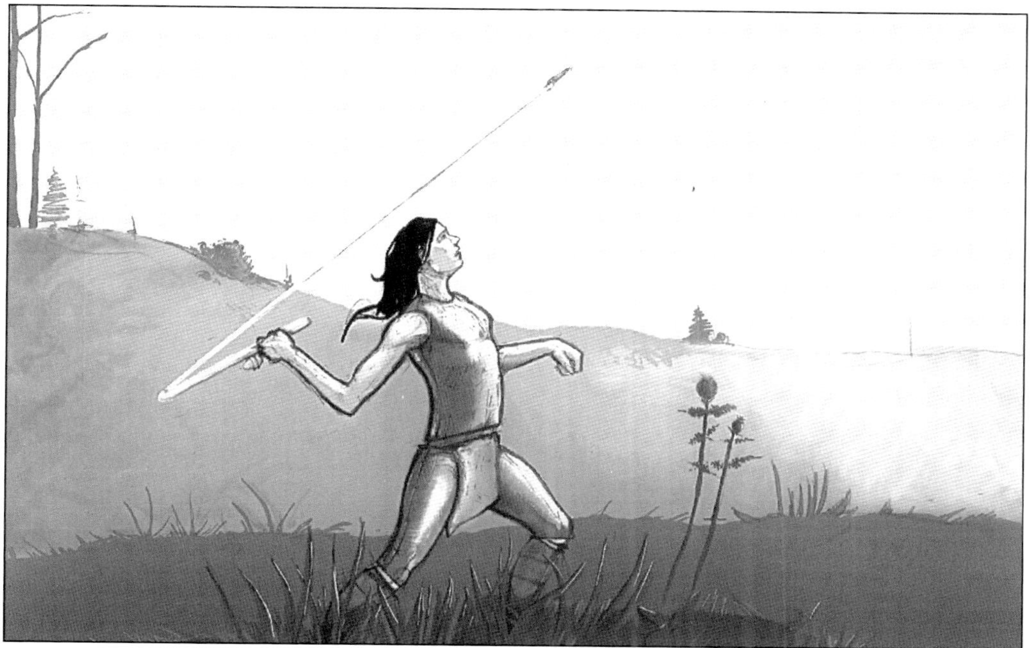

Native Americans discovered that spears could be thrown straighter and with more force by using an atlatl, a wooden or bone device that supported the spear. This drawing by Justin Miller of the Public Archaeology Facility at Binghamton University demonstrates the proper use of the atlatl or spear thrower.

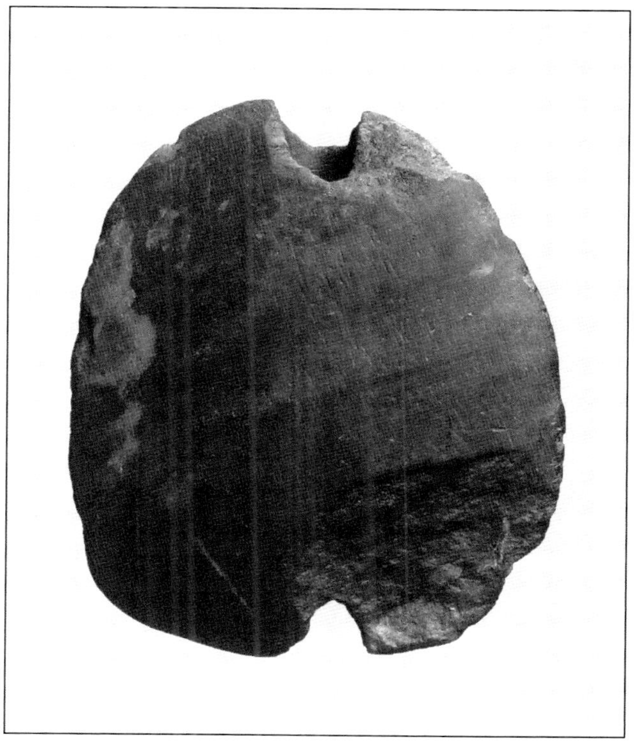

Not only did the atlatl improve trajectory over a handheld spear, but by adding a weight or bannerstone, the spear could be thrown farther and with greater force. An atlatl weight was created by using sand and a stick to drill a hole through a stone. The weight could be then slipped over or tied to the atlatl shaft. This atlatl weight was found at the Castle Gardens site. (Courtesy of David Tuttle.)

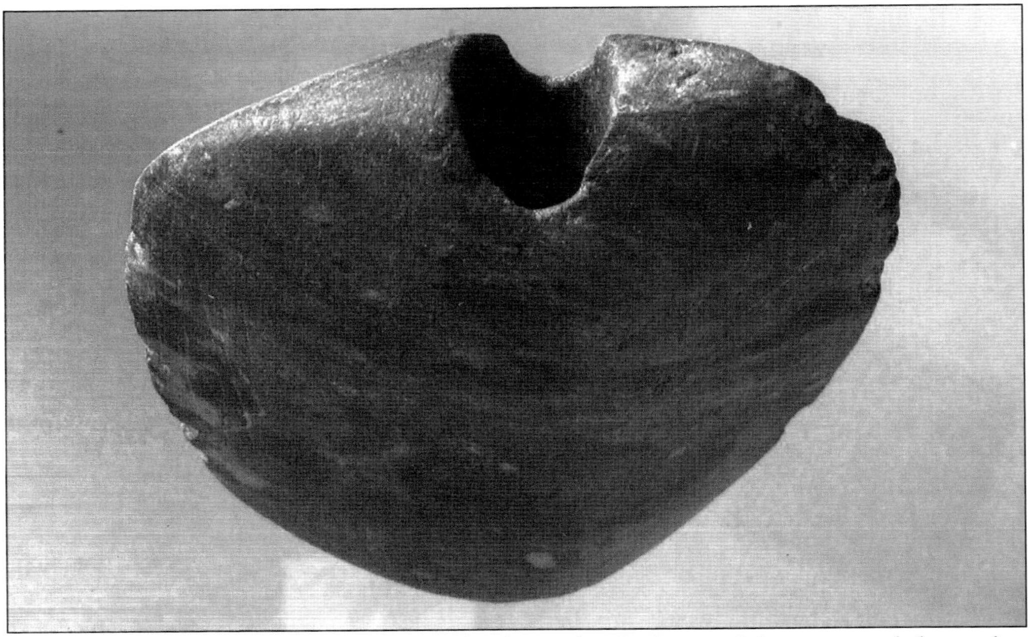

This view of the polished slate atlatl weight shows the thickness of the stone and the perfect hole drilled through the center. Time and patience combined with skill were required to create this rarely found artifact. (Courtesy of David Tuttle.)

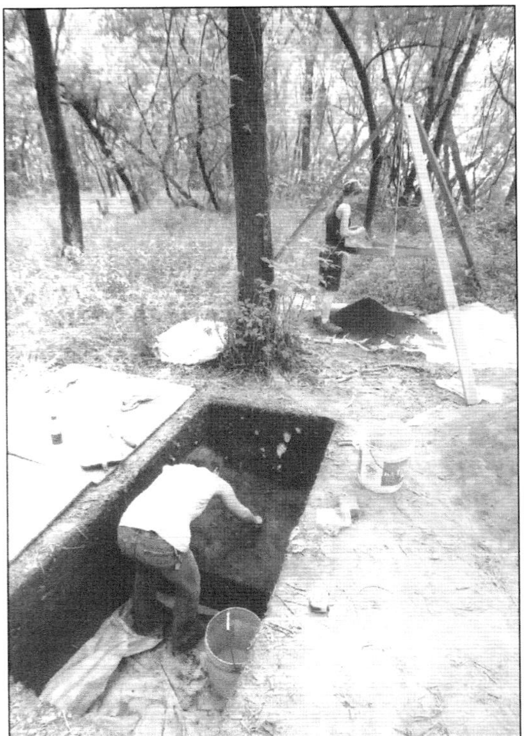

A Binghamton University archaeology student excavates this one-by-two-meter unit in five-centimeter layers. Each layer of dirt is screened to look for artifacts such as projectile points, fire-cracked rock, and pottery pieces. Even tiny flakes that result from knapping projectile points and stone tools are recovered, bagged, and labeled according to the level at which they were found.

The fire-cracked rock of a hearth was discovered in this Castle Gardens unit in July 2003. Soil is carefully excavated to retain the form of the feature, just as it was left by the individuals who used it centuries ago. Features are diagramed and photographed to document their location and depth.

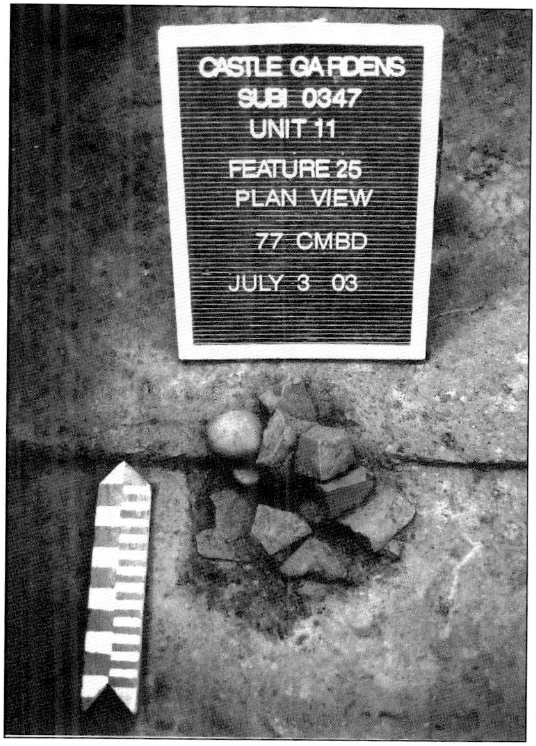

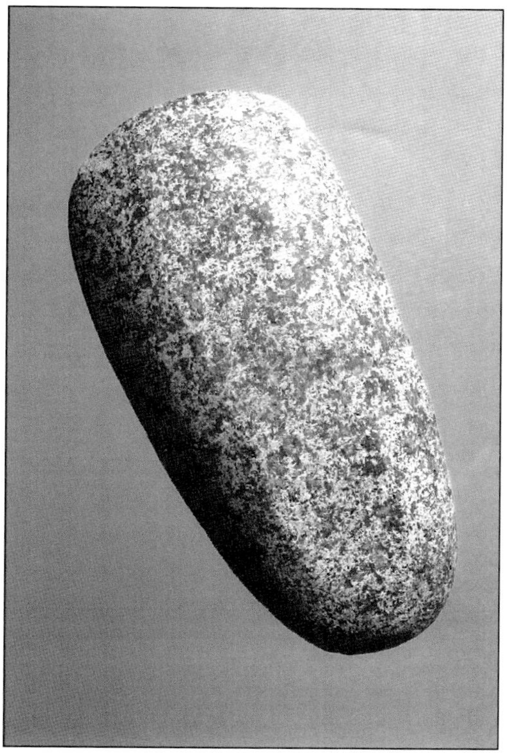

A celt is a lithic, or stone tool, that is used as an ax or pick. This excellent specimen, also found at the Castle Gardens site, shows highly polished beveled edges.

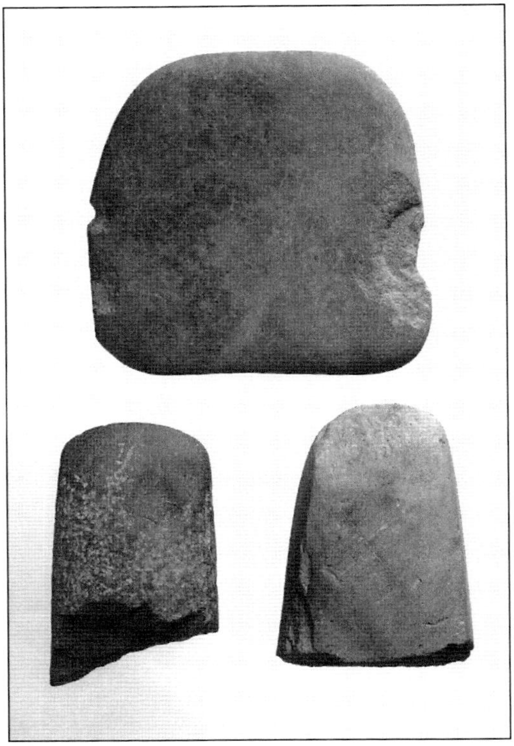

In early spring, shad, a saltwater fish related to the herring, swam up the Susquehanna River to spawn. Native Americans caught the fish in nets weighted down with net sinkers. Sinkers were held in the net by wrapping cord around the side notches of the sinkers as the net was tied. Net sinkers with deeper notches are also found. The celt on the left was probably broken during construction, as its pitted surface has not yet been smoothed. The finished celt on the right may have broken during use. Notice the precisely tapered bit end. To make an axe or pick, the celt was hafted to a handle.

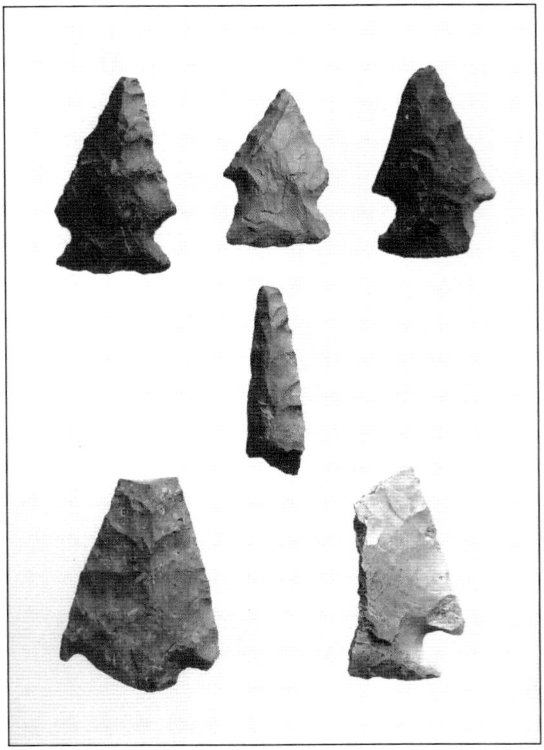

Vestal points, found at the Castle Gardens site, date from the Late Archaic Period, 3000 to 2000 BC. This small corner-notched point type, which radiocarbon dates to 2140 (plus or minus 100 years) BC, was first identified and described at the Castle Gardens site. It is thought the "shoulders" of these small-notched points would have been very efficient for spearing fish caught in weirs. The top three points are all Vestal points. The pointed end of the drill at the center can be used to pierce holes in hides in preparation for sewing. The two bottom points are broken Vestal points from the site.

Two

VESTAL

The central area of Vestal, sometimes referred to as the hamlet or village of Vestal, is located at the intersection of Main Street and the Vestal Parkway.

Before the first wooden bridge over the Susquehanna River was built in 1851, Jacob Crane operated a ferry at the end of Pumphouse Road to transport passengers and livestock across the river. When the Delaware, Lackawanna and Western Railroad (DL&W) tracks were built through Vestal in 1880, North Main Street dead-ended at the tracks. A viaduct was built to cross the tracks, providing access to Vestal Road and the Vestal-Endicott Bridge over the Susquehanna River.

Until 1967, the intersection of Main Street and Route 17 had a fifth "leg," Front Street. It was popularly known as the Five Corners. Traffic congestion resulted in numerous accidents, forcing the reconfiguration of the intersection. Route 17, a two-lane road from Tioga County to the Five Corners, was extended to Binghamton, replacing the Binghamton-Vestal concrete highway, or Vestal Road, as the main east-west route through the town.

In 1969, Route 17, the Vestal Parkway, became Route 434 and the property along its 5.5-mile length grew in value. Businesses purchased the farmland and established themselves along "the Golden Mile." Harpur College bought the former 347-acre Hazard Lewis Farm in 1955 for its beautiful new campus, now Binghamton University. Once a barren stretch of concrete, both sides of the Vestal Parkway experienced unprecedented growth from the former Five Corners to the Binghamton city line.

For years overshadowed by Ross Corners and Vestal Center, Vestal survived the explosion associated with a train wreck in 1901 and a major fire in 1927 to evolve into the heart of the township.

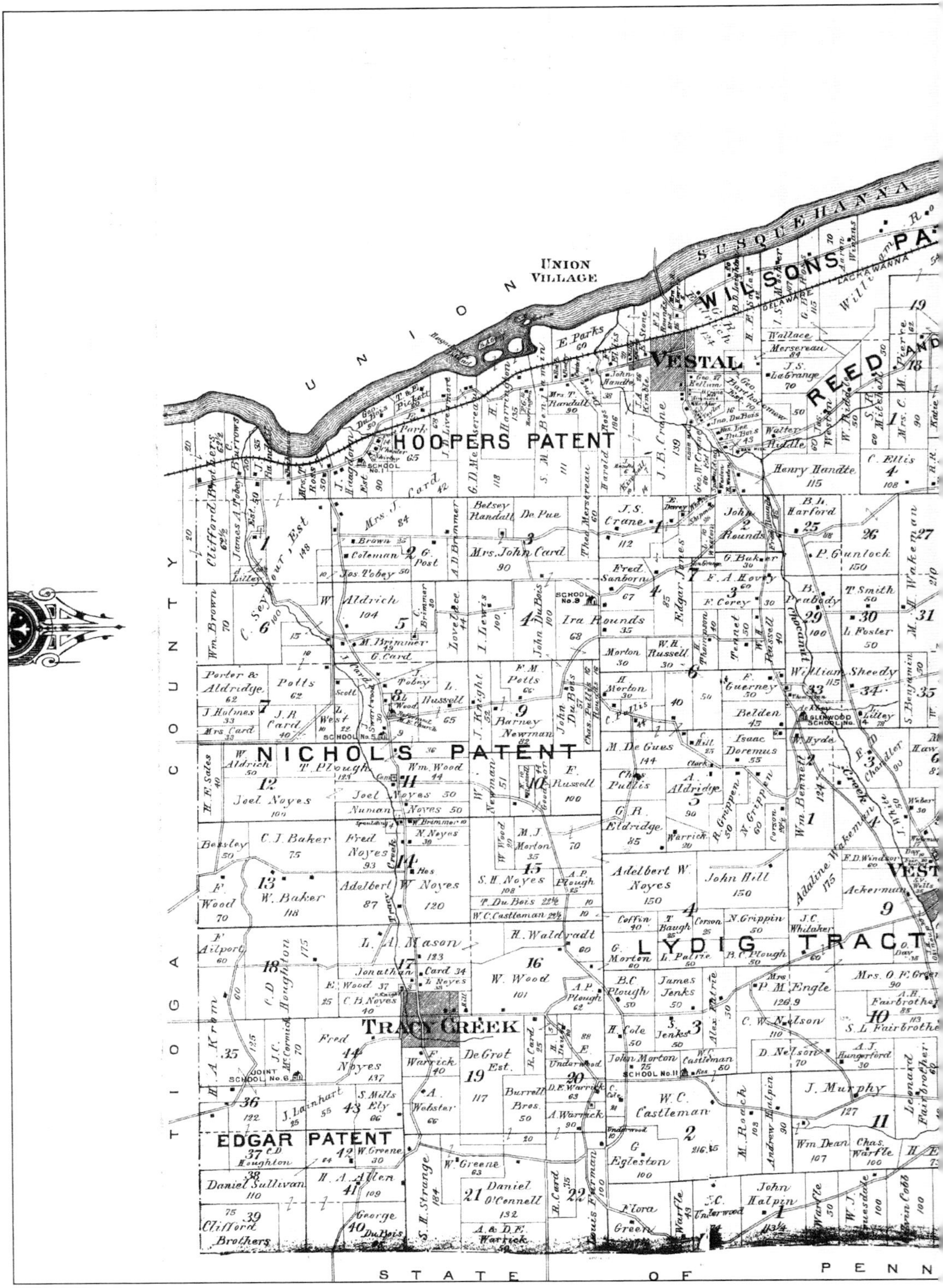
UNION VILLAGE
UNION
SUSQUEHANNA
WILSONS PA
REED AND
VESTAL
HOOPERS PATENT
NICHOL'S PATENT
LYDIG TRACT
TRACY CREEK
EDGAR PATENT
TIOGA COUNTY
STATE OF PENN

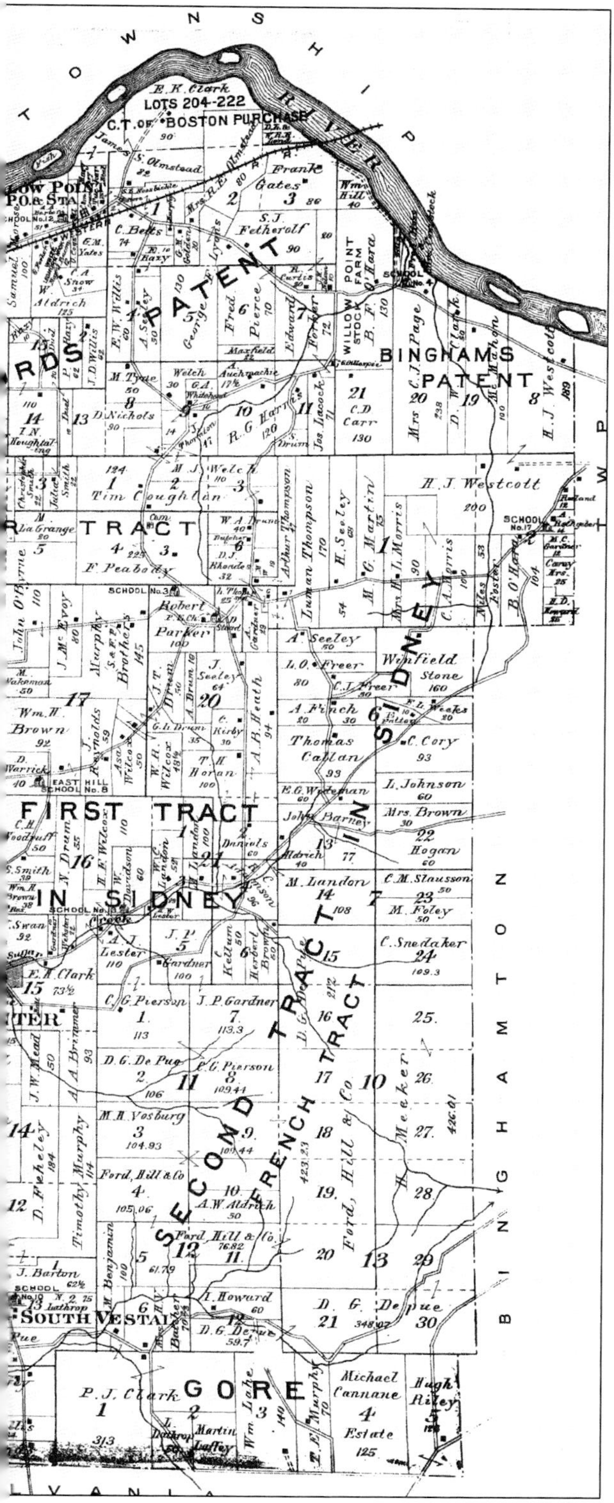

The 1908 map provides an overall picture of the hamlets and areas within the town as well as the names of residents and building locations.

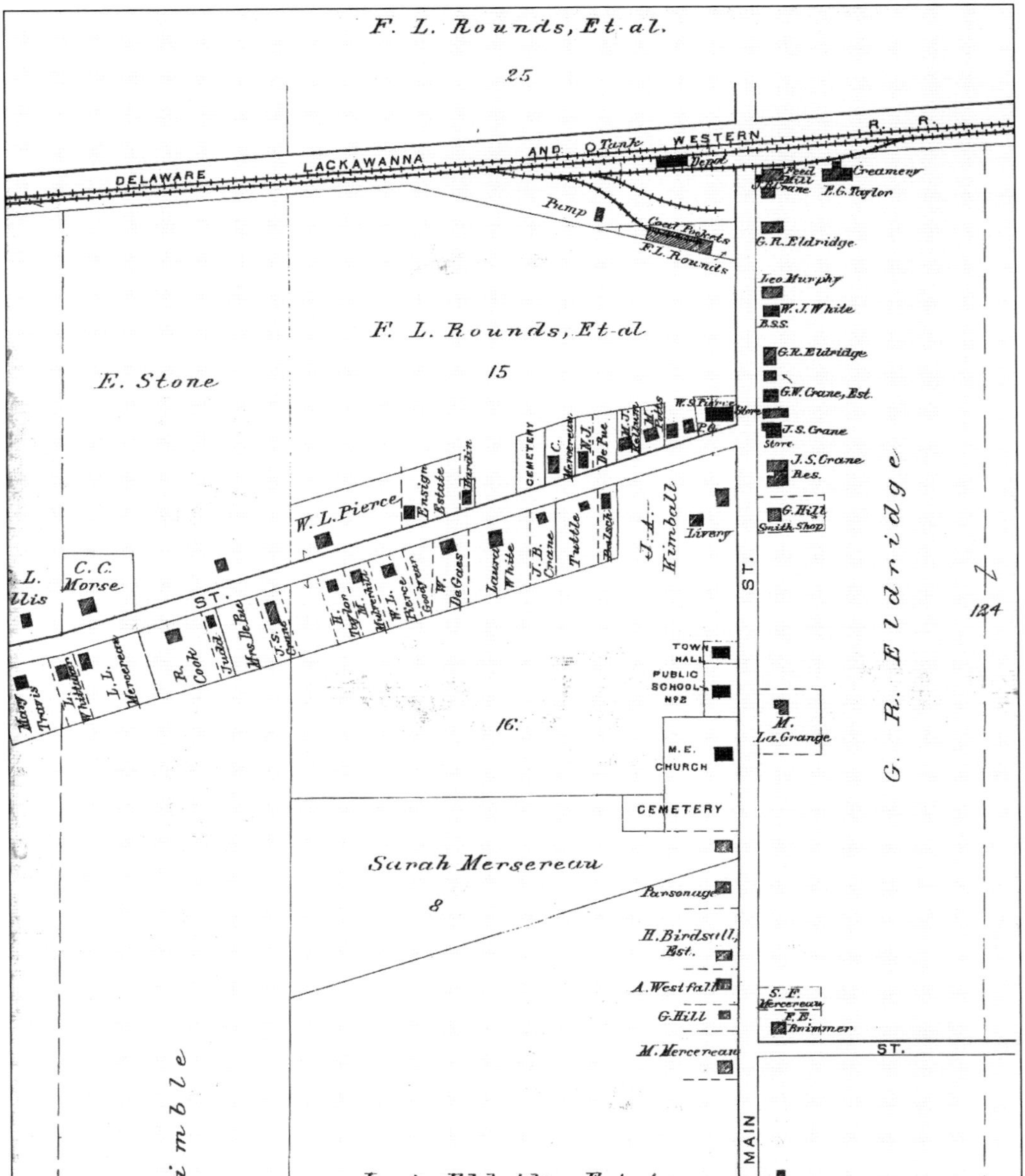

Vestal's business district in 1908 is shown in this detail. Front Street is the road running left from Main Street near the top. The DL&W tracks to the north separate the Rounds House, Drover's Inn, and the Susquehanna River from the main part of town.

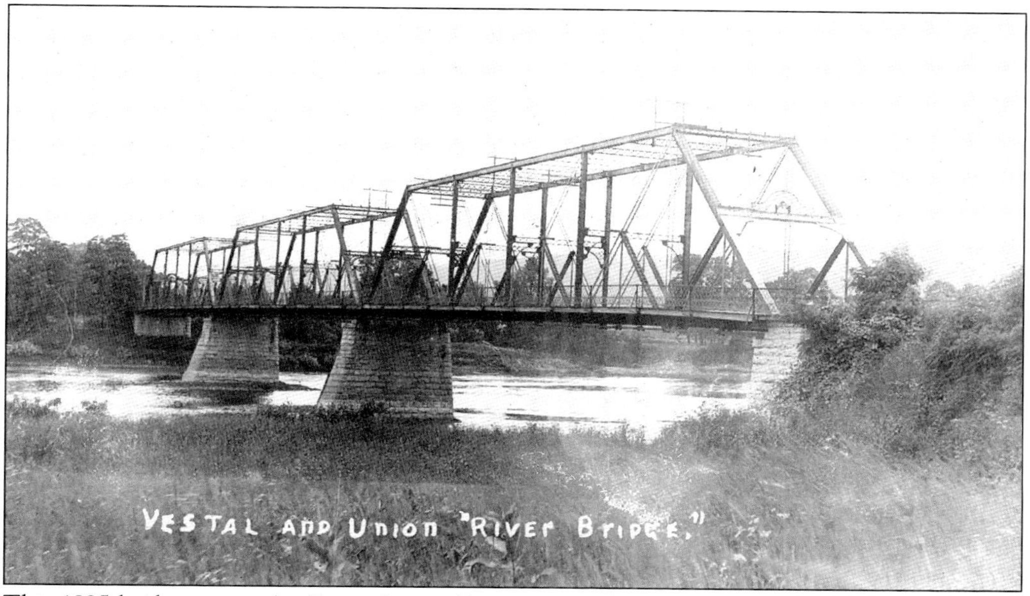

This 1895 bridge across the Susquehanna River was replaced in 1936 with a similar span built slightly to the east. In summer when the river is low, the original foundations of the 1870 bridge can be seen.

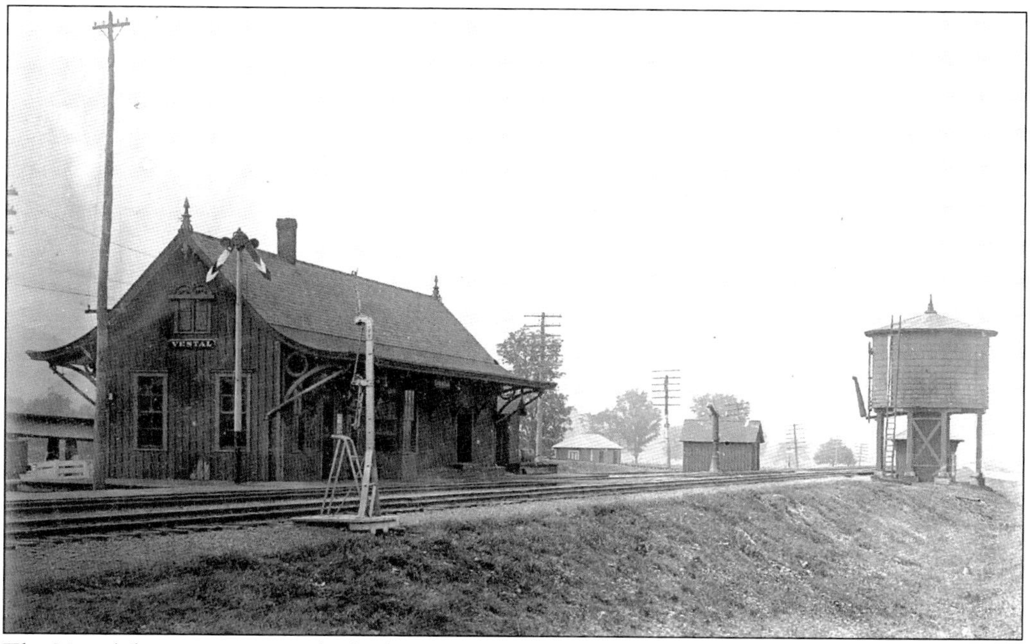

The Vestal depot is seen as it looked at the beginning of the 20th century. On that fateful night of June 8, 1901, a long freight train was taking on water from the tank at the right of the picture when a fiery accident occurred.

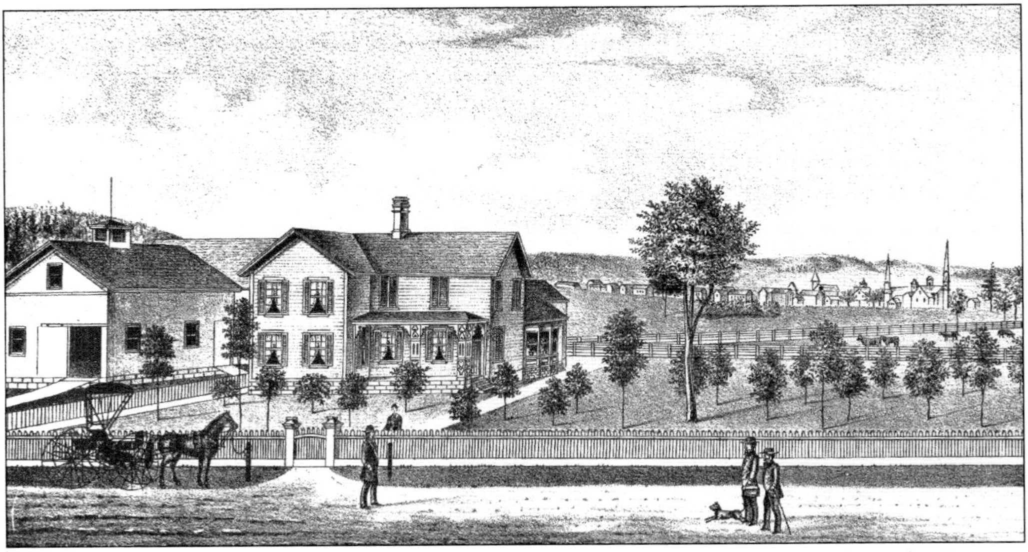

The residence of naval officer L. T. Safford is shown in this 1876 engraving from the Broome County atlas. Safford married Lucy Whitney Morse in 1867 and purchased the homestead of Kate Winans in 1874, moving there in 1876. Deafness forced his retirement from the U.S. Navy in 1881, the year before he built his shirt factory. Remodeled and no longer behind a fence, the original Safford residence maintains a presence on Front Street.

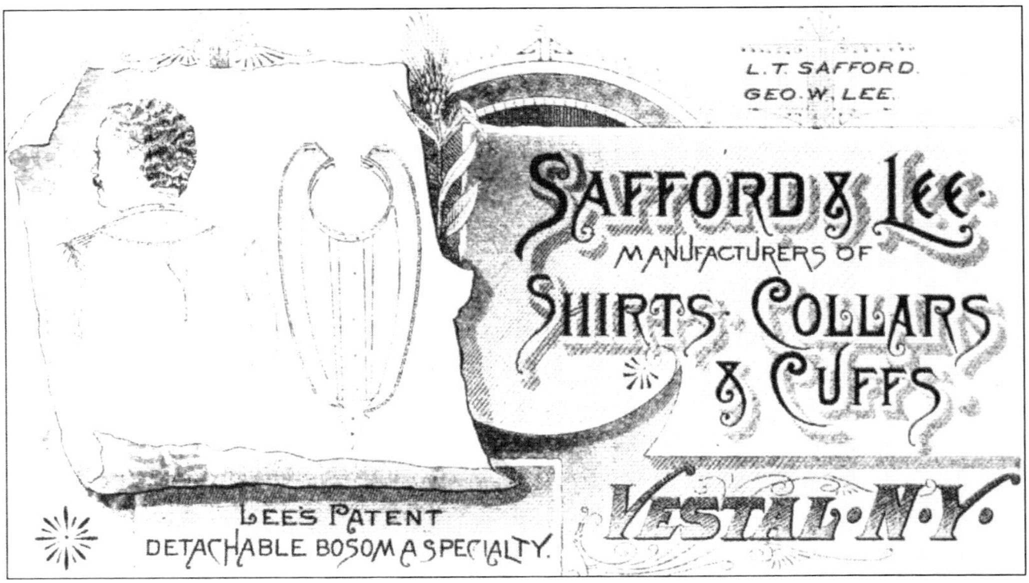

Safford, along with George W. Lee, built and operated a factory across from his Front Street residence that manufactured shirts, collars, and cuffs. A detachable bosom, patented by Lee, was their specialty. Historical references are also made to Safford owning an overall factory at the same site from 1880 to 1885. He is said to have built four small houses or cottages for the employees.

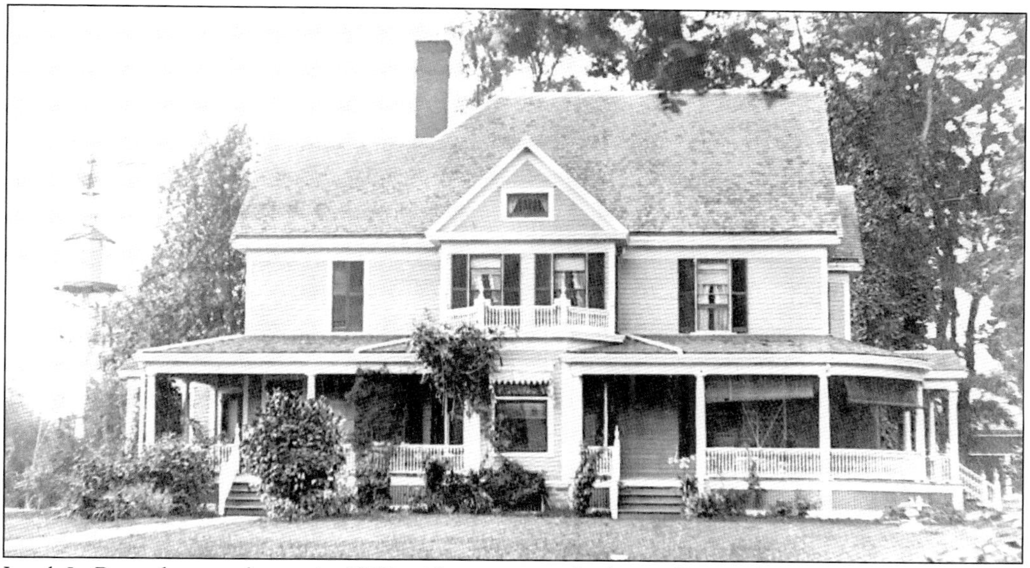

Jacob L. Rounds passed away in 1889 without seeing the large, Queen Anne–style home his son Fayette L. Rounds would build across the street in 1895. A large tower was added to the west elevation in about 1912. Fayette and his wife, Susie Knapp Rounds, raised their six children in the 15-room, 7-bedroom home, which was occupied by daughter Hilah Rounds until her death in 2001. The windmill on the left is in the backyard of the Rounds House. Designated a local landmark, the Rounds House has been partially restored.

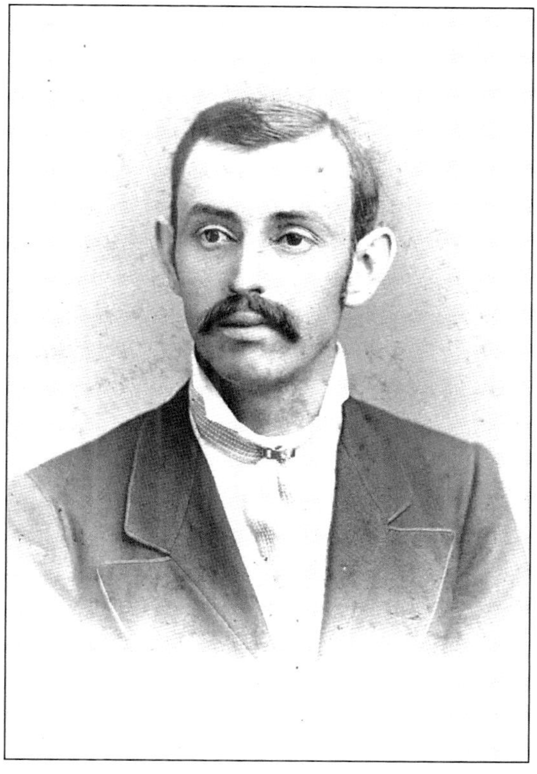

Born in 1858, young Fayette Rounds was Vestal's first stationmaster and eventually opened the Rounds Coal Company, which sold coal and later fuel oil until 2001.

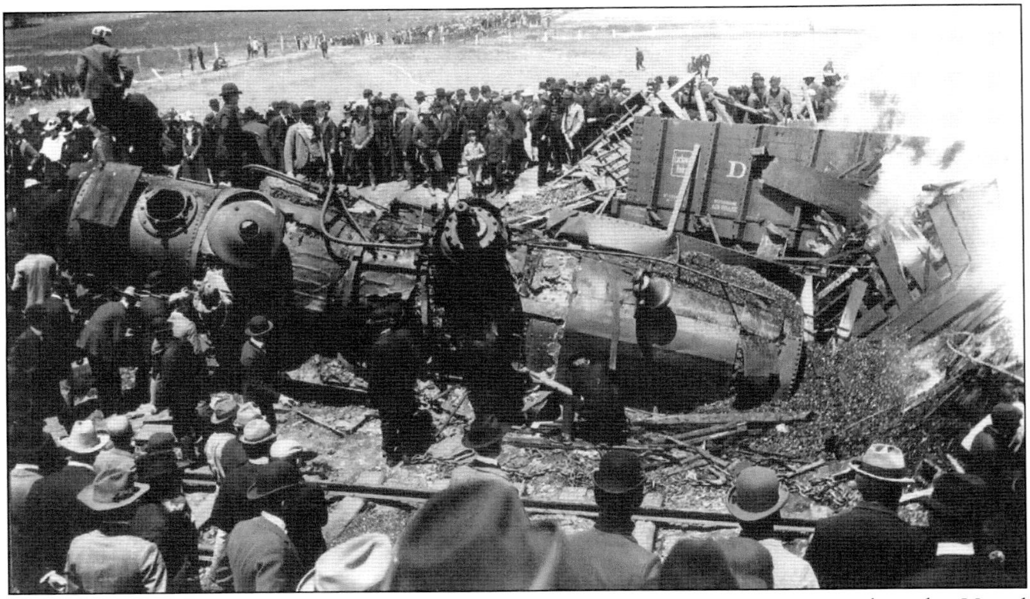

At approximately 9:45 p.m. on June 8, 1901, DL&W train No. 61 was stopped at the Vestal depot, taking on water. The 700-foot-long freight train was carrying five tons of dynamite in a boxcar just ahead of the caboose. As the flagmen were about to set flags along the track behind No. 61, a fast-moving, two-engine wildcat train, unable to stop, hit the caboose of No. 61. The resulting explosion was heard 30 miles away. It was reported that more than 10,000 people traveled to the site. Here onlookers view the twisted metal of the wildcat engine.

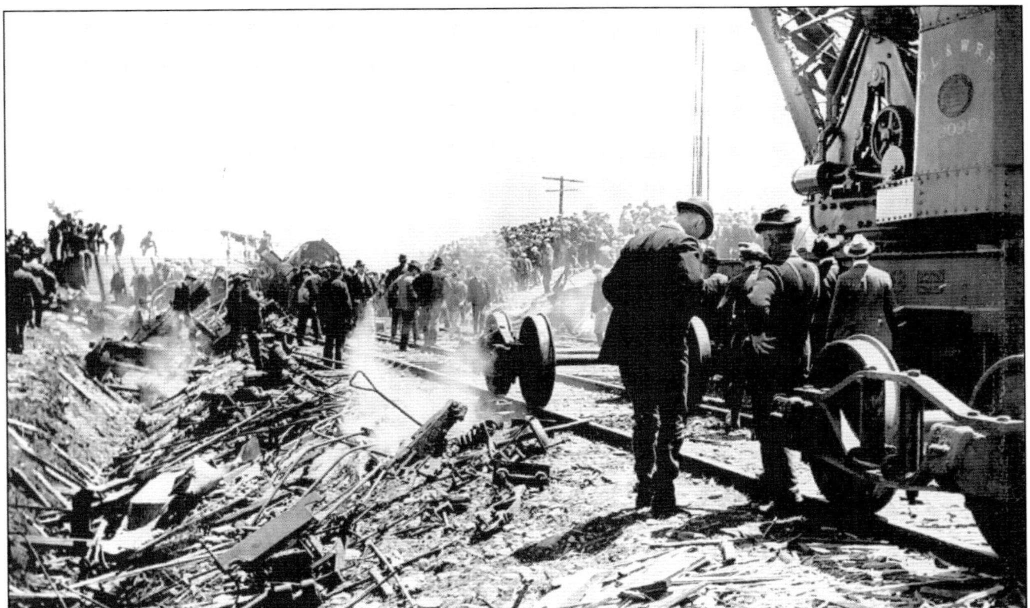

A large fire ensued as the spilled coal ignited. Men from No. 61 and the wildcat train attempted to jump to safety, but the explosion was so large that five trainmen were killed, three were seriously injured, and four others received minor injuries. The crews of both trains were from Elmira.

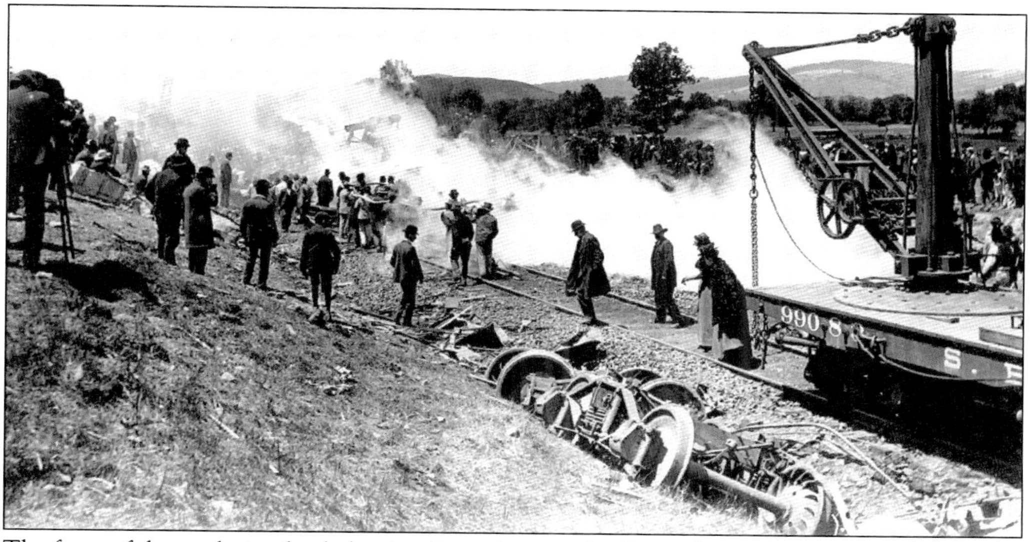

The force of the explosion hurled twisted metal across the Susquehanna River, imbedding it four feet in the ground in the stadium behind the current Union-Endicott High School. Surprisingly, within 24 hours of the accident, enough debris had been removed to repair the tracks and the fires had been extinguished, allowing train travel to resume through Vestal.

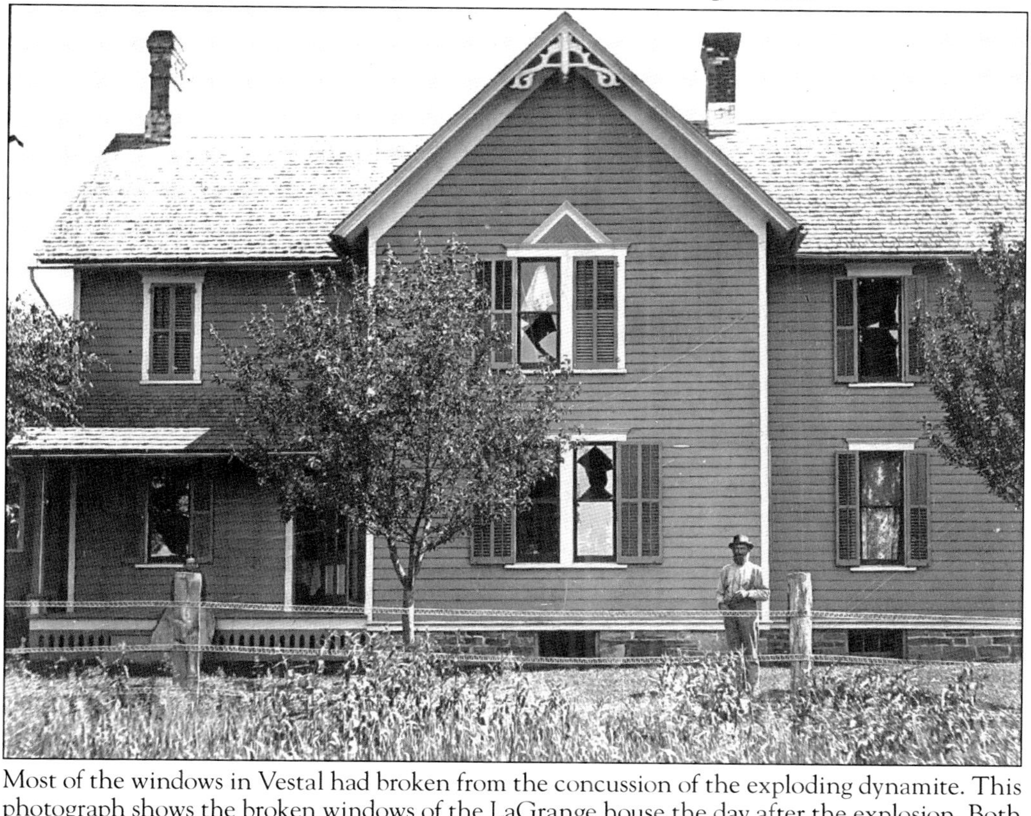

Most of the windows in Vestal had broken from the concussion of the exploding dynamite. This photograph shows the broken windows of the LaGrange house the day after the explosion. Both chimneys survived the blast, but many in town did not.

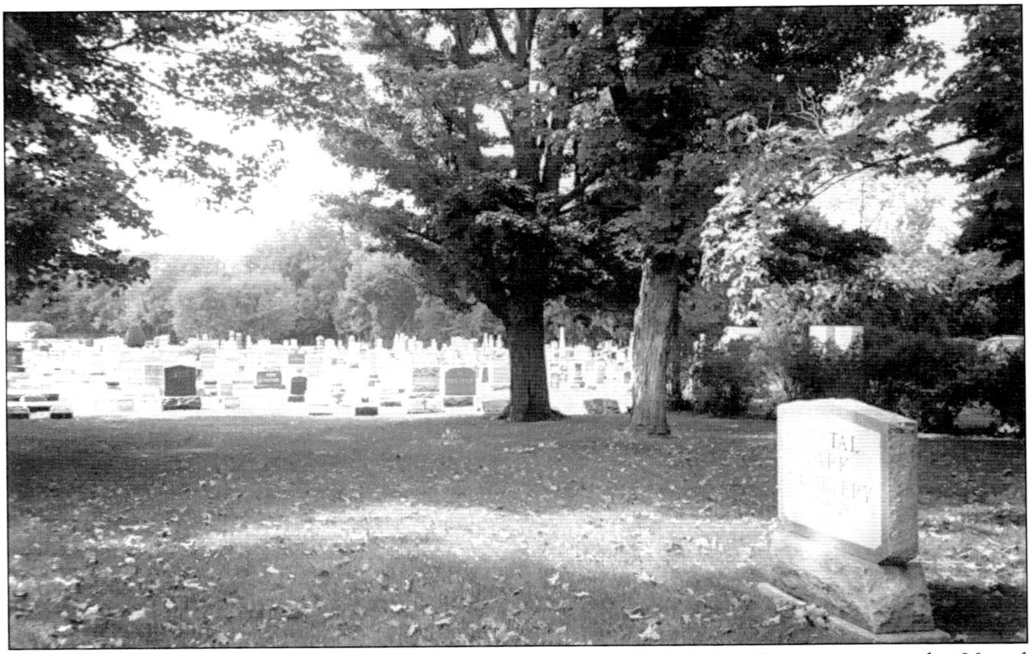

Established about 1826, the Vestal Park Cemetery located on Main Street next to the Vestal Methodist Church contains the graves of Revolutionary War soldiers who pioneered the development of the area. Cemetery tours are occasionally given by members of the Vestal Historical Society.

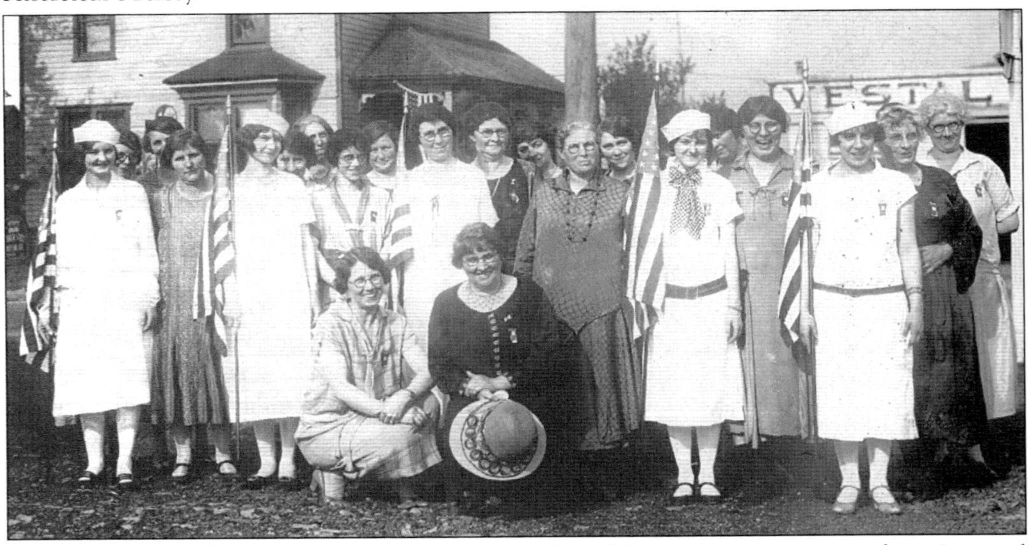

The Daughters of the Union Veterans of the Civil War celebrate the organization's first Memorial Day in 1926. They are, from left to right, (first row, kneeling) Maud Wells Hoffman and Cleo Morse Ellis; (second row, standing) Lillian Brearly Walker, Lulu Johnson, Susie Weston Cross, Bess Morse Ellis, Antoinette Gibbs, Mrs. William Carron, Grace Williams Gould, Lulu DeShatter Taylor, Luella Chandler, Elizabeth Jenner Drake, Estelle Jenner, Julia Owen, Anna Murphy, Louise Jenner Brooks, Della Wood Letson, Leona Jenner Landon, Esther Drum Brimmer, Elena Owen Denman, Kathryn Drumm, and Julia Gibbs.

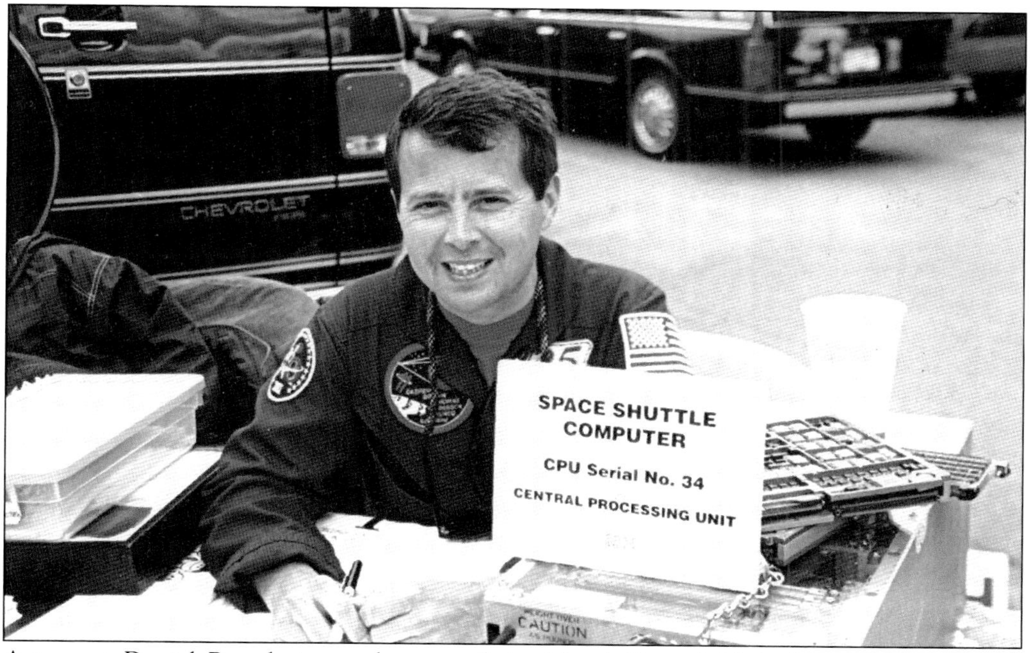

Astronaut Daniel Bursch is an alumnus of the Vestal Central High School class of 1975. Commander Bursch returned to serve as grand master of the annual Vestal Festival Parade. Here he signs autographs and displays the IBM processor that accompanied him on the space shuttle.

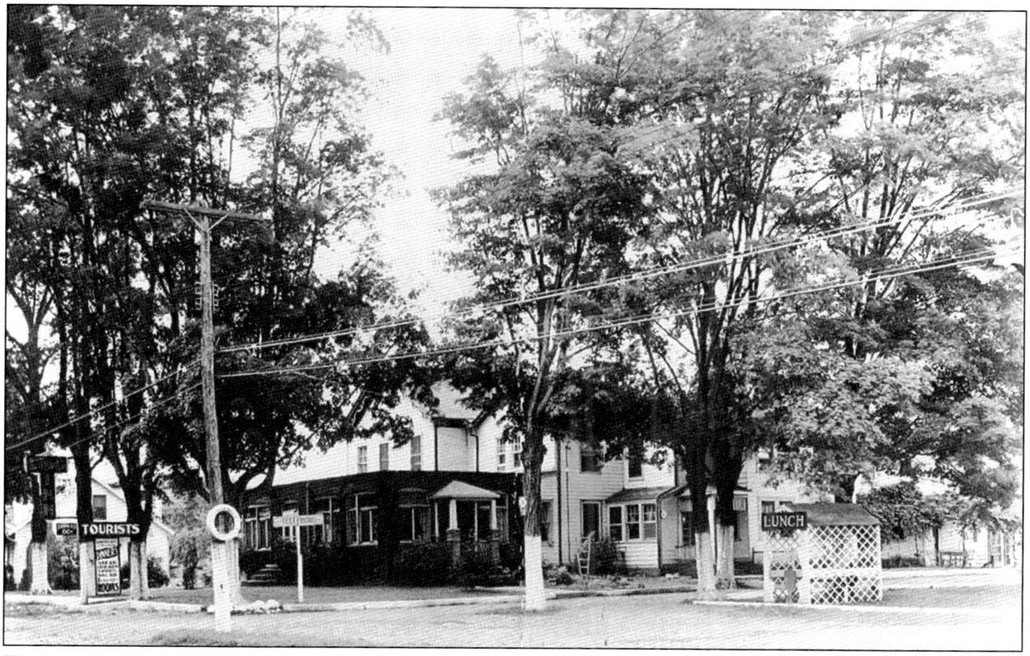

Tourists staying at the Lido Inn in the 1920s and 1930s could enjoy a dinner of steak, chicken, or chops with salad and beverage for 60¢. The inn, which was on Vestal Road, was operated by Lou Laviani. The sign on the corner advertises a public telephone.

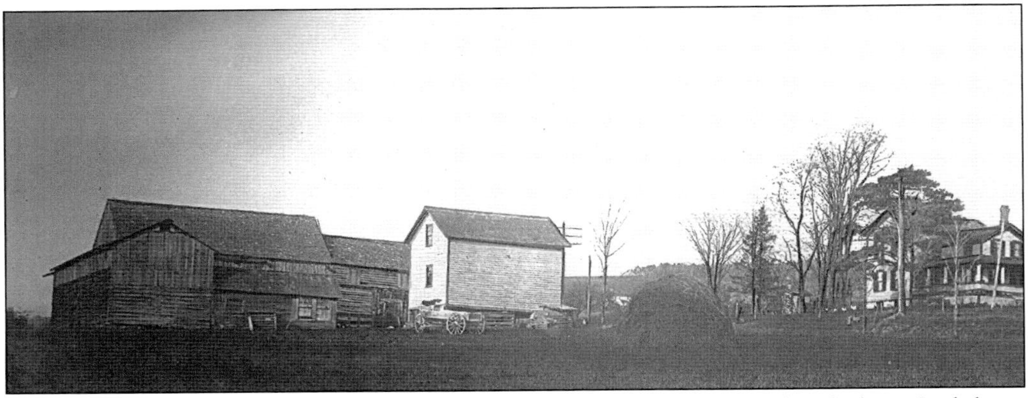

On the northeast corner of Sheedy Road and Route 26 sits the former Sheedy farm. Irish-born William Sheedy migrated to the United States in 1866, where he and his wife, Pennsylvania-born Elizabeth, raised eight children. The farm consisted of several barns and the house, which was built about 1850. The farmhouse, which has been remodeled and enlarged over the years, enjoys an excellent view of the Choconut Valley.

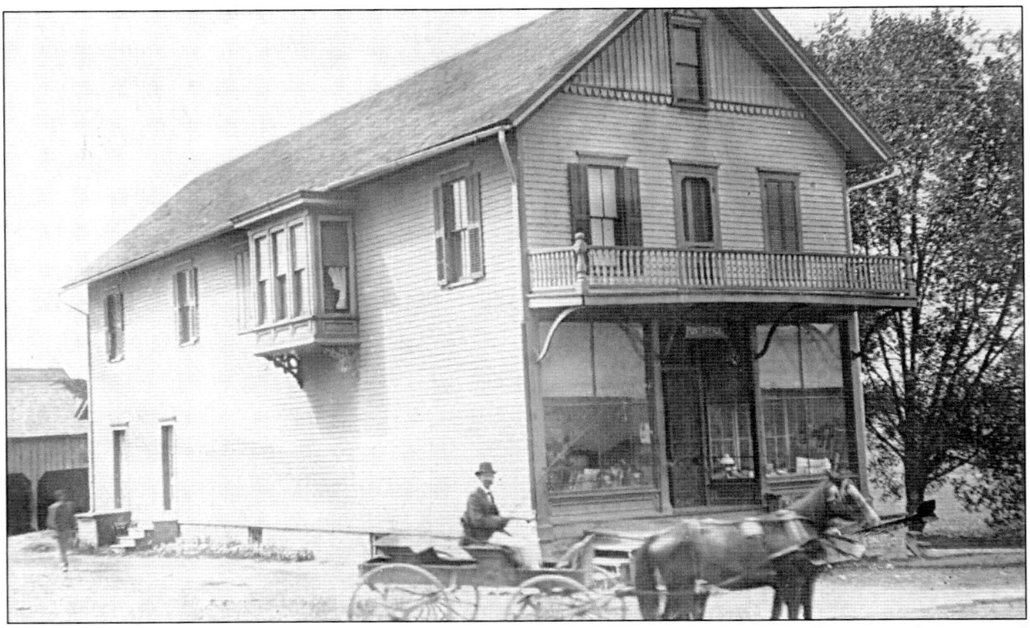

William S. Pierce, born in Union Center, moved to Vestal before 1892 and operated a general store at the northwest corner of Front and Main Streets. This photograph was taken before a roof was added over the second-floor porch. The store, which was across from J. S. Crane's store, was destroyed in the 1927 fire.

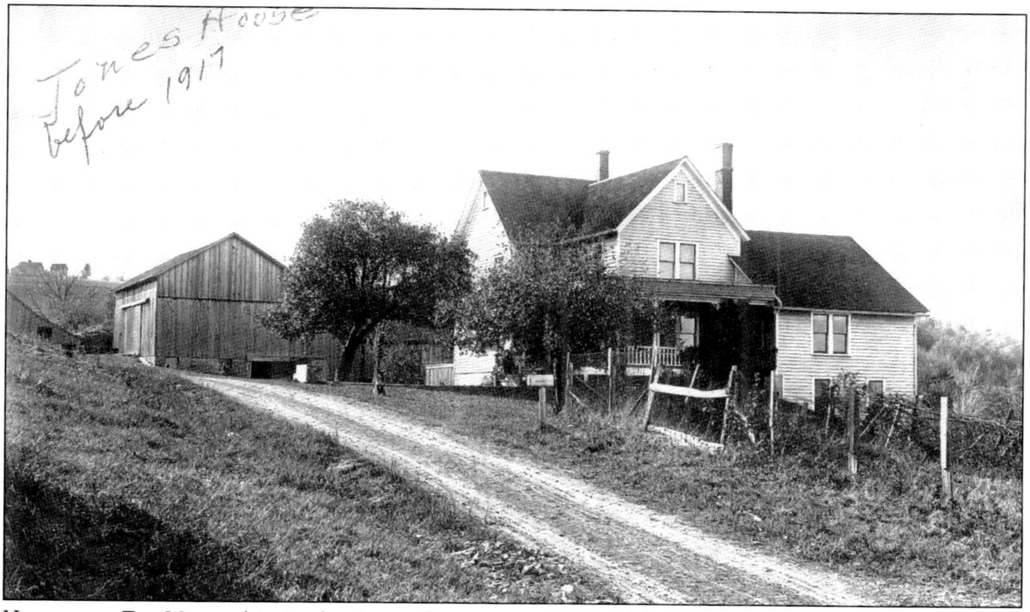

Known as Far View, this is the Jones farm as it appeared before 1917. The road, then barely a wagon path, passed close to the house and barn just as Jones Road does today. Edgar and Jane Jones's descendants have occupied this farmhouse for over 100 years. They are currently restoring the barn.

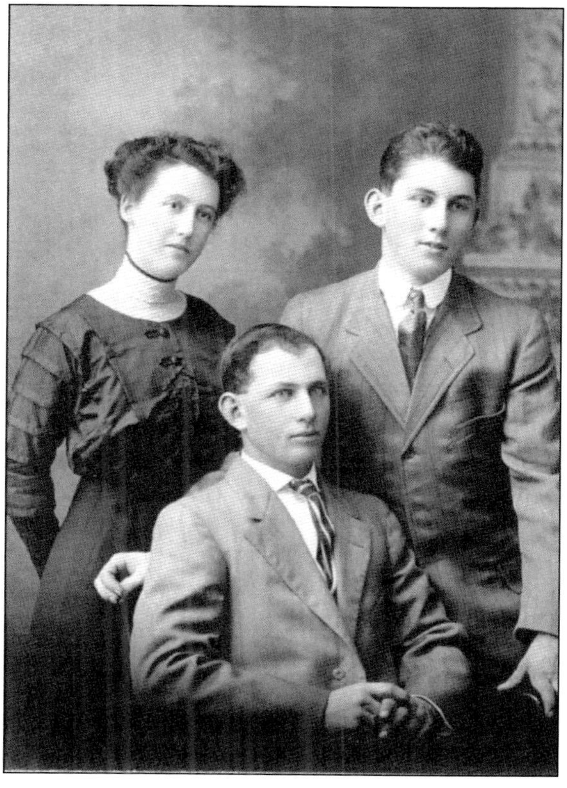

In 1884, Edgar Jones, originally from Pennsylvania, purchased the farm, later called Far View, from Frederick Aldrich. The following year he married Jane and brought her to the farm where they raised their three children, Katherine, James, and Leland.

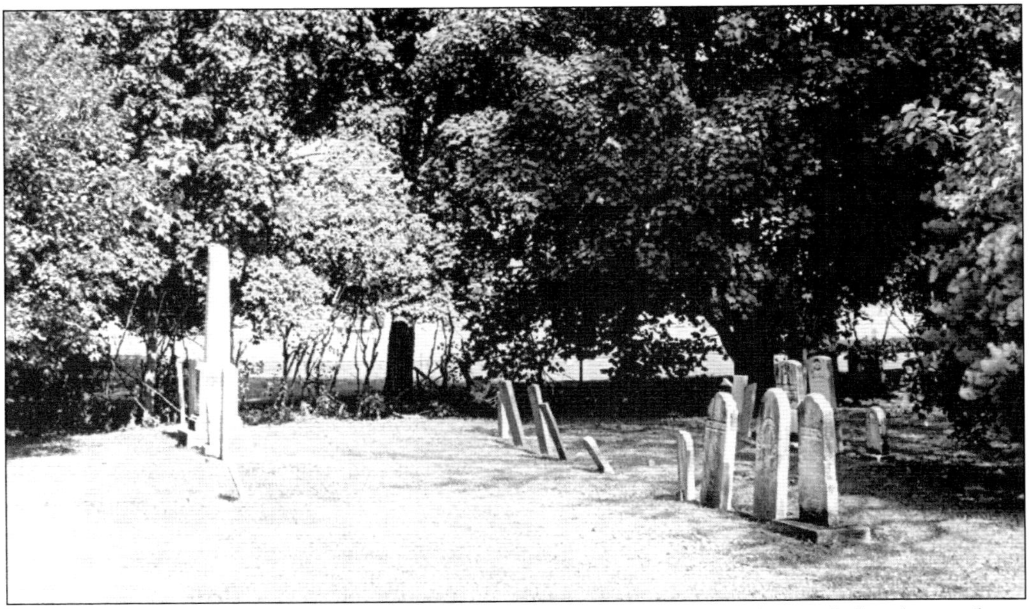

Gravestones in the Rounds Cemetery on Front Street bear the names of Rounds family members, their spouses, and their friends. Pioneers Alford and Rachel Rounds, as well as William Jones, an early proprietor of Drovers Inn, are buried here.

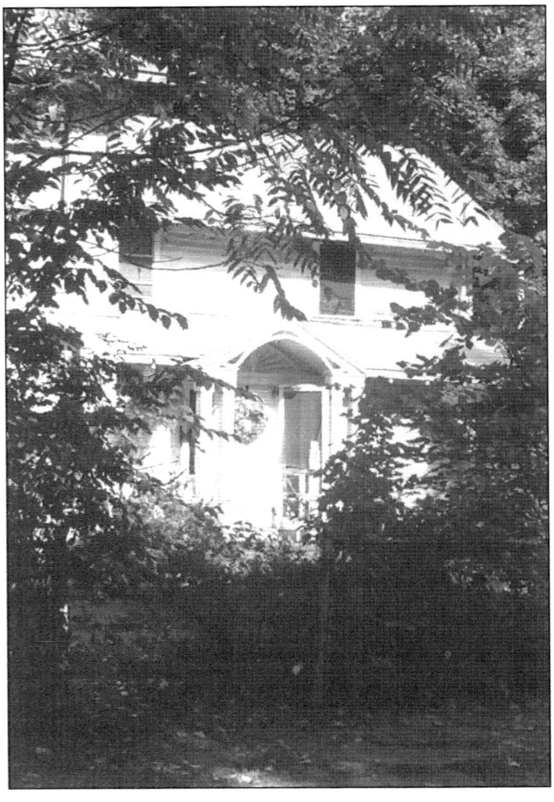

Walter L. Johnson, son of George F. Johnson, the owner of Endicott-Johnson Shoe Company, moved from Union to this large house in Vestal. After Walter's death, the house was sold and divided into apartments. It has since fallen into disrepair, and the carefully tended plantings have become overgrown. Walter and his wife, Julia, had three children, William, Mabel, and Jane.

Susie Gunglach was a prominent Vestal teacher who taught in several of Vestal's one-room schools. An avid historian, Gunglach kept scrapbooks of articles about her students and the town in general. She wrote that when she began teaching at the two-room schoolhouse on Powderhouse Road in 1908, her contract was for 32 weeks at $8 per week.

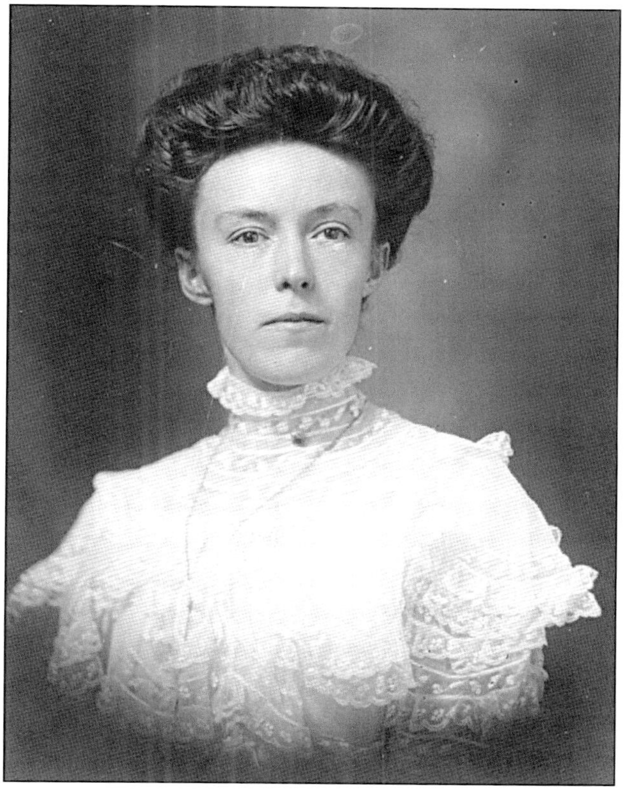

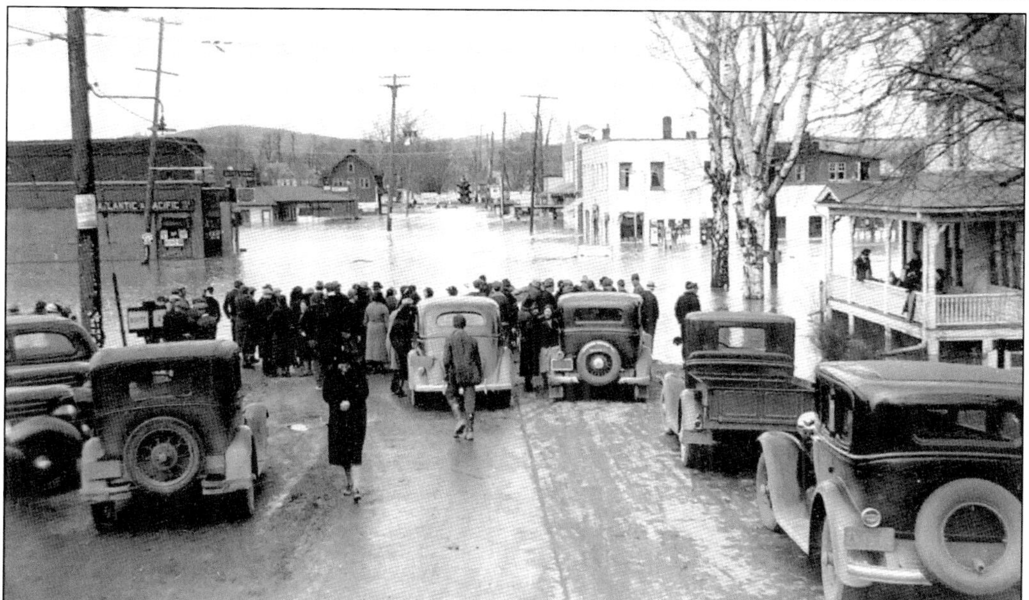

Prior to flood control, spring frequently meant flooding along the Susquehanna River. During the 1936 flood, water crept through the main intersection. Onlookers stand on South Main Street at the edge of the advancing water.

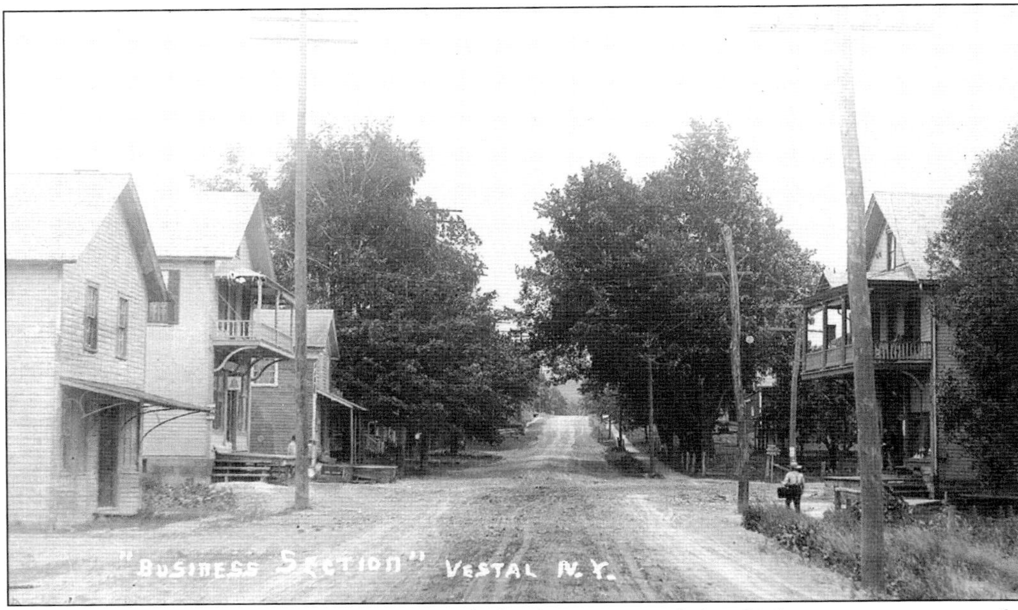

This was Vestal's business district around the beginning of the 20th century, so peaceful compared to the traffic problems of the Five Corners 40 years later. The second building on the left with the second-floor porch was Jesse Crane's store; across the street on the right-hand corner was William Pierce's store and the post office.

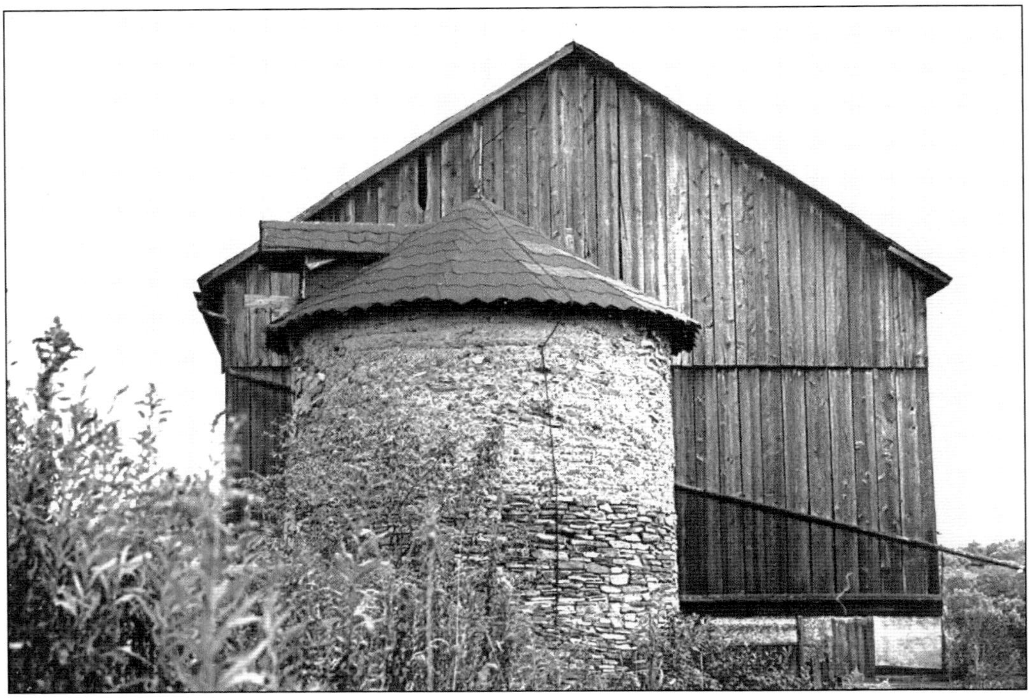

A magnificent stone silo stands strong against this barn located high on Echo Road. Fortunately Gordon Allen took this prize-winning photograph, because both barn and silo are gone.

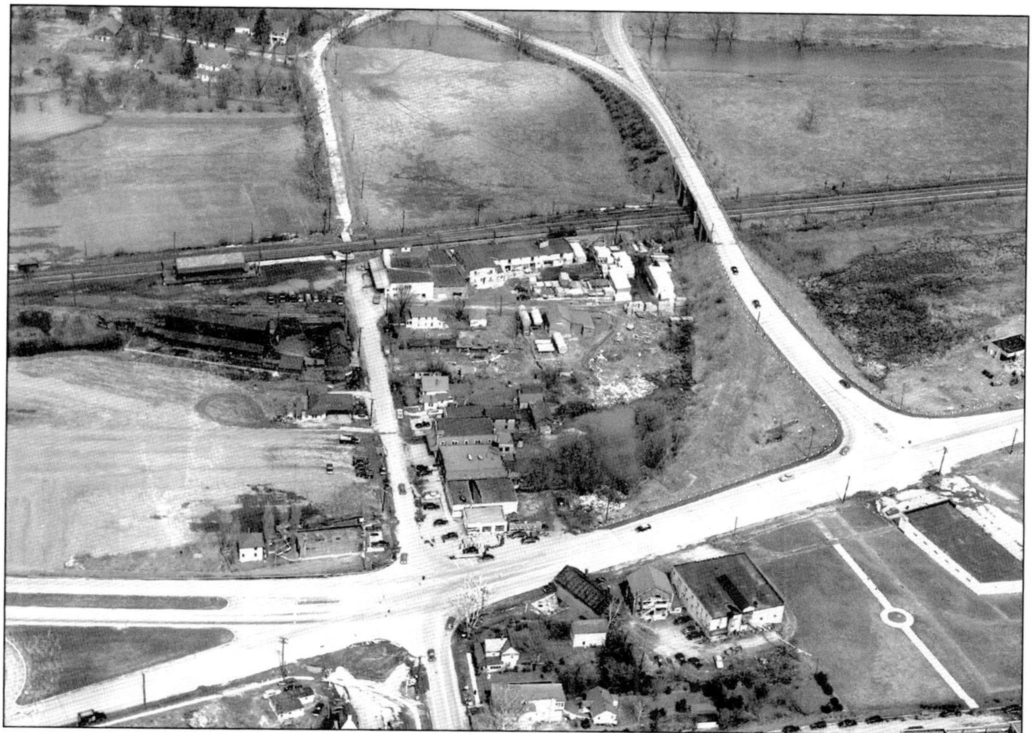

This 1950 photograph shows the hazardous Five Corners, the depot, and the Rounds coal business along the DL&W tracks, and the viaduct that carried traffic over the tracks north to the Vestal-Endicott Bridge or east to Vestal Road. The road just left of the bridge ends at the approximate location of Crane's Ferry. By 1969 North Main Street reopened, eliminating the need for the viaduct. (Courtesy of Ed Aswad.)

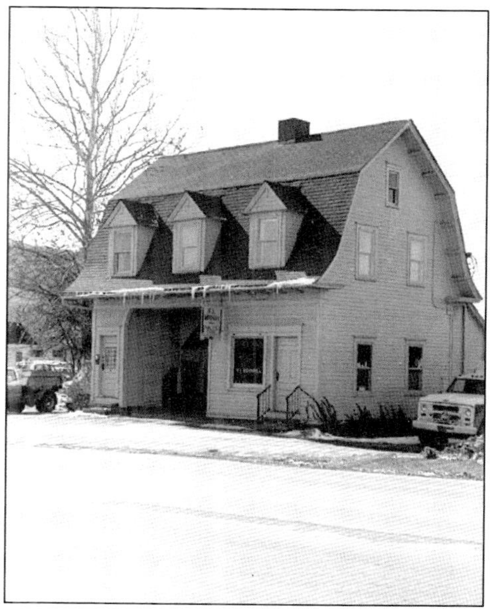

The Rounds Coal Company building, owned by Fayette L. Rounds, was built in 1908. Designed by architect C. A. Olmstead, coal trucks drove through the center arch over a five-ton Jones Scale to be weighed empty. After being filled from the coal pockets behind the building, the truck would exit through the arch to be reweighed. The office was on the right, while stairs to the second floor were located on the left. The building was designated a local landmark and moved in 2006 to a location straddling the Rail Trail.

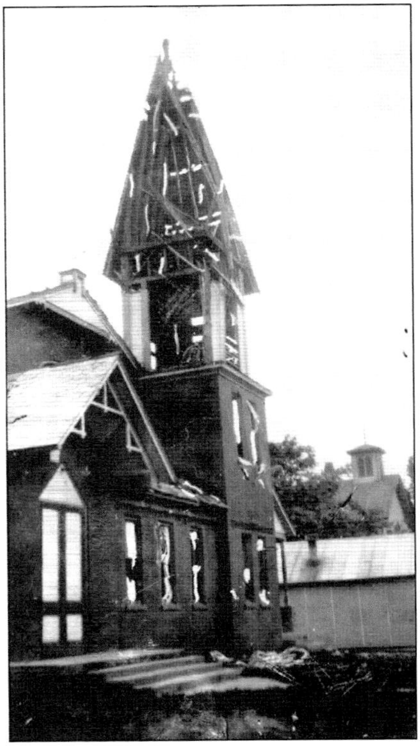

This 1845 church was built on one acre of land purchased in 1834 from Daniel and Abigail Foster at a cost of $100. A tall wooden steeple graced the Vestal Methodist Church on Main Street until a storm severely damaged the structure. Repairs were made, and the tower was redesigned. A large portion of the acre was subsequently used for the Vestal Park Cemetery. (Courtesy of the Broome County Historical Society.)

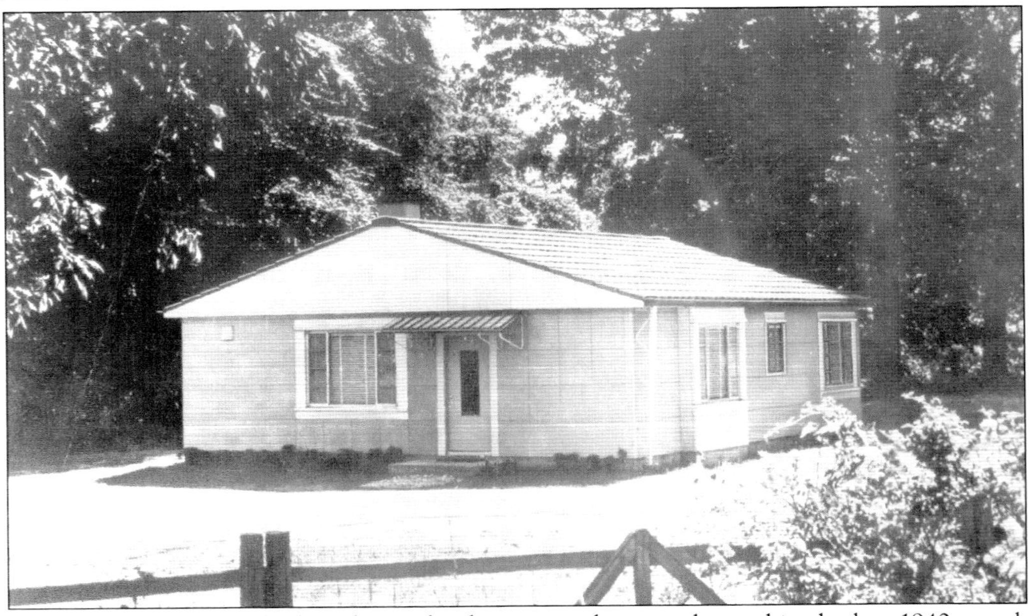

The Lustron Company had a solution for the postwar housing demand in the late 1940s: steel. The tiny houses, constructed entirely of enameled steel inside and out, were advertised as the "houses of tomorrow." During 1948 through 1950, the three years the company was in business, it sold about 2,680 homes and 2 of them are in Vestal on the Vestal Parkway across from the Town Square Mall. (Courtesy of the Broome County Historical Society.)

In addition to dry goods and groceries, Jesse Crane's store carried specially formulated livestock feed by Dr. Gilbert Hess, a physician and veterinary surgeon. Orin J. White of Willow Point paid $19.15 for 1,600 pounds of feed for his animals on December 27, 1904.

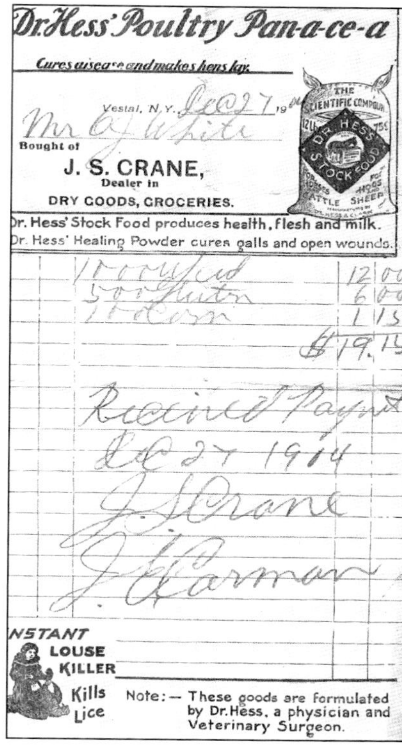

Dr. Hess' Poultry Pan-a-ce-a

Cures disease and makes hens lay.

Vestal, N.Y. 19

Bought of

J. S. CRANE,

Dealer in

DRY GOODS, GROCERIES.

Dr. Hess' Stock Food produces health, flesh and milk.

Dr. Hess' Healing Powder cures galls and open wounds.

INSTANT LOUSE KILLER Kills Lice

Note:— These goods are formulated by Dr. Hess, a physician and Veterinary Surgeon.

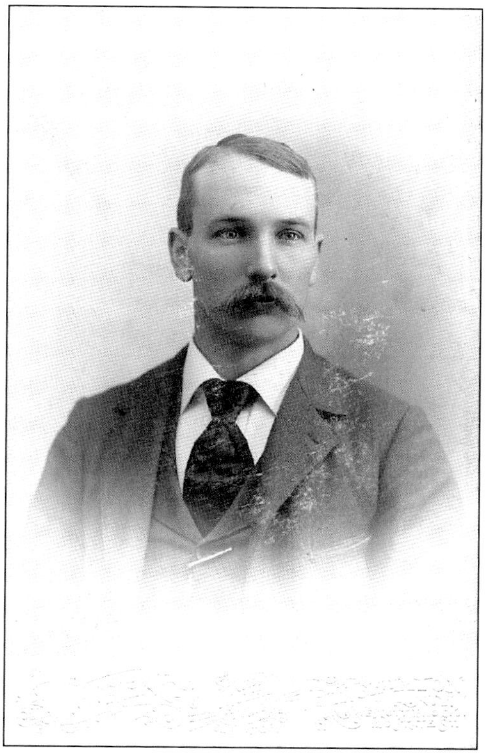

Handsome Crane owned one of the two general stores in central Vestal. Like other early settlers who believed in the importance of civic duty, Crane served as supervisor and postmaster. It was at Crane's store in 1906 that a group of citizens formed the Vestal Grange No. 1073.

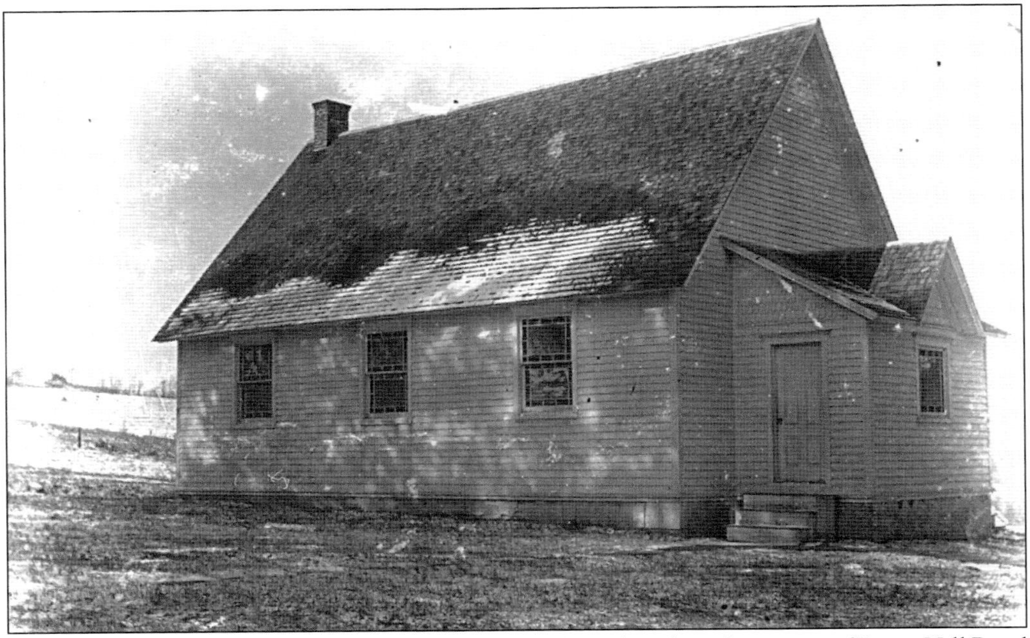

Originally established in 1897, the Reformed Methodist Church at the corner of Bunn Hill Road and Coughlin Road was known as the "Little White Church in the Pines." The church, now almost double in size, is the Bunn Hill Baptist Church.

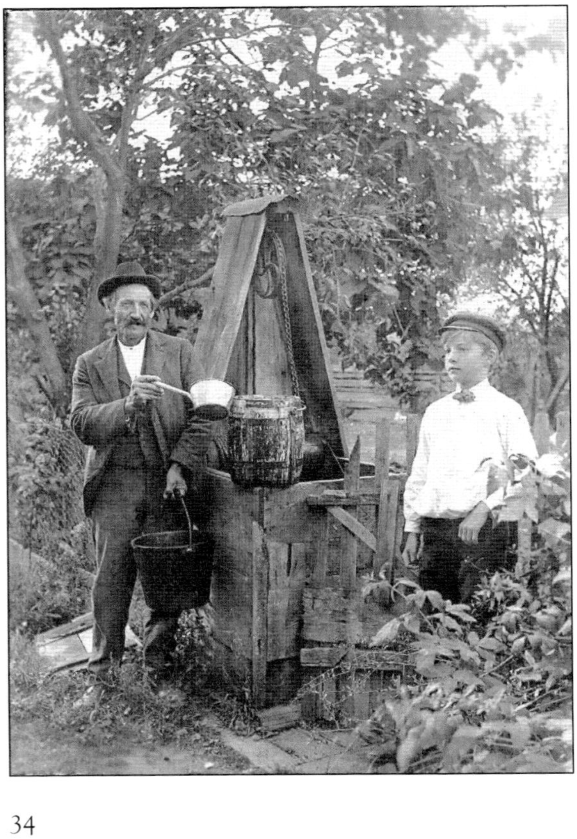

Nine-year-old Harry Clark was living with his grandfather Albert Westfall when this photograph was taken in 1905 as they fetched water from the well. Notice the simple A-frame roof protecting the pulley and stout chain used to raise and lower the small barrel. The Westfall house was located on Main Street just south of the Methodist church.

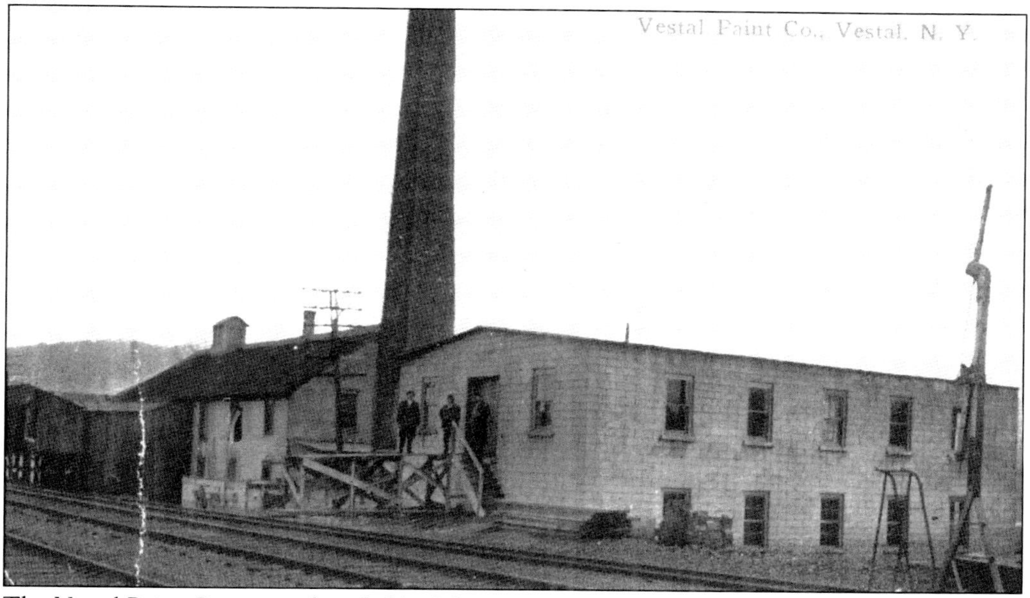

The Vestal Paint Company, founded by Jake Crane, was located along the DL&W tracks at the site of the Vestal Lumber Company. The stock certificate below certifies that John J. Weidman is the owner of two shares of Vestal Paint Company stock at the price of $5 each. The company was established about 1900 and closed soon after this stock was purchased in 1911. A safety pin manufacturer occupied the building for a short time before being disbanded, causing considerable loss to its investors.

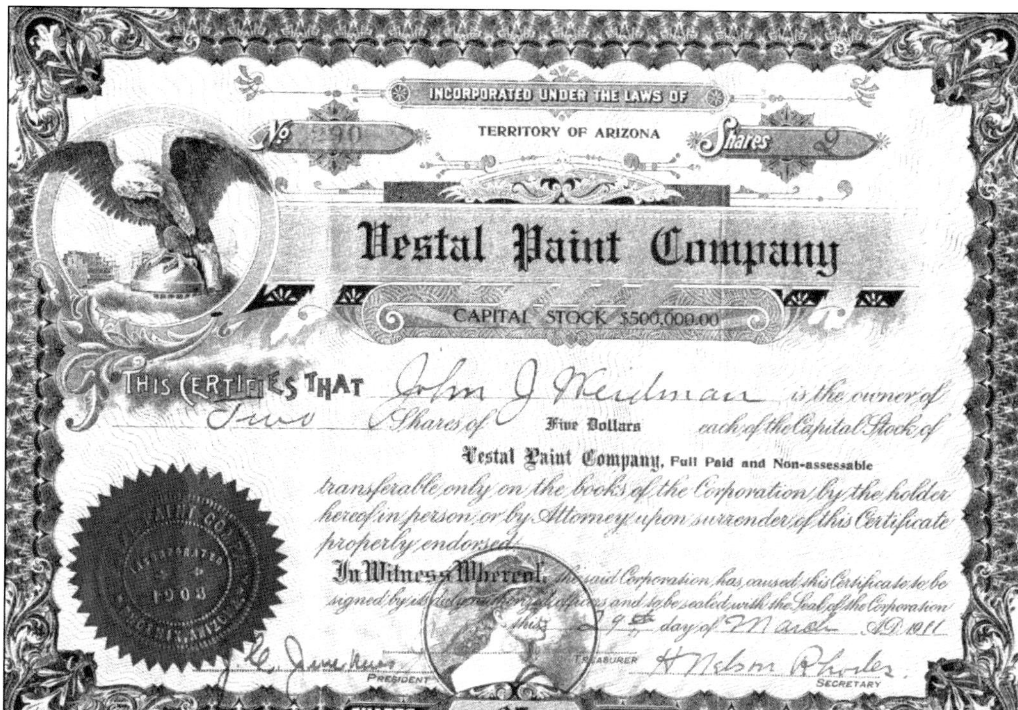

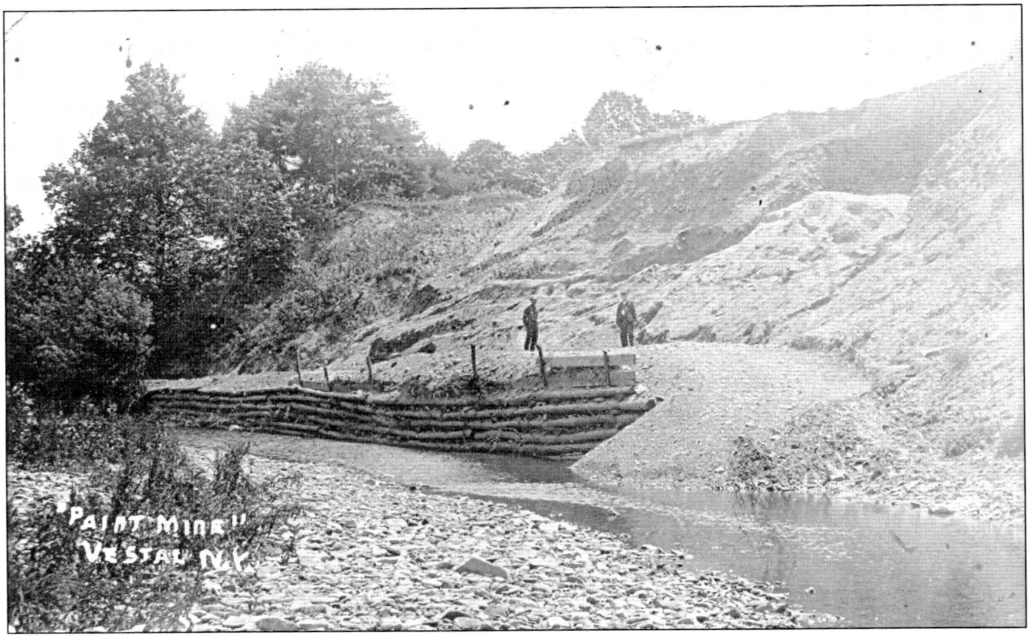

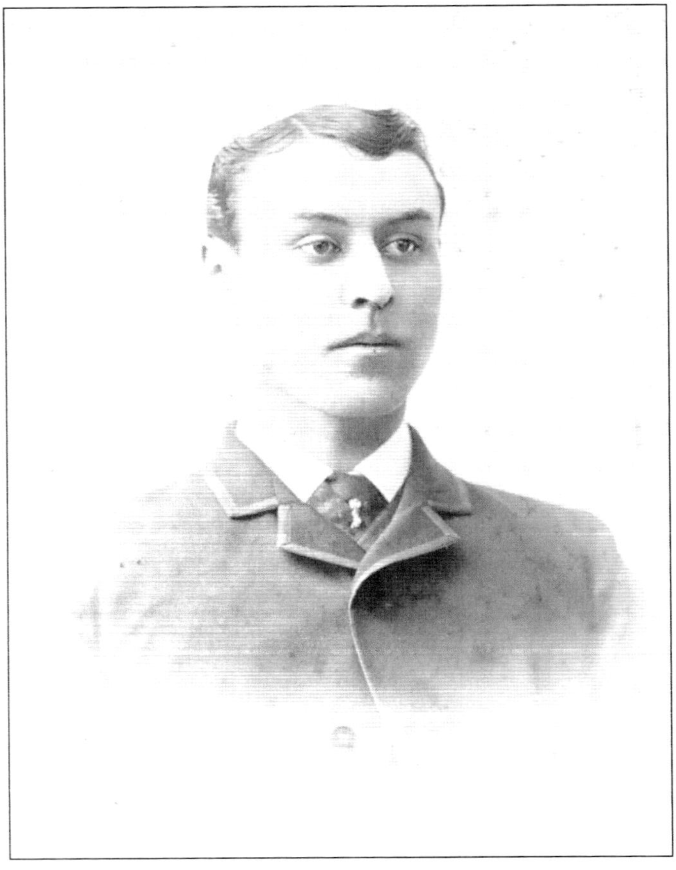

Jake Crane used clay from the Choconut Creek bank on his farm to make the paint at the Vestal Paint Company. Logs were used to shore up the hillside where the clay had been removed. Seen here is a "cartes de visite" of entrepreneur Jake Crane.

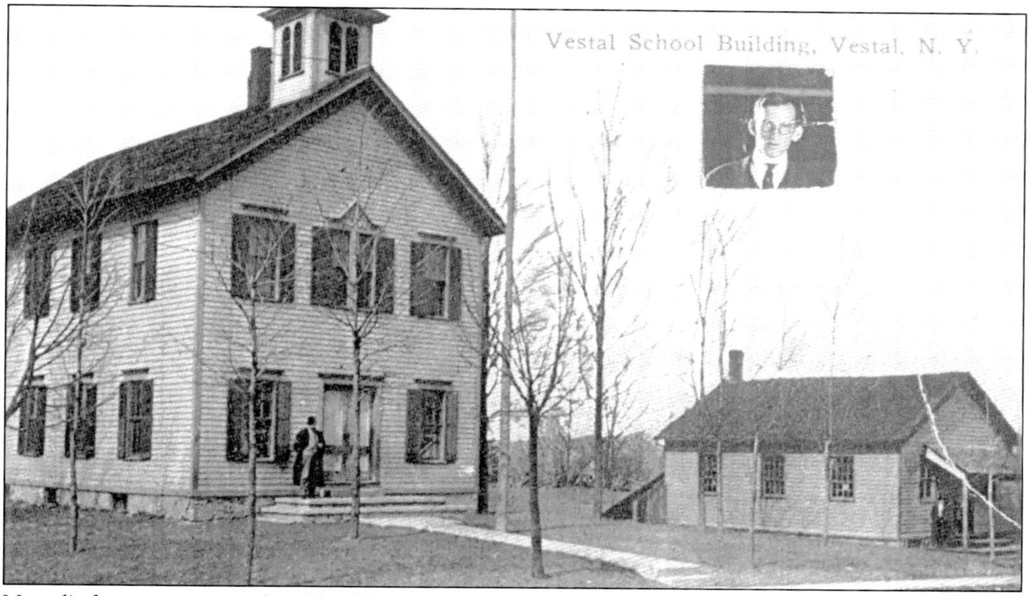

Vestal's first two-story school building on the west side of Main Street was built in 1881 by Silas Twilliger. Containing two classrooms on the first floor and a recitation room upstairs, it housed grades 1 through 9. It became a community hall in 1924 when the new Intermediate Building was finished on the east side of Main Street. Teacher Duane O. Croffut's picture is inset.

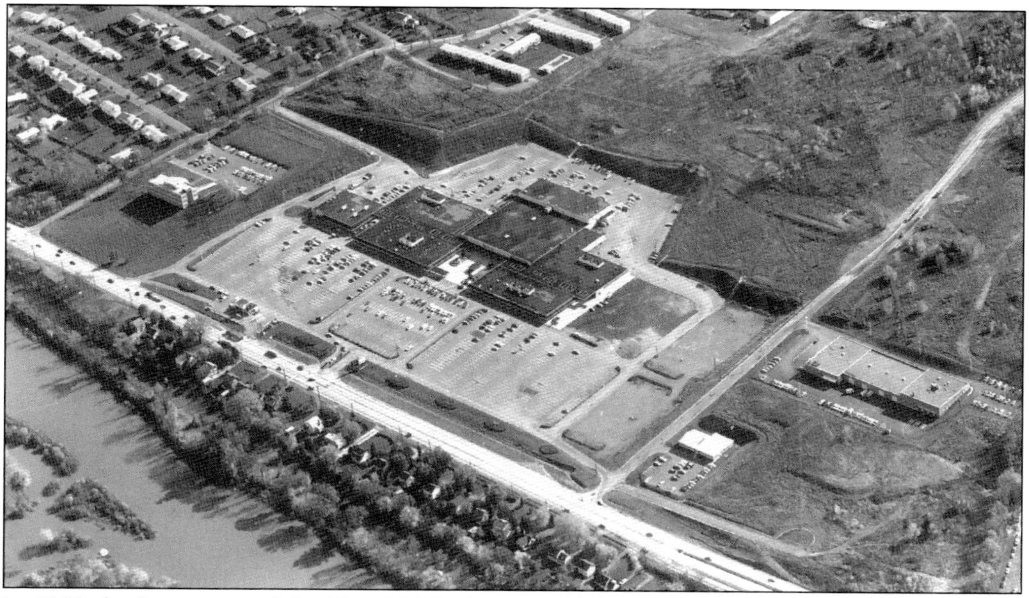

In 1957, the former site of the Vestal Hills Country Club was purchased for the construction of the Vestal Plaza. Considered large at the time, the plaza would include 20 to 30 stores and provide parking for 3,000 cars. The lines of homes between the Vestal Parkway and the Susquehanna River, known as Rivercrest, were originally built as summer homes for Binghamton residents who wanted to get out of the city. A small section of the Chenango Canal remains behind the homes.

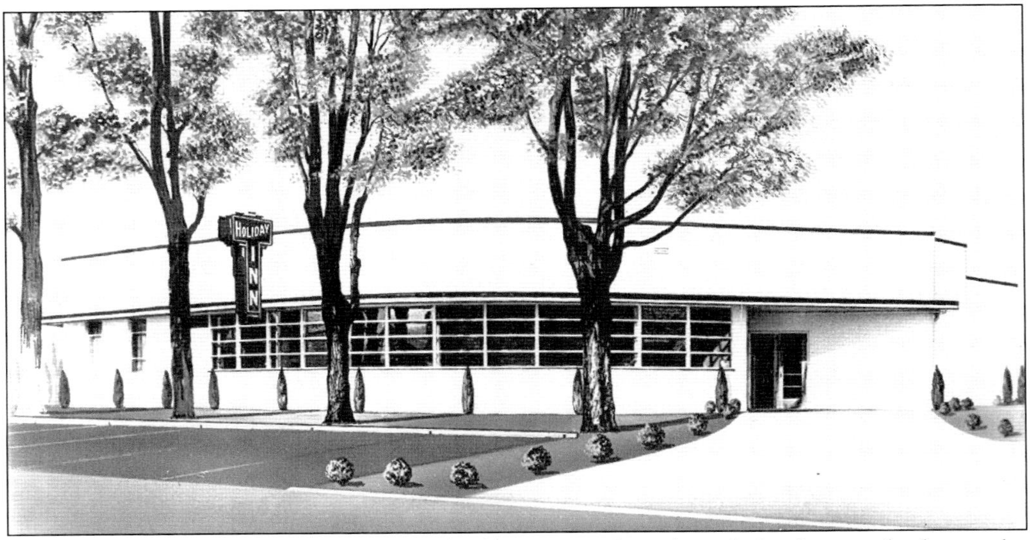

The sweeping curve of the white stucco building was reflected inside by the circular bar at the Holiday Inn on Vestal Road. Advertised as the "place with the Country Club atmosphere," it was sold in 1950 to the Vestal American Legion Post 89, which occupied it until it was demolished for the construction of the Thomas J. Watson Memorial Bridge.

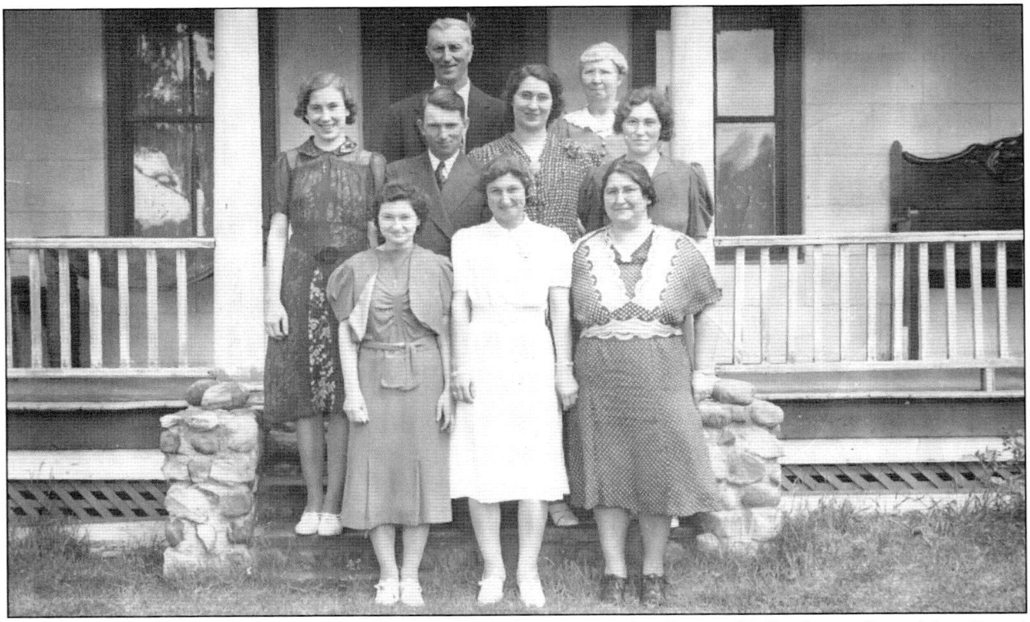

Harry and Mae Dodd owned a dairy farm at the top of the Bunn Hill where Coughlin Road meets Dodd Road. Harry cut ice from the small pond west of the house to keep the milk cold until Crowley's picked it up. Harry also sold eggs, chickens, and vegetables in Binghamton and Johnson City. All seven children helped with the milking, haying, and other chores. The children walked down Coughlin Road to the one-room Bunn Hill School No. 3, where Miss Pomeroy, a teacher from Endicott, taught a full classroom. The Dodd family stands in front of their 1890 farmhouse about 1930; they are, from left to right, (first row) Jennie, Gertrude, and Ruth; (second row) Verna, James, Mabel and Nellie; (third row) Harry and Mae.

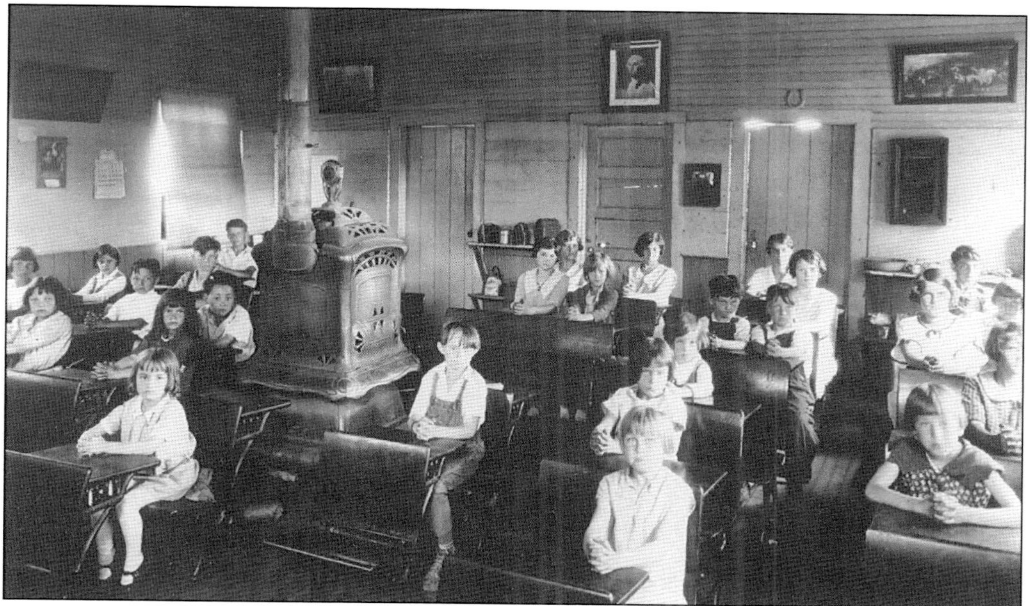

The 1932 Bunn Hill School class sits obediently with folded hands for this class picture. Pictured front to back beginning at the far left: Beverly LaMont, Evelyn Whitehead, and Donald Stanley; second row, Angie Blewer, George Swartwood, and Ralph Miller; third row, Eda Benedict and Bob Swartwood; fourth row, Beulah Stanley; fifth row, Ronald Cahill; sixth row, Betty Drum, Beatrice Benedict, Thelma Whitehead, James Rhodes, Wesley Miller, Doris Miller, and Doris Pomeroy, teacher; seventh row, Verna Dodd, Rachel Benedict, Nancy Benedict, Frances LaMont and Bert Prince, and back middle row, first seats, Jennie Dodd and Marjorie Stanley, and second seats, Hazel Miller and Gertrude Dodd.

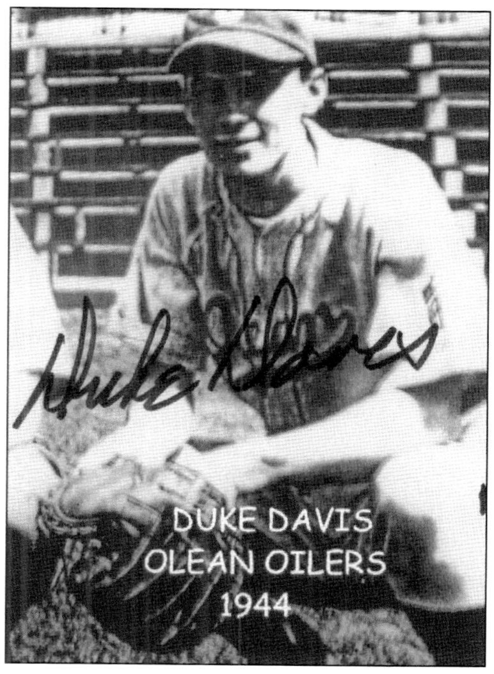

Howard "Duke" Davis started his minor-league career in 1944 as a catcher for the Brooklyn Dodgers. His .361 batting average while playing in the Industrial League got him signed as the starting catcher for the Olean Oilers. By 1945, Davis was playing for the Dodgers' Thomasville Tommies in the Carolina League where he played against the fabled Durham Bulls. Duke was inducted into the New York State Section IV Hall of Fame.

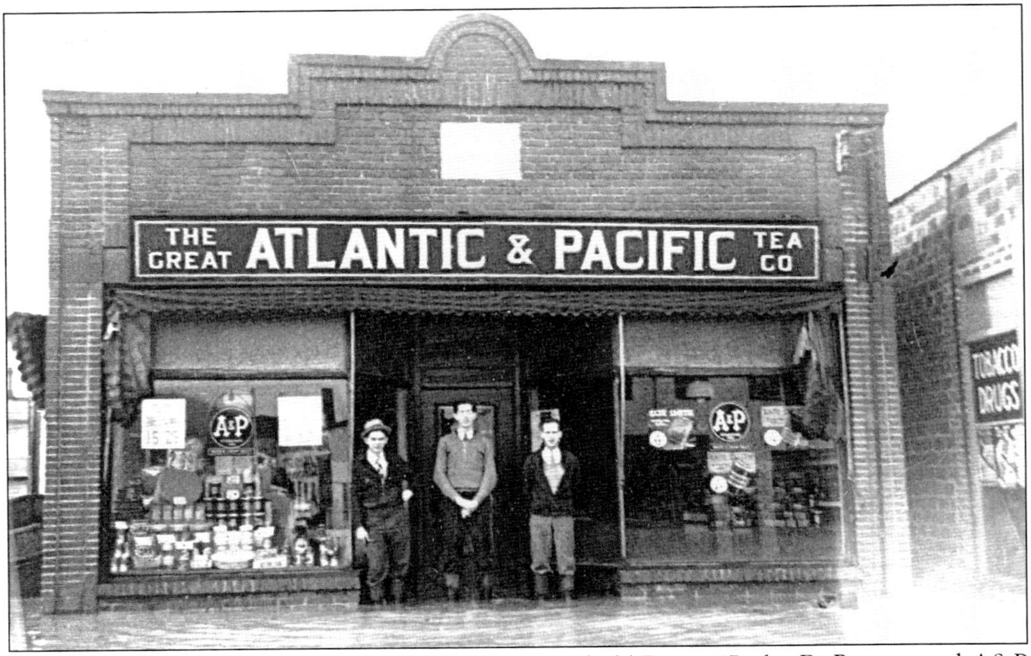

Located at the northwest corner of Main Street and old Route 17, the DuBois-owned A&P store is seen here during the 1936 flood. These stores were the forerunners of the popular A&P grocery stores.

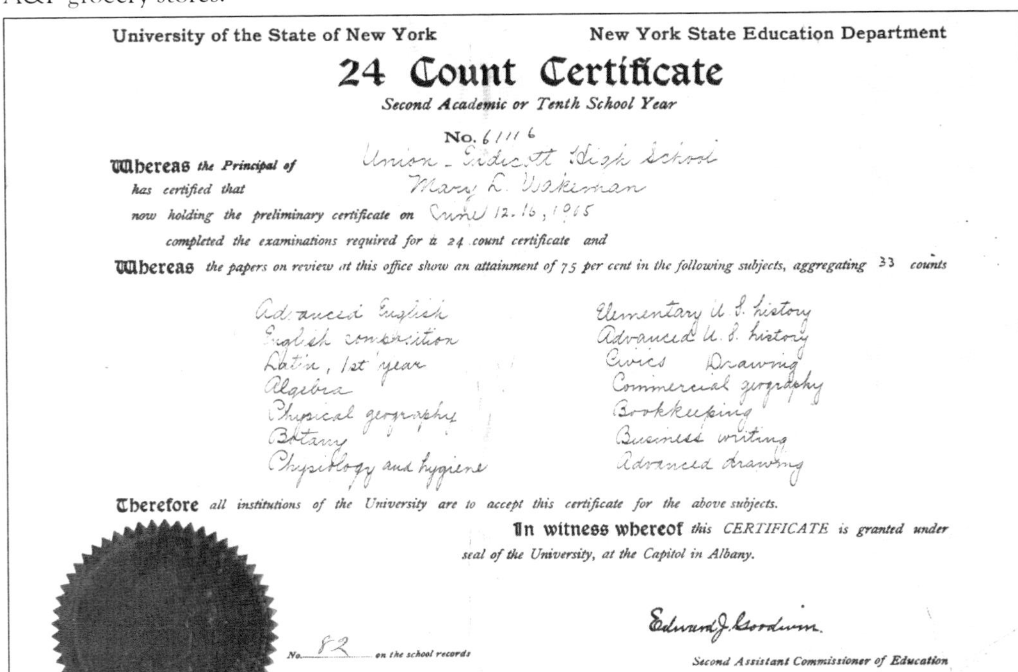

University of the State of New York **New York State Education Department**

24 Count Certificate

Second Academic or Tenth School Year

No. 61116

Whereas *the Principal of* Union - Endicott High School *has certified that* Mary L. Wakeman *now holding the preliminary certificate on* June 12. 16, 1905 *completed the examinations required for a* 24 *count certificate and*

Whereas *the papers on review at this office show an attainment of* 75 *per cent in the following subjects, aggregating* 33 *counts*

Advanced English
English composition
Latin, 1st year
Algebra
Physical geography
Botany
Physiology and hygiene
Elementary U. S. history
Advanced U. S. history
Civics Drawing
Commercial geography
Bookkeeping
Business writing
Advanced drawing

Therefore *all institutions of the University are to accept this certificate for the above subjects.*

In witness whereof *this CERTIFICATE is granted under seal of the University, at the Capitol in Albany.*

No. 82 *on the school records*

Edward J. Goodwin
Second Assistant Commissioner of Education

Vestal students attended the Union-Endicott High School for grades 9 through 12 until 1939, when the Vestal Central High School was built. Mary L. Wakeman's "24 Count Certificate," dated June 1905, lists the courses she had completed during her sophomore year.

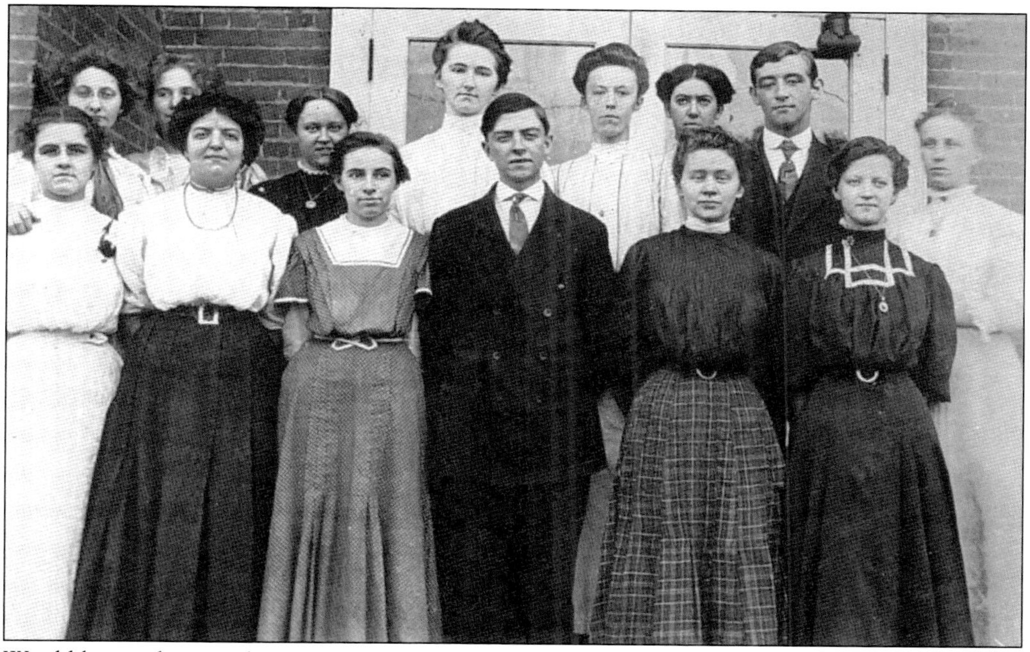

Would-be teachers in the Vestal districts attended training at the Union-Endicott High School. Here 14 new teachers attend the 1907–1908 training class. Susie Gunglach is the fifth from the left in the second row.

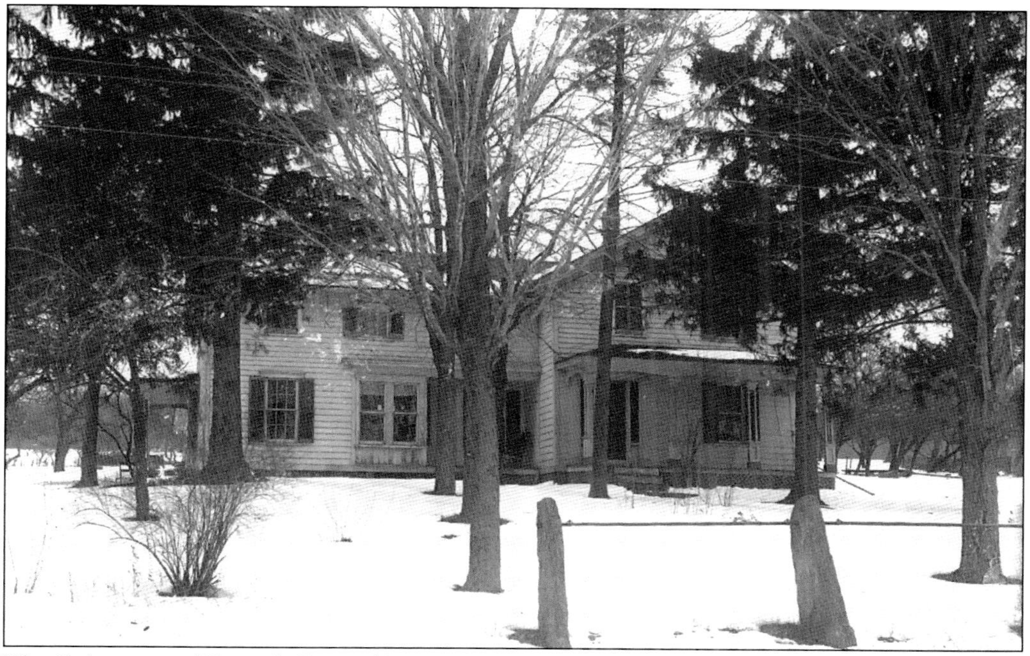

The Coleman and Daniels Funeral Home on Main Street in Vestal was once the home of John DuBois, and later Frank and Lena DuBois Harrington. The left wing was removed when the building was owned by the Moat Funeral Home. The stately Colonial home has weathered the years well.

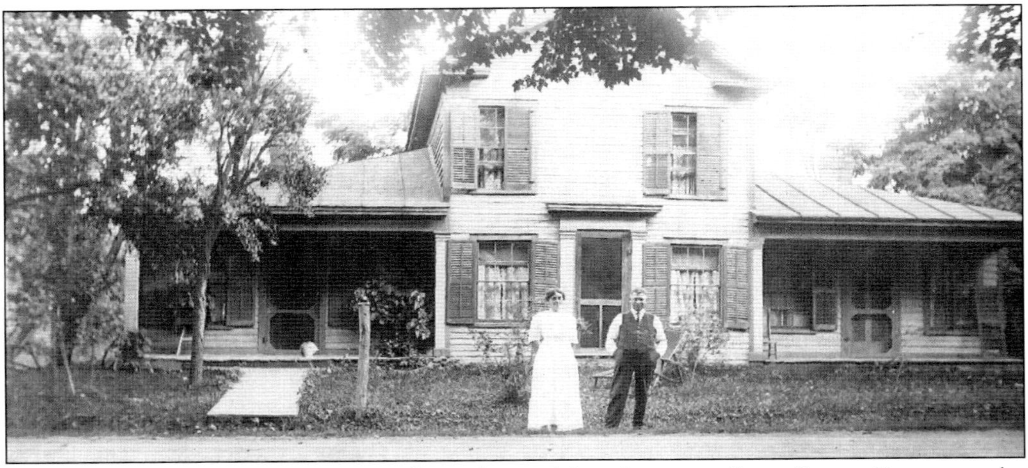

Jacob and Sophia Layton stand proudly in front of their home on Front Street. Known as the "Old Layton Homestead," it had an unusual design with two side wings and three front entrances, all topped with a metal roof. For a time, there was a barbershop in the home.

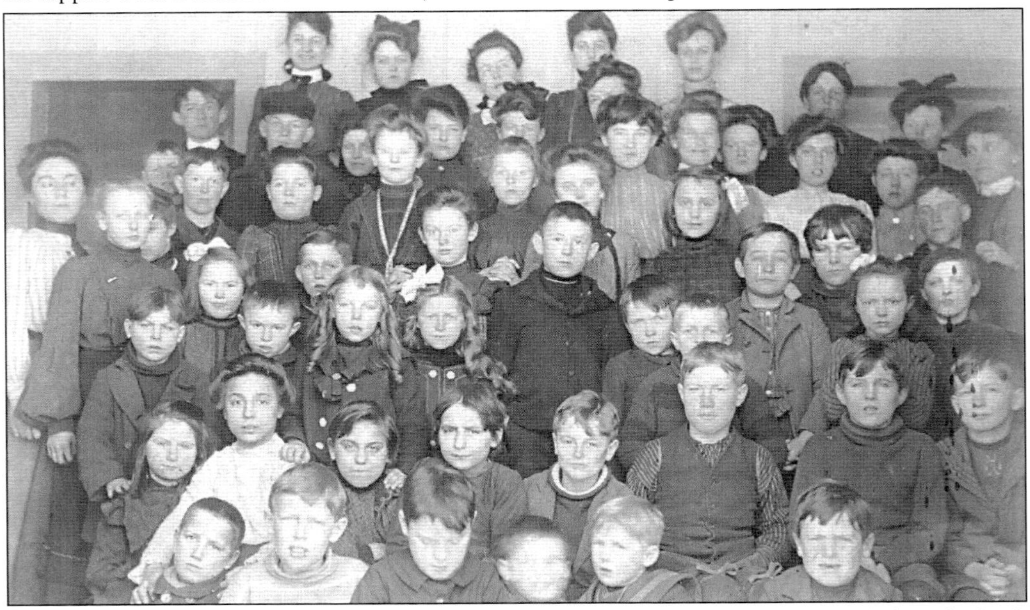

The names of the students in this 1903–1904 Vestal School class were neatly penciled on the back of the photograph. They are, from left to right, (first row) Ralph Riddle, Arthur White, Lansing Rounds, unidentified, Robert DuBois, and Theodore Rounds; (second row) ? Carrig, Victoria Gimmie, Lucy Gimmie, Rose Gimmie, Howard Leighton, Merritt Guiles, Clayton DuBois, and Harry Clark; (third row) Tony Gimmie, ? Carrig, Hazel White, Irene Weston, Charles Campbell, ? Holden, unidentified, and Charley Riley; (fourth row) Alice Guiles, unidentified, Mable Rounds, ? Carrig, Jesse Weston, Otis Potts, and Almond Weston; (fifth row) Virginia Niemire, Ethel Brady, Irving Guiles, Hazel Pierce, Agnes Estes, Grace Mersereau, Rose Weston, and Ad Crane; (sixth row) Clarence Weston, Clay Holden, Ella Riley, Susie Pierce, Mamie Carrig, Susie Gunglach, Agnes Carrig, Grace Castle, Martha Estes, Florence Fairbanks, Irene Pierce, and Jane Goodnough, primary teacher; (seventh row) James Carrig, Louise Crane, Ethel Kellum, Nina Pierson, Florence Crane, Jim Riley, Harriet Estes, and Minnette Pierson.

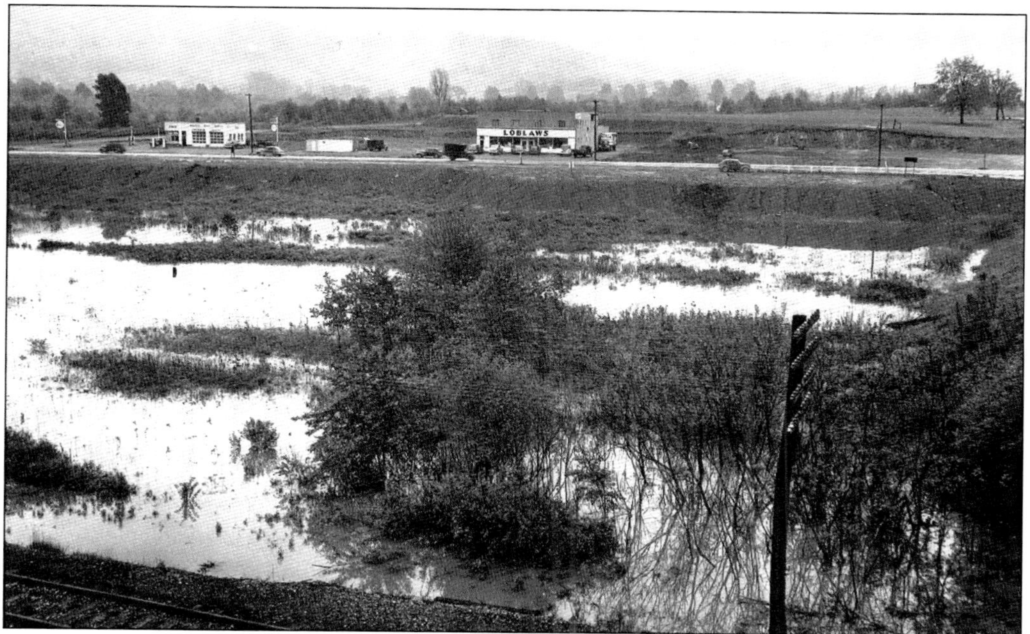

The photographer stood on the DL&W tracks to take this May 1948 photograph of the floodwaters. More interesting than the water is the lack of buildings along two-lane Route 17. The gas station at the left is on the corner of Clayton Avenue. Both sides of the highway and the land behind these two lone businesses would be filled within 10 years.

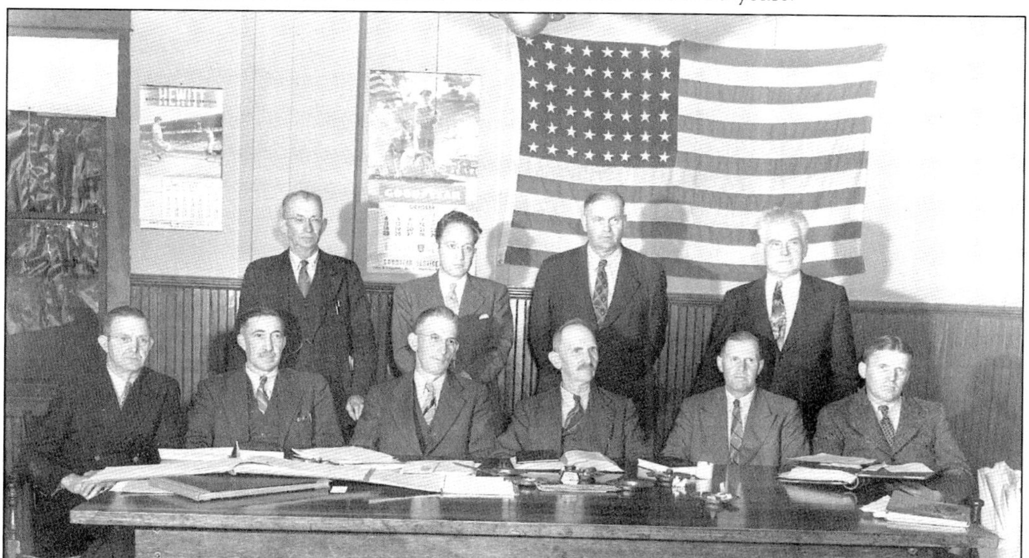

The Town of Vestal officials shown here in 1942 are, from left to right, (seated, first row) justice of the peace W. Edward Bennett, George P. Foster, supervisor Leland L. Jones, justice of the peace Edward J. Zimmer, Arthur W. Plough, and town clerk Lester O. Kretschmar; (second row, standing) welfare officer Dean J. Denmon, town attorney Emory Resseguie, highway superintendent Earl Webster, and water superintendent Leon Gibbs. Jones served as town supervisor from 1933 to 1962.

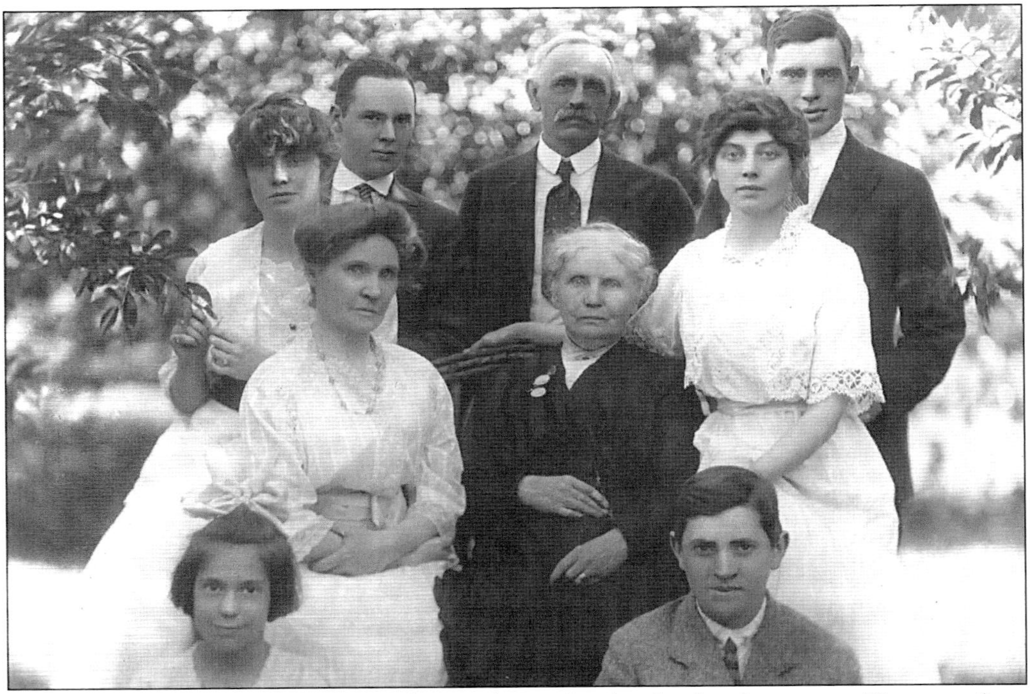

Three generations of the Rounds gather in the garden for this family portrait. They are, from left to right, (first row) Hilah Rounds and Robert Rounds; (second row) Susie Knapp Rounds, grandmother Annie Todd Knapp, and Anna Rounds; (third row) Mabel Rounds, Lancing Rounds, Fayette Rounds, and Theodore Rounds.

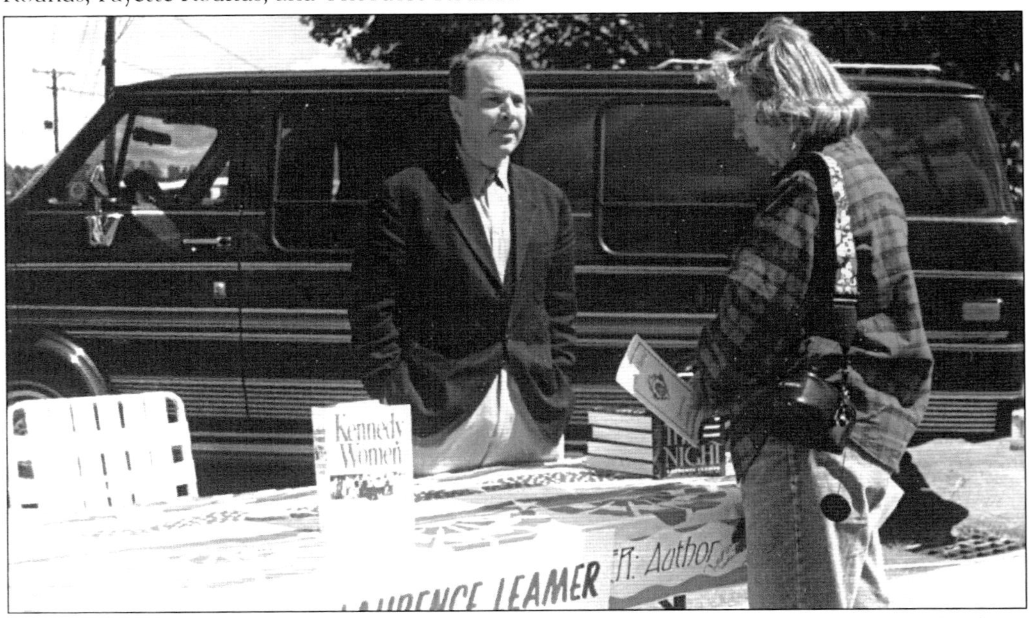

Author Laurence Leamer, a graduate of Vestal High School's class of 1959, autographs books at Vestal's 175th anniversary celebration. Leamer is the author of books about the Kennedy family, the Reagans, and other well-known celebrities.

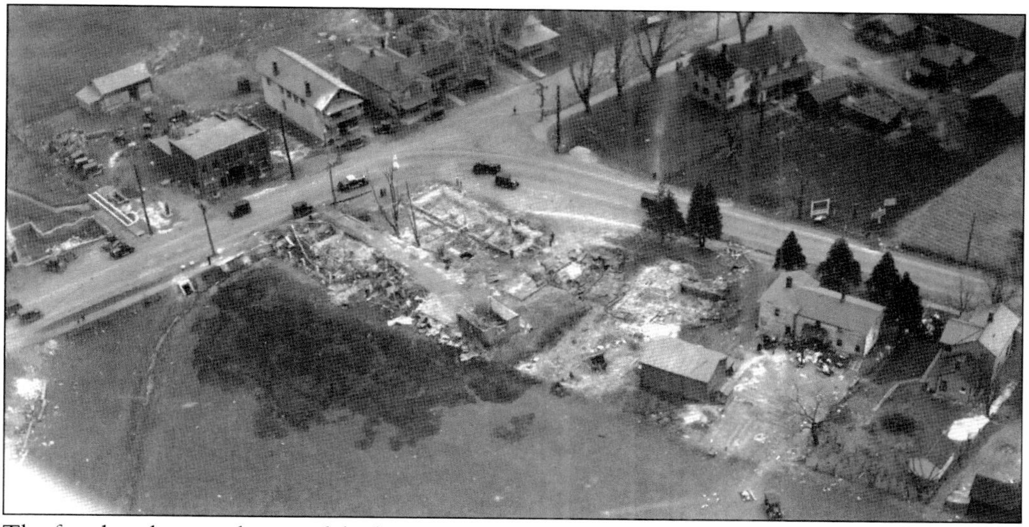

The fire that destroyed most of the business section of Vestal in 1927 was the driving force in the establishment of a municipal water supply soon after.

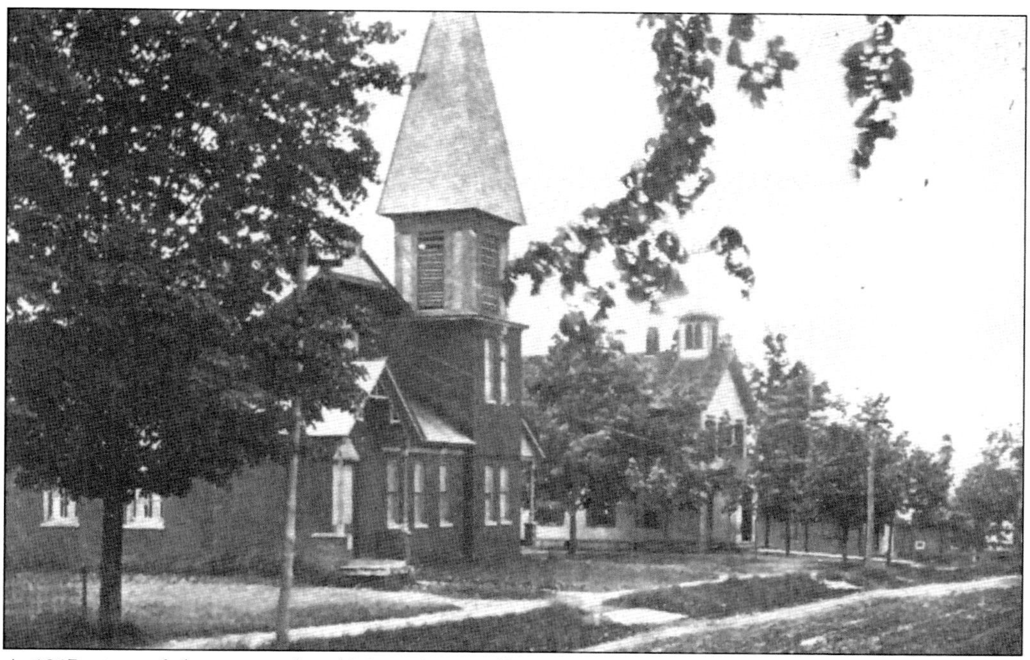

A 1917 view of the west side of Main Street illustrates the proximity of the Methodist church and Schoolhouse No. 2. Both roadway and walking path were compacted dirt until about 1930, when the road was paved.

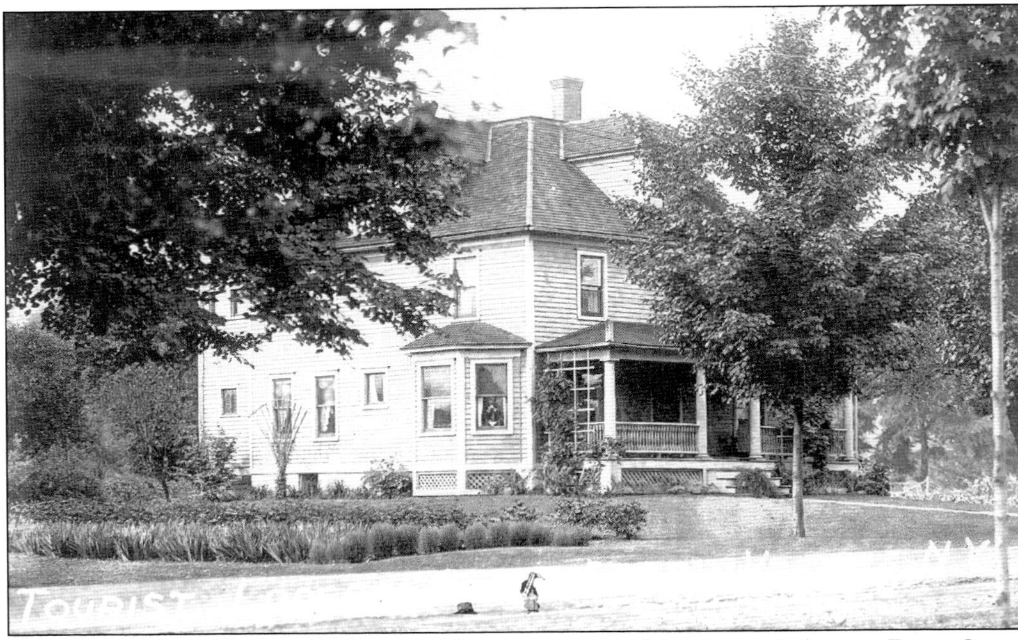

George Diehl and his wife, Ila, owned and operated this tourist lodge on Front Street during the 1920s. George was a machinist in a tabulator factory, perhaps employed by the Computer-Tabulating-Recording Company in Endicott, the company that became IBM. Ila and George had three daughters, Kathryn, Jane and Lois.

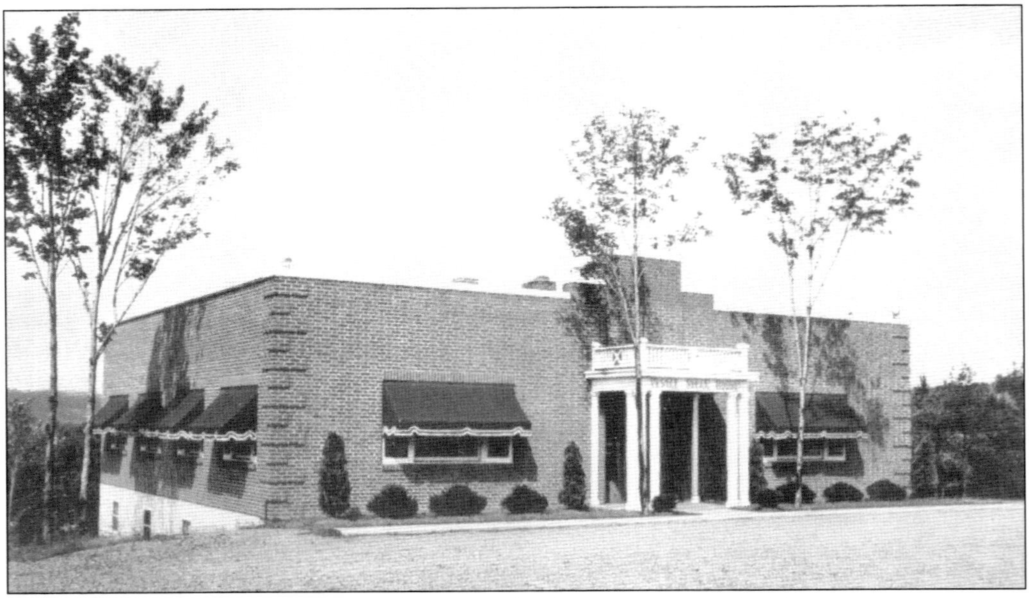

The Vestal Steak House, owned and operated by Morris and Rosalind Protage, was a popular restaurant on the Vestal Parkway for over 50 years. To residents, former residents, and visitors alike, the name evokes an image of a huge bull atop a large porte cochere. In the early 1950s, the restaurant, minus the bull, was among the first businesses on the Vestal Parkway.

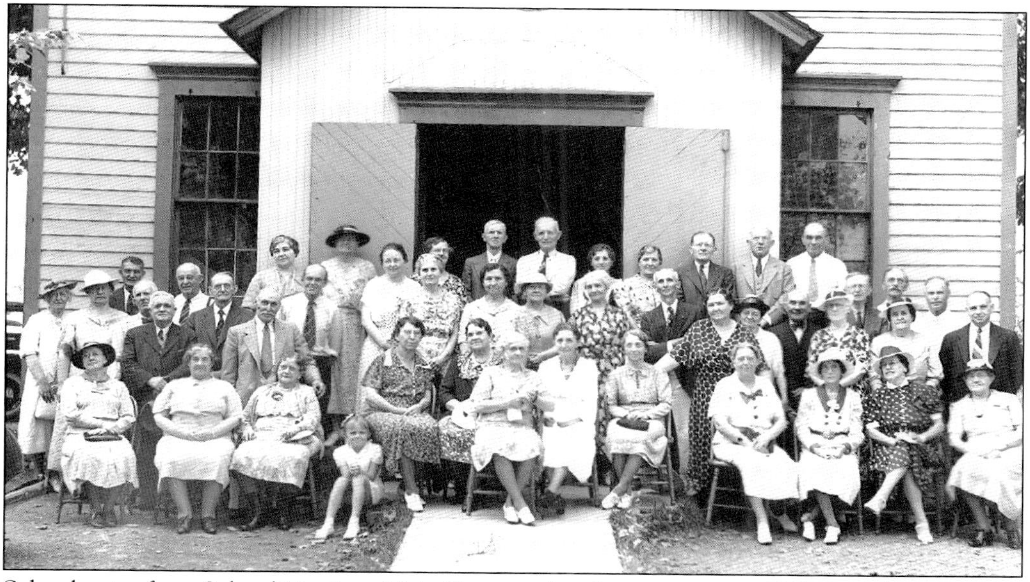

Schoolmates from School No. 2 on Main Street gather for a reunion in 1937. Seen here are (first row) Mrs. Elmer Casler, Anna Peabody, Mrs. J. B. Crane, Susie LaGrange Bunn, Bessie Potter, Vesta Mersereau, Freddie Zimmer, Helen Clark, Bertha Oliver, Ellen Peck, Hattie Leighton, and Mimmie Gillespie; (second row) Anna Wild, Mrs. George Wilkinson, George Wilkinson, Sam Wilkinson, Lee Winans, Jake Crane, Len Par, Mabel White, Delight Luce, Doris Baty, Permelia Bunn, John Simmons, Nellie Layton Westfall, Mrs. John Simmons, Albert Casler, May Peabody, Mary Eldridge Stevens, and Adelbert LaGrange; (third row) Charles Bunn, Dwight Birdsall, Mrs. Len Park, Mrs. Dwight Birdsall, Mrs. Adelbert LaGrange, Mrs. John Rounds, Mrs. Ray Garrison, Mrs. Fay Garrison, Ray Garrison, Fay Garrison, Elmer Casler, Frank Peabody, Del Zimmer, and Burt Leighton.

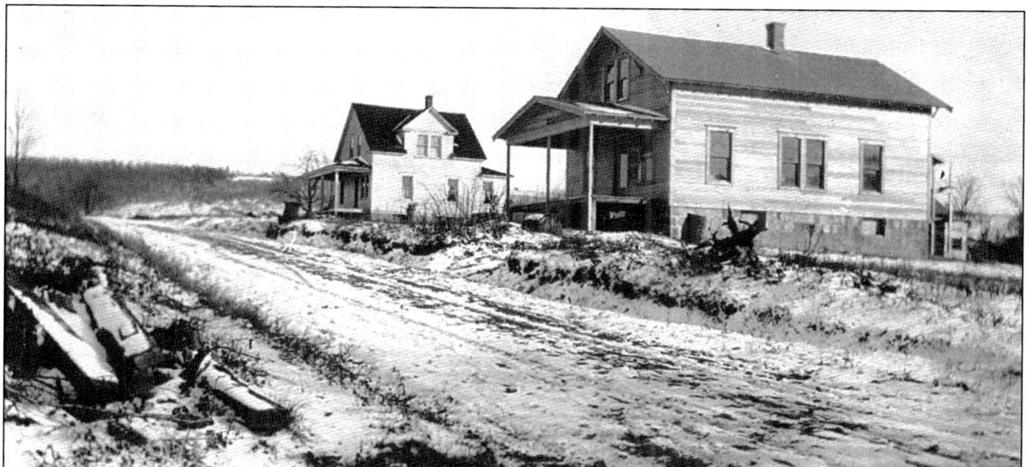

Looking east along the south side of LaGrange Street, these two houses were among the earliest built on the street. The Hiram Knapp house on the left was built in 1915 and is still in the Knapp family. The newly constructed house on the right dates from about 1930. Most of the side streets would remain unpaved for a time. The street is named for the LaGrange farm beyond these houses at the eastern end of the road.

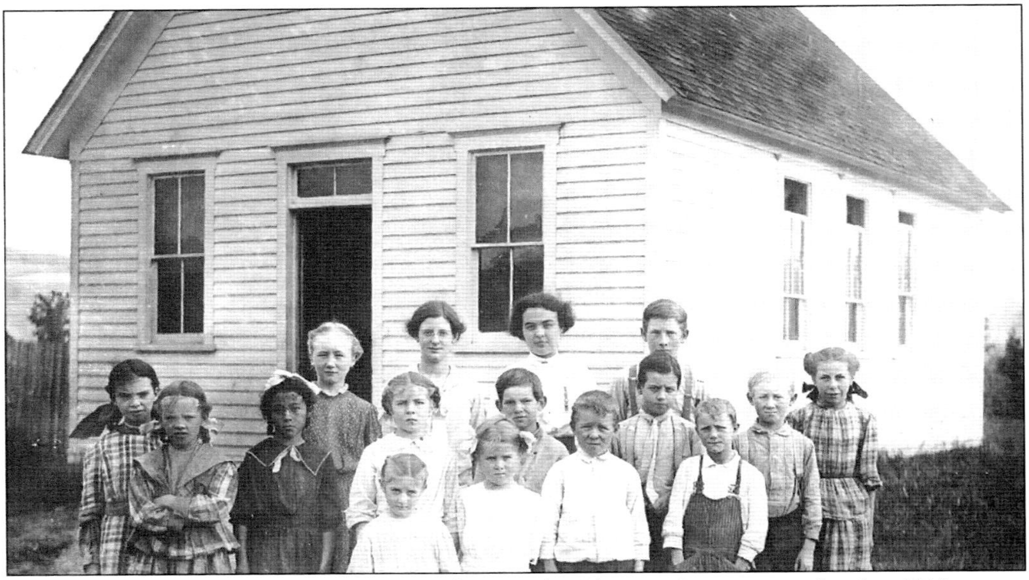

Another school year begins, and these students at the Glenwood one-room school in 1913 appear bored with the routine. School No. 14 was located on the east side of Glenwood Road near the intersection with Grippen Hill Road.

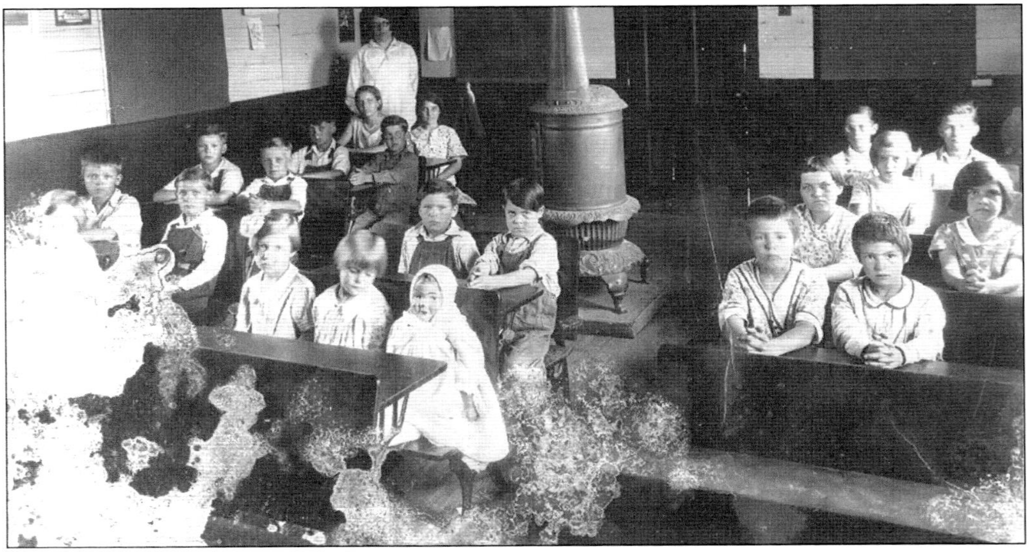

The small school at the intersection of Bunn Hill and Sheedy Roads was East Hill School No. 8. Consolidation of the 16 Vestal school districts in 1936 eliminated the need for these one-room schools. No longer needed, East Hill School was purchased and converted to a home. Students attending East Hill in 1932 sat quietly at bench-style desks. Mary Parker was the teacher standing at the rear of the room. The students on the left side are, from left to right, (first row) Virginia Lewis (who is partially obscured), Betty Bartlow, Louise Cummings, and Betty's doll; (second row) Francis Carman, Arthur Warrick, Douglas Jump, and Thomas Nesmith; (third row) Dick Langstaff and Lindsey Bartlow; (fourth row) Jack Bartlow and Norman Nesmith; (fifth row) Florence Warrick and Doris Nesmith. On the right side, in rows one through four, are Mabel Carman, Letha Carman, Anna Warrick, Jean Nesmith, Jane Lewis, Robert Drum, and John Warrick.

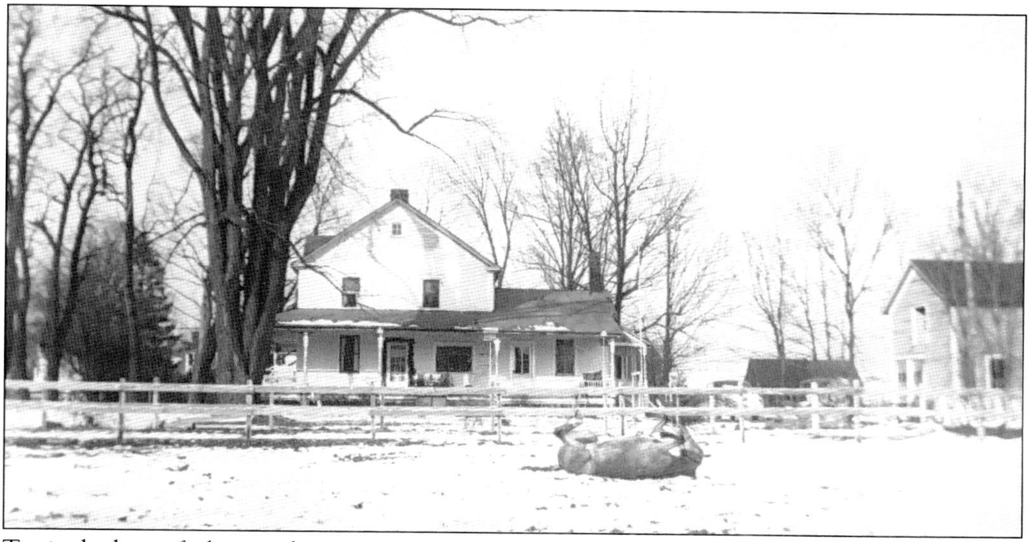

Tessie the horse frolics on the snow-covered pasture next to the home of Lee and Lela LaGrange DuBois. Our Lady of Sorrows School building now occupies the property on Main Street where the home and farm were located. Lee was a descendant of Revolutionary War veteran Mathias DuBois, one of Vestal's earliest settlers.

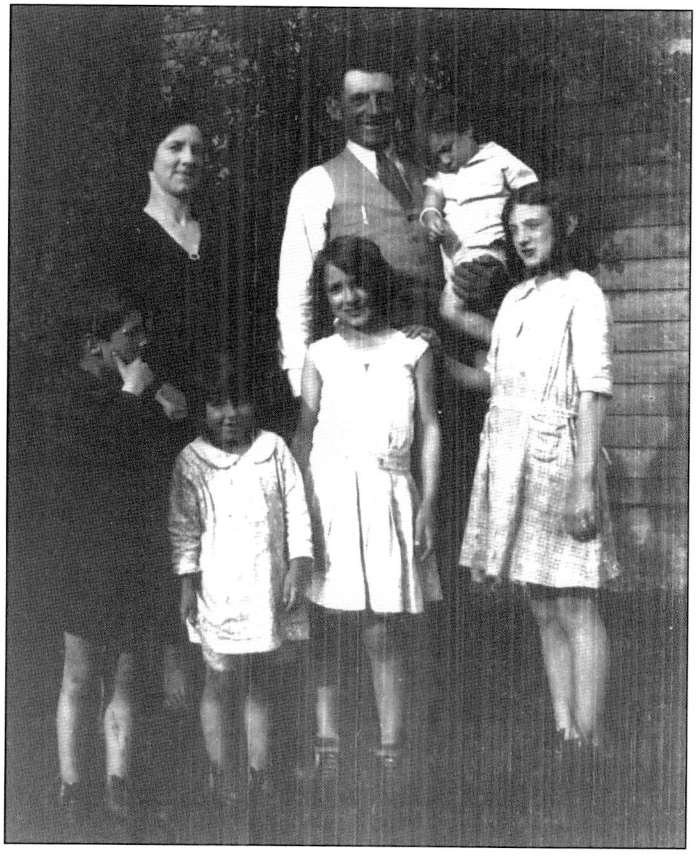

Italian immigrant Peter Vallese arrived in the United States in 1909 with his wife, Hazel, and daughter Cora. They joined the long list of owners of the former John S. LaGrange farm. The Vallese family, from left to right, includes (first row) Harold, Pauline, Florence, and Cora; (second row) Hazel and Peter Vallese holding son Peter.

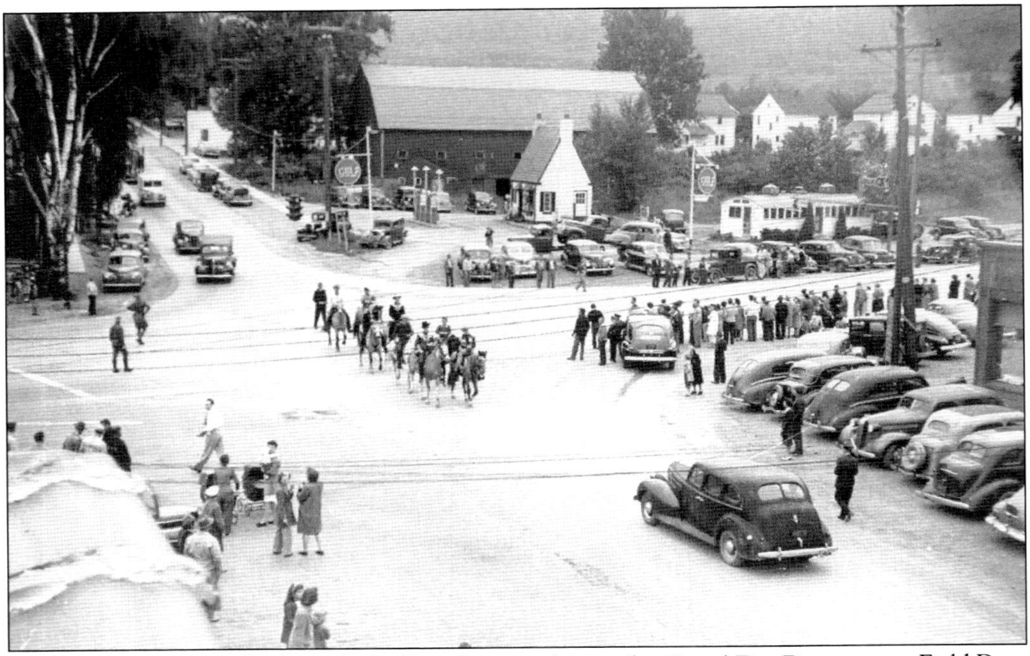

Bands and riders parade through the Five Corners during the Vestal Fire Department Field Days in 1950. Of note is the large Kimball barn on South Main Street, the quaint Gulf gas station on the corner, and the popular Vestal Diner to the right of the Gulf station. The reconfiguration of this corner in 1967 would eliminate these buildings.

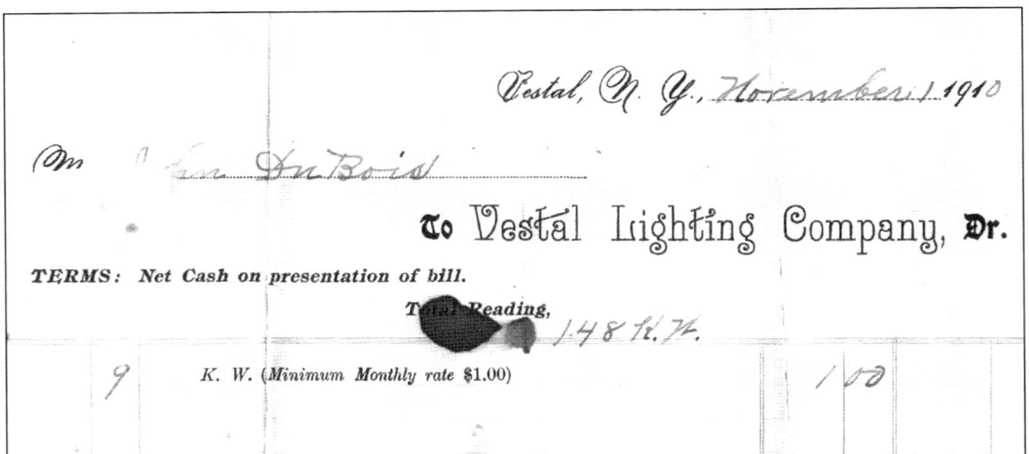

Vestal, N. Y., November 1 1910

M [illegible] DuBois

To Vestal Lighting Company, Dr.

TERMS: Net Cash on presentation of bill.

Total Reading, 148 K.W.

9 K. W. (*Minimum Monthly rate* $1.00) 1 00

Received Payment, Nov 8th 10

[illegible] *Treas.*

Vestal resident John DuBois used 148 kilowatt hours of electricity during the month of October in 1910 at a cost of $1, the minimum rate at the time. How times have changed.

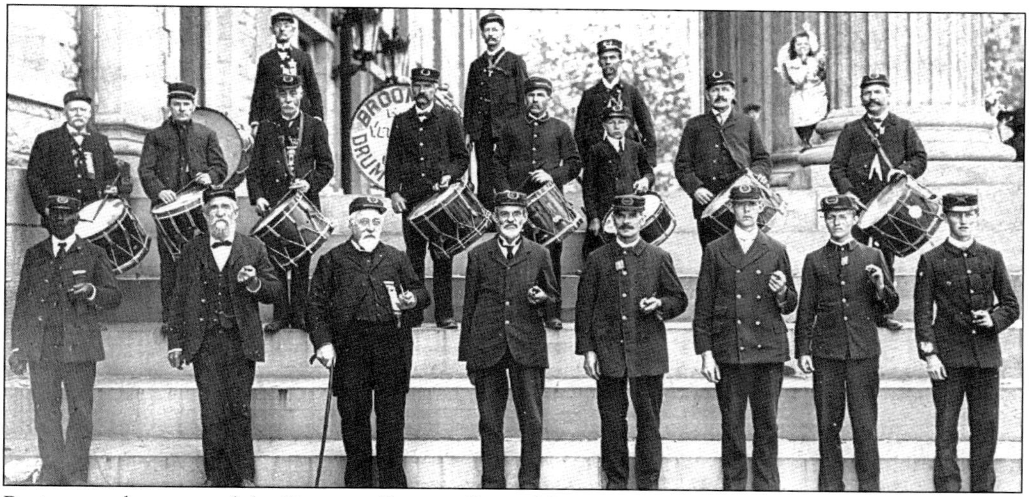

Posing on the steps of the Broome County Court House in 1903 is the 19-man Broome County Veterans' Fife and Drum Corps. The gentleman in the first row, far left is Christopher "Kip" Smith, a veteran having served in Company B of the 26th New York Colored Troops. The Smiths, Bartons, Purvises, and other African American families owned farms in an area called Grand View, at the top of Houghtaling Road, now African Road.

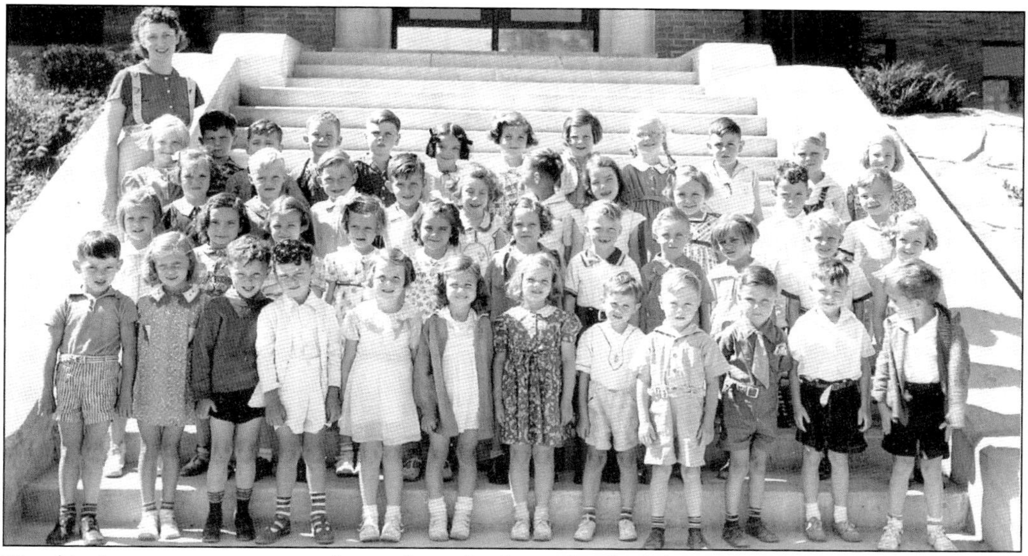

Two kindergarten rooms were located on the lower level of the new Vestal High School built in 1939. This is the first kindergarten class. They are, from left to right, (first row) David Hildebrandt, Ruth Pyluck, unidentified, Rudolph Vallese, Audrey Hinrichsen, June Fisher, Mary Jane Conklin, Blaine Ellis, Donald Ackley, Ralph Stephens, George Gilg, and Clyde Thompson; (second row) Mary Summers, Jean Denmon, Jane Harned, Marilyn Noyes, Delores Yoder, Ilene Beam, Roger McManus, Roger Wick, Rose Barnett, Richard Hoyt, and Gloria Kneen; (third row) Beverly Vandermark, Keith Willis, Kenneth Bidwell, Keith Terry, Myrna Youmans, Richard Hill, Eleanor Nelson, Sarah Hoadley, Rolland Vallese, and Lawrence Brearley; (fourth row) Sally Snyder, Robert Maas, Donald Middleton, Albert Slottje, Richard Hunsinger, Louise Avis, Jean Anderson, Martha Lisenby, Marion George, Herbert Carter, Neil Robinson, and Mavis Cheney. The teacher was Maude Glann.

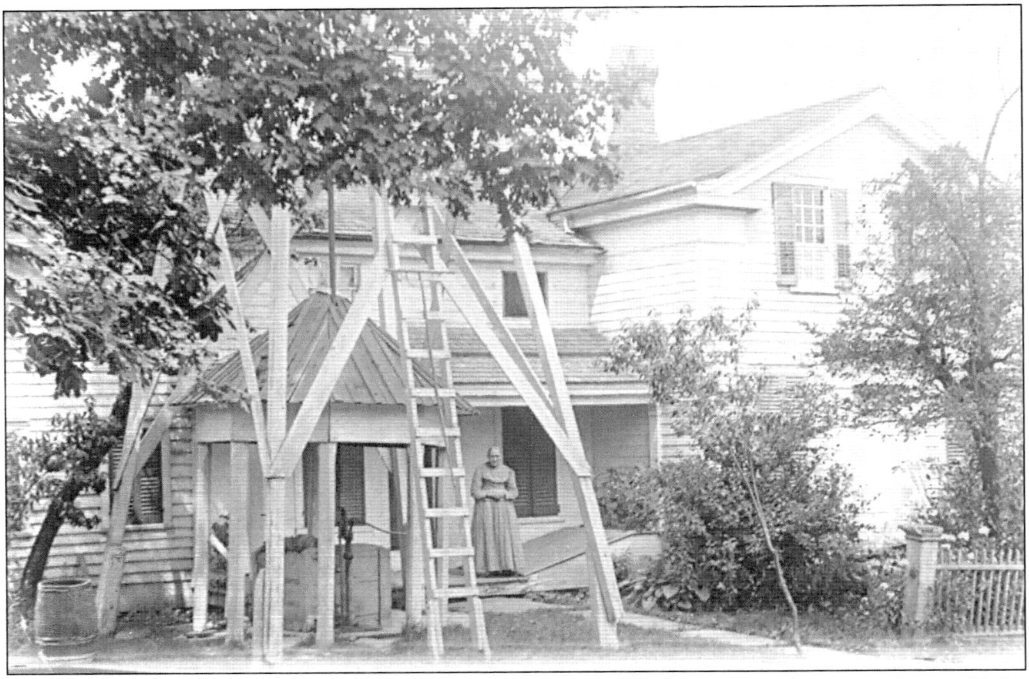

It appears that an elaborate structure was constructed to hold up the oak tree in front of Jake Crane's house. Actually a closer look reveals the structure is a windmill over the well. The house was located on Main Street across from the intersection of Hazel Drive.

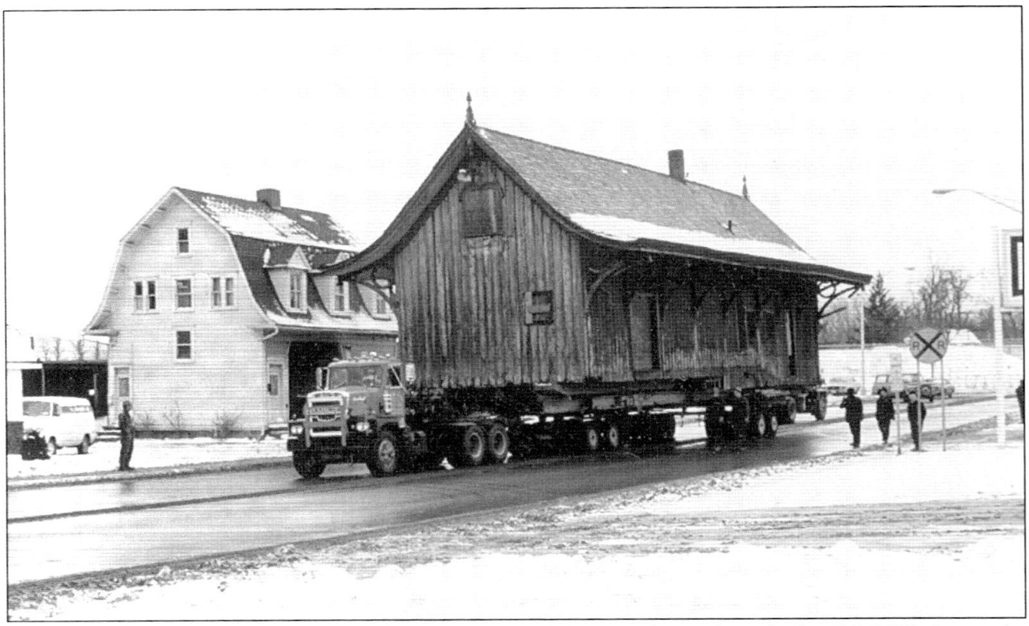

Abandoned and rapidly deteriorating, the Town of Vestal purchased the DL&W depot for use as the town museum. In 1972, the depot was transported to the current location and renovations began. In 1976, the town turned over the operation of the new museum to the Vestal Historical Society.

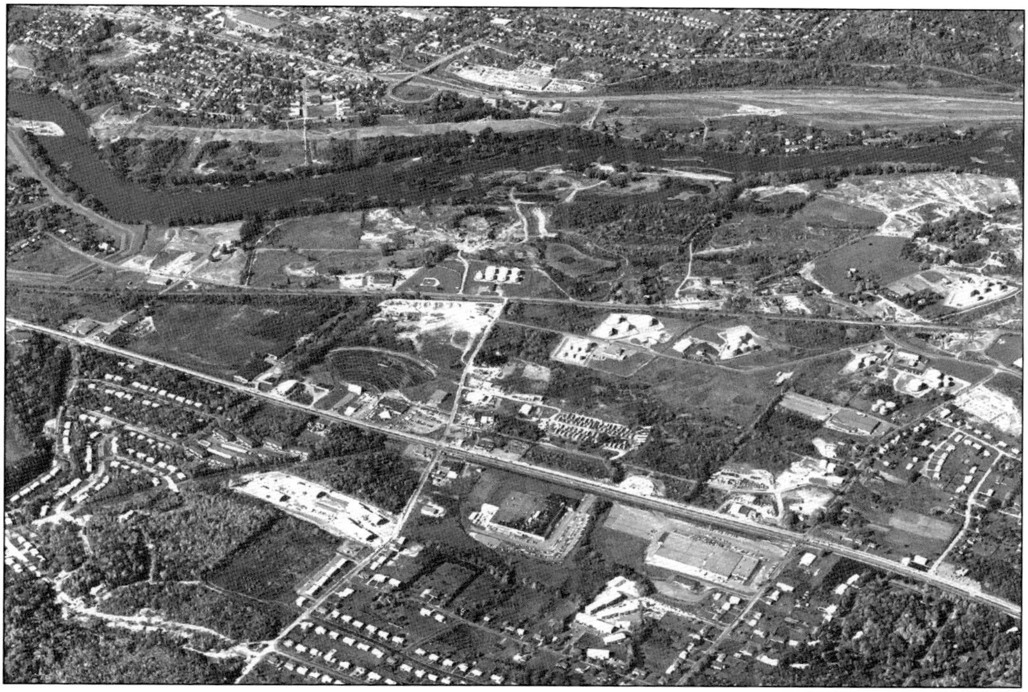

In this aerial photograph of the Vestal Parkway from 1966, the V-Drive In is left of the center. The former outdoor theater is now the Town Square Mall. (Courtesy of Ed Aswad.)

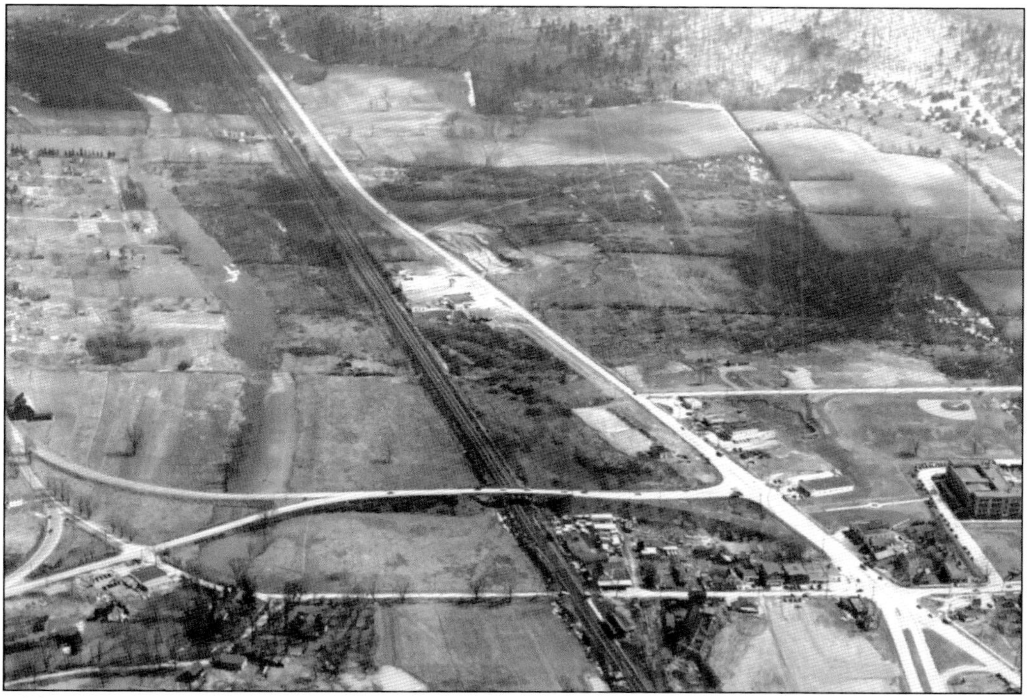

Old Route 17, now the Vestal Parkway, slices eastward through the countryside. In a few short years, the property values would increase as businesses flourished. (Courtesy of Ed Aswad.)

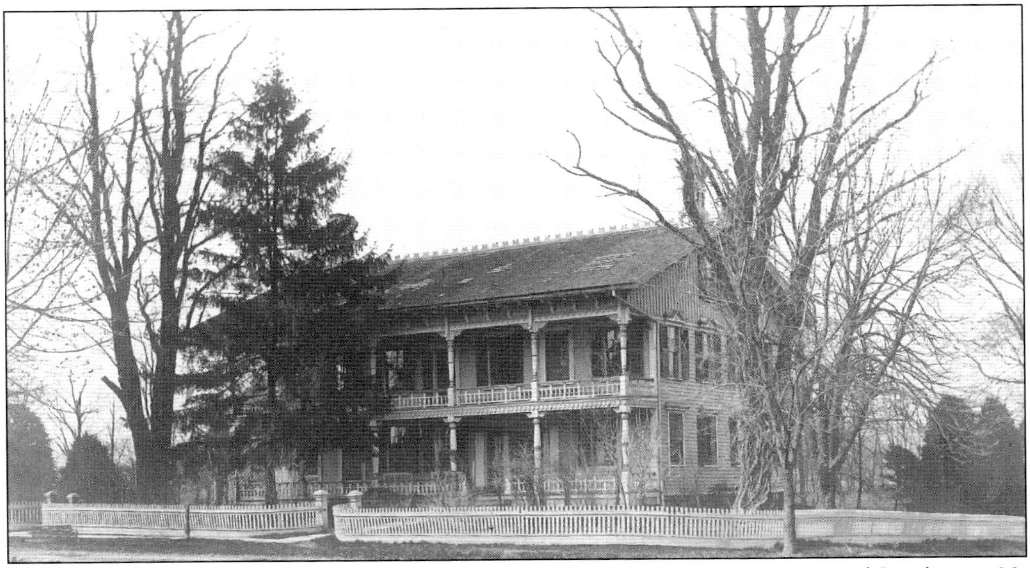

When Jacob Rounds Sr. died at the young age of 42, his sons John, age 22, and Jacob, age 20, tore down the old Rounds Tavern and built a new Rounds Turnpike Tavern in 1844. The tavern opened with a "Polka Ball" victory celebration for U.S. president-elect James K. Polk. The name is believed to have changed to Drovers Inn after it became a favorite overnight stop for drovers who were driving their livestock to market. The popularity of the inn continued after 1851, when the first covered Vestal-Union toll bridge was built. During the 1850s, the inn was closed and made into a private residence by Jacob Lansing Rounds.

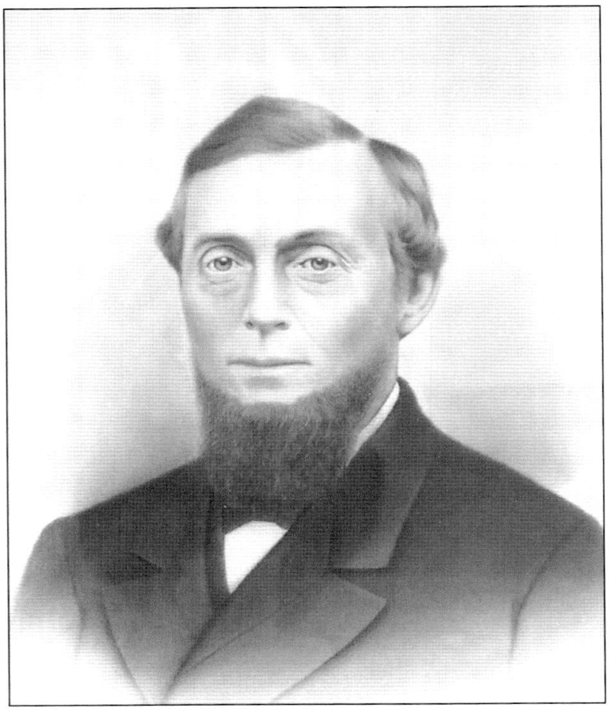

Jacob L. Rounds, grandson of Vestal pioneer Alford Rounds, built the Inn on Pumphouse Road in 1844. Jacob served several terms as Town of Vestal supervisor and one term as Vestal postmaster. Jacob and his wife, Amanda Crandall Rounds, raised their four children there.

Three

Ross Corners

Part of the Hooper Patent, the hamlet of Ross Corners, located at the western portion of the township, was named for prominent lumberman David Ross who settled there. Between 1835 and 1850, Ross rafted huge quantities of lumber down the Susquehanna River, more than 20 rafts in a season. This prosperous business employed between 25 and 30 men in a season. In addition to the lumber business, Ross opened a general store. Son George Ross continued the lumber trade for a number of years.

Methodist preacher John B. White was also a blacksmith in Ross Corners as early as 1835. Charles Crocker, another blacksmith, served the community for over 10 years before turning over the business to son Warren Crocker.

Early settler Samuel Murdock arrived in Ross Corners from Connecticut in 1812. Elected in 1823 as Vestal's first supervisor, he was elected to the position three additional times before 1846.

Ross Corners grew from a few residents to 80 families by 1939. The original one-room schoolhouse was replaced in 1925 by a two-classroom schoolhouse where Grace Camp and Hazel Steenburg were teachers.

Although some of Vestal's earliest settlers chose Ross Corners for their farms and mills, today it is one of the smaller, less populated hamlets of the town.

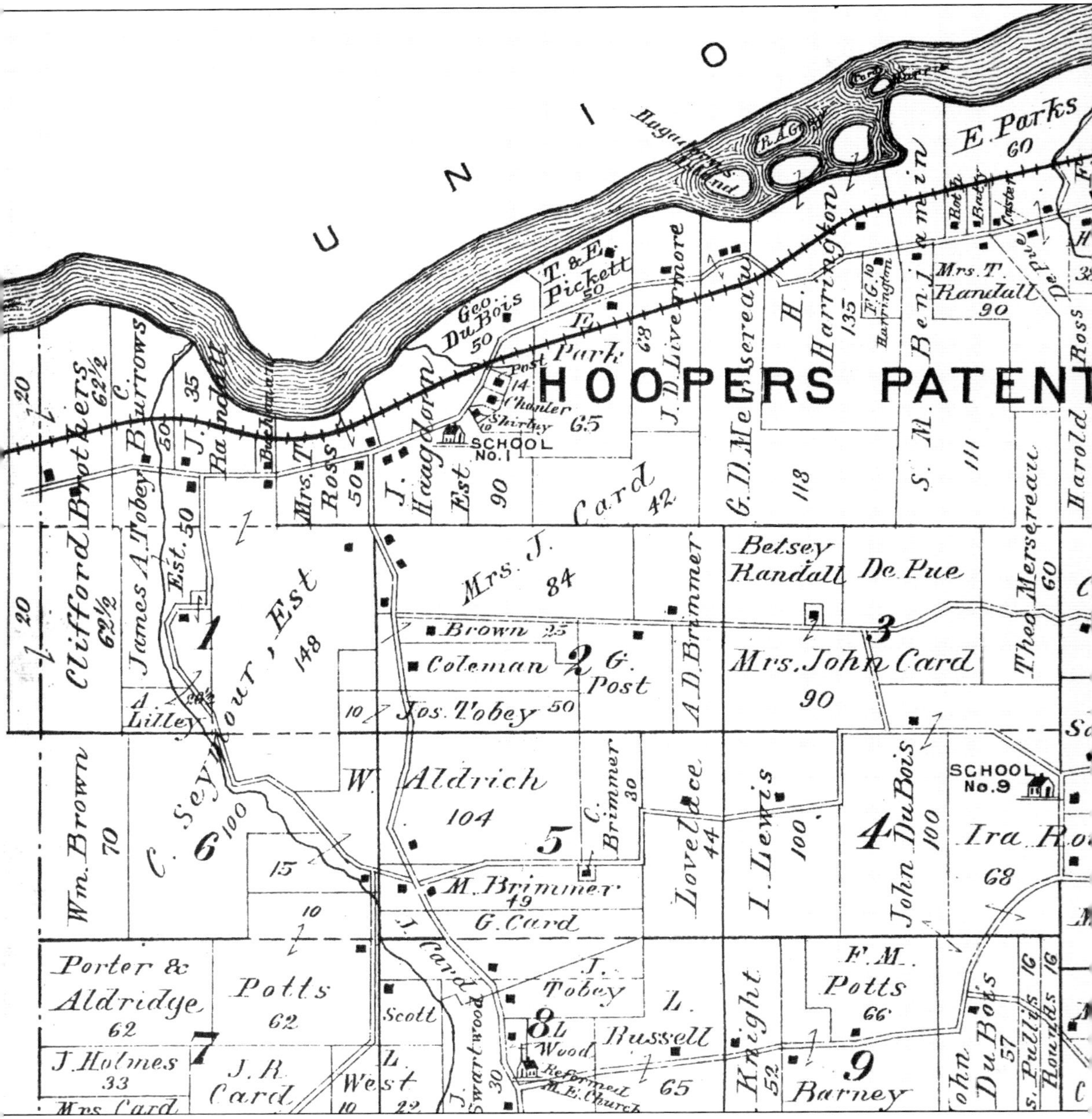

As shown on this 1908 map, the hamlet of Ross Corners is in the northwest corner of the town of Vestal.

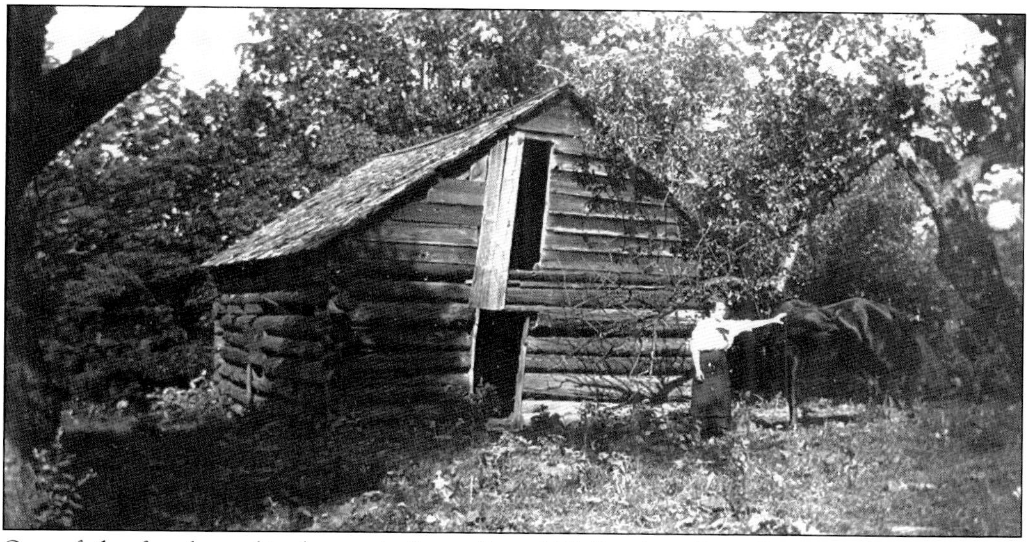

One of the first log cabin homes built on Ross Hill Road in Ross Corners, this homestead belonged to either the Seymours or the Harringtons.

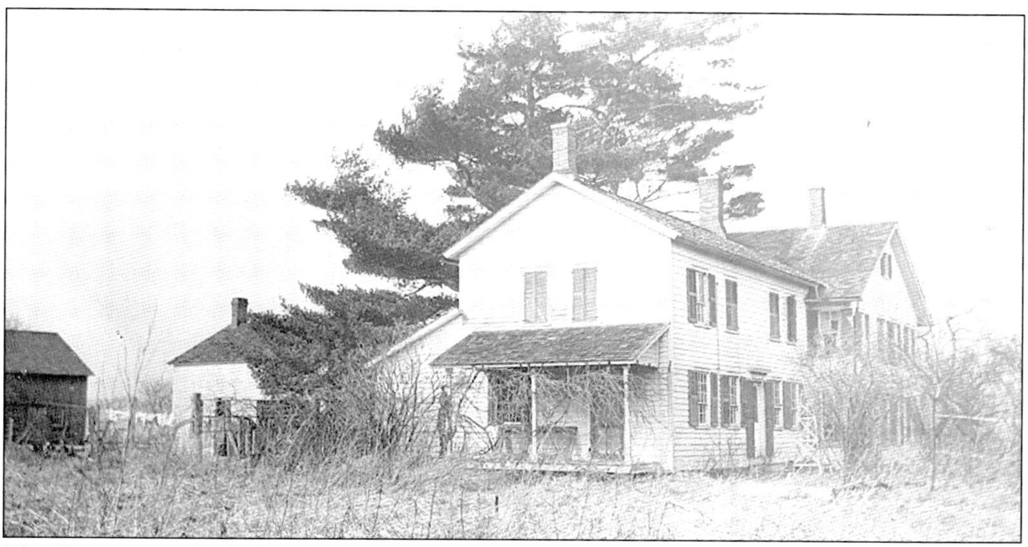

The Harringtons built this farmhouse on Ross Hill Road, which provided the space needed for this extensive family. The home has remained in the Harrington family.

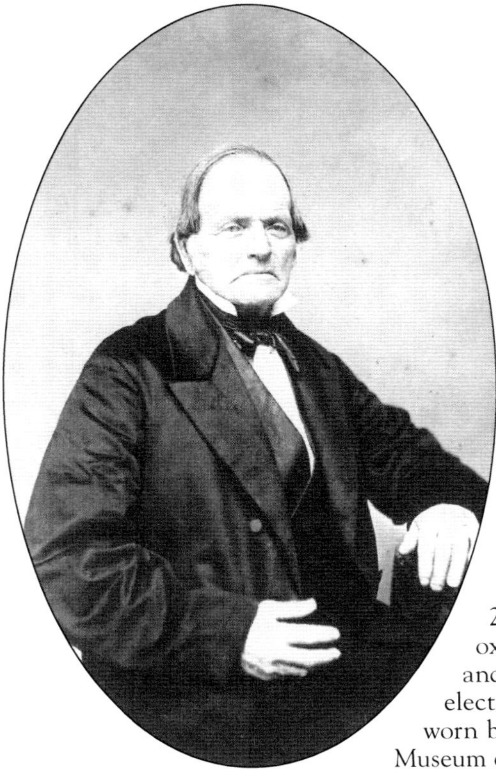

Samuel Murdock, born in Connecticut in 1787, was an early pioneer who became a prosperous farmer. After building a cabin high on the ridge of Ross Hill Road in 1812, he returned to Connecticut to marry Charlotte. Their 200-mile trip to Ross Corners was made in an oxcart containing their possessions, a table, chair, and chest. A Jacksonian Democrat, Murdock was elected as Vestal's first supervisor in 1823. Clothing worn by the Murdocks has been donated to the Vestal Museum collection.

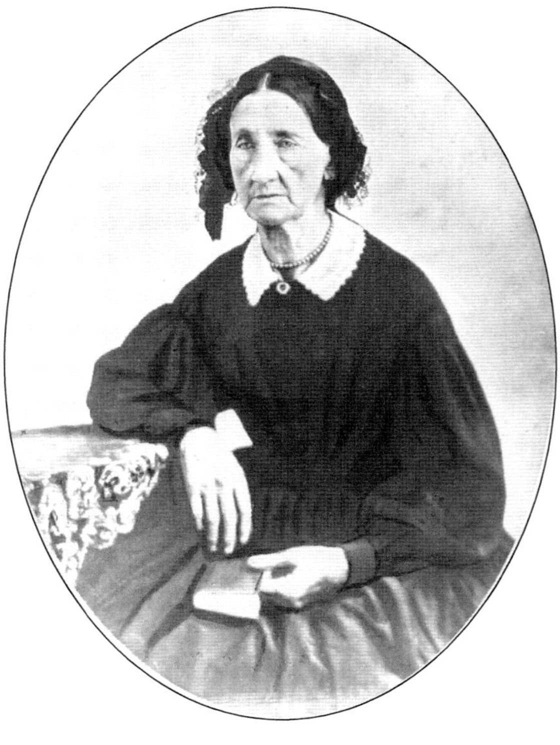

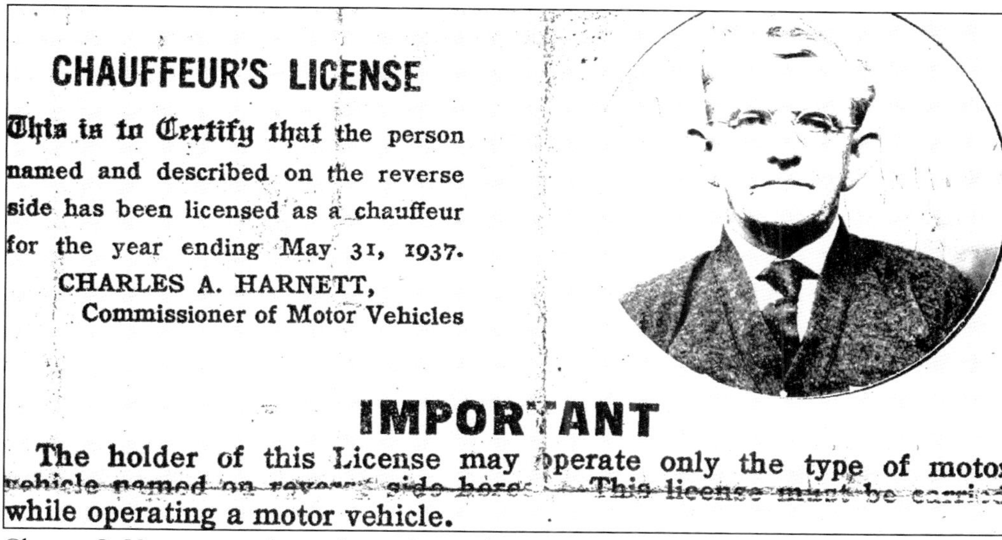
CHAUFFEUR'S LICENSE

This is to Certify that the person named and described on the reverse side has been licensed as a chauffeur for the year ending May 31, 1937.

CHARLES A. HARNETT,
Commissioner of Motor Vehicles

IMPORTANT

The holder of this License may operate only the type of motor vehicle named on reverse side hereof. This license must be carried while operating a motor vehicle.

Chester S. Harrington, descendant of one of Ross Corners' first settlers, operated Vestal's first cab service from 1917 to 1946. Harrington met all passenger trains at the Vestal depot and still managed to ferry passengers arriving at nearby railroad stations. Shown here on his chauffeur's license, Harrington was described on the reverse side as 5 feet 6 inches tall, weighing 178 pounds, with gray eyes and brown hair.

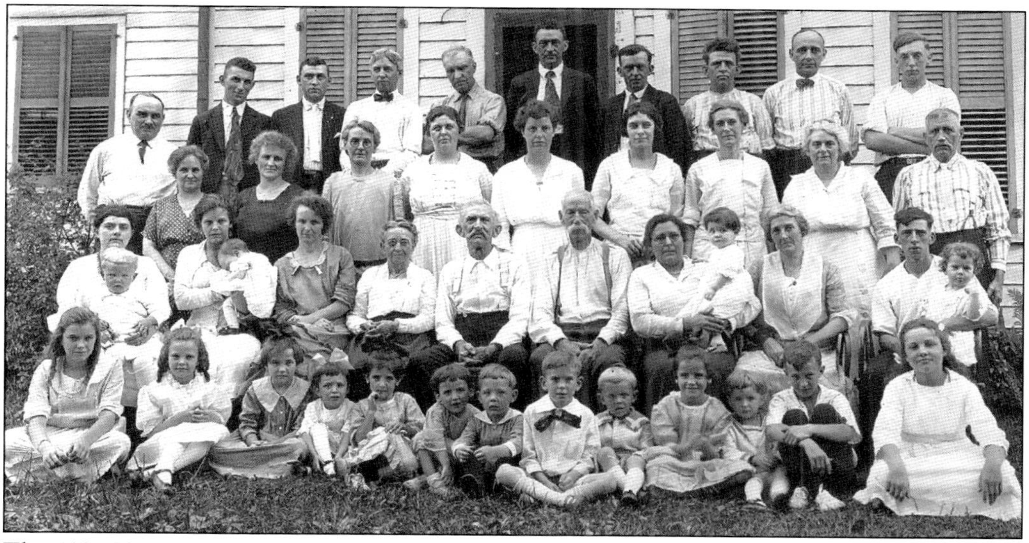

The 1921 Harrington reunion brought together the extended family of four generations. Seen here are, from left to right, (first row) Dorothy Casler, Eleanor Harrington, Leona Harrington, Katharine Jones, Margery Harris, Evelyn Harris, ? Cooper, Howard Casler, Howard Brown, Dorothy Harris, Richard Harrington, Maurice Harrington, and Lela Harrington; (second row) Edna Cooper and son, Hazel and Zena Steenburg, Estella Harrington, Emeline Harrington, Henry Harrington, Walter Riddell, Estella and Rheba Jones, Mary Yetter, and Earl and Elsie Steenburg; (third row) Mrs. Henry Church, Florence Harris, Jennie Rhodes, Hazel Brown, Lena Harrington, Florence Casler, Clara Casler, Flora Brown, and Edgar Brown; (fourth row) Elmer Casler, Leland Jones, George Brown, Henry Church, Nelson Rhodes, Harry Harrington, Frank Harrington, Seymour Harrington, Royal Cooper, and Floyd Rhodes.

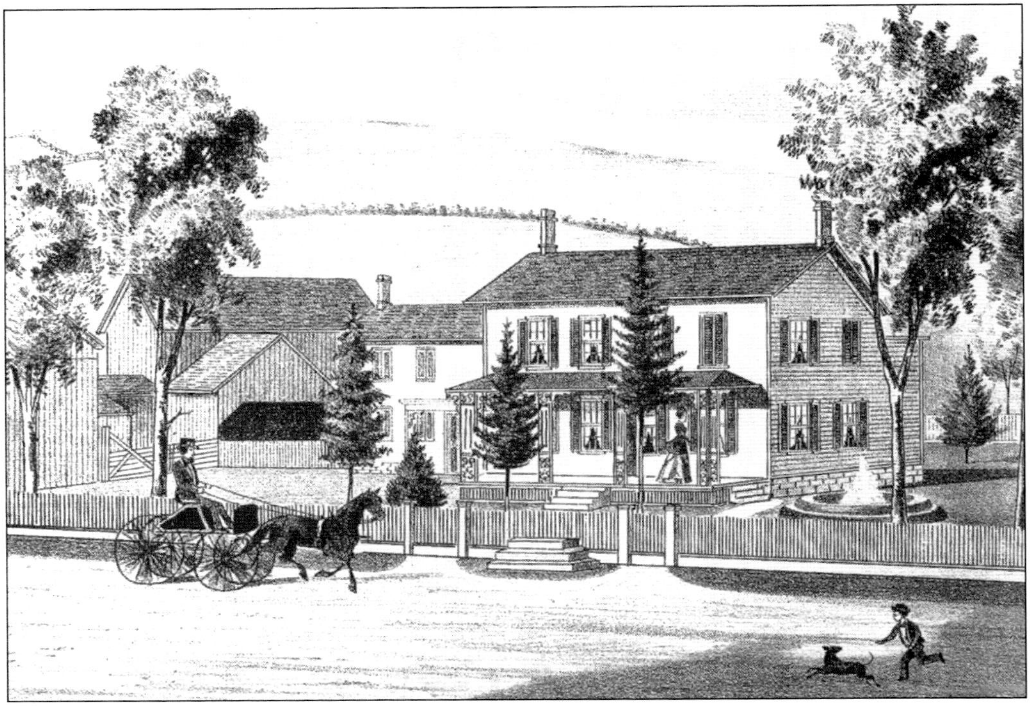

David Ross, wealthy lumberman and merchant after whom Ross Corners was named, was the original owner of the residence identified in the 1876 atlas map of Broome County. Son George E. Ross was listed as the head of the house in 1860 and lived there with his wife, Catherine.

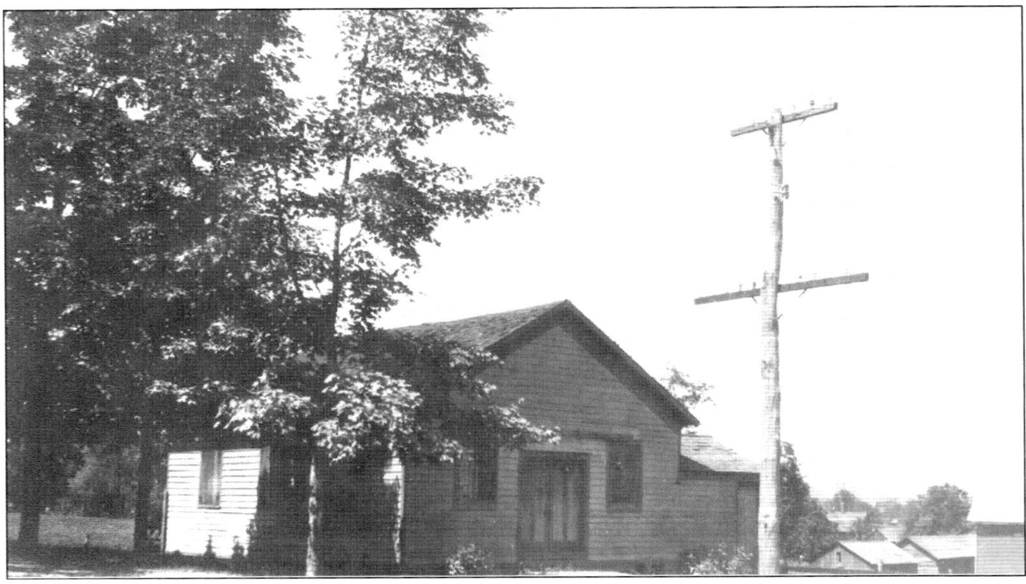

This Ross Corners one-room school was School No. 1. Some of the names that would have appeared in the teacher's grade book were Ross, Randall, Crocker, Murdock, Brimmer, Seymour, DuBois, Parks, Layton, Fox, and Garrison. (Courtesy of the Broome County Historical Society.)

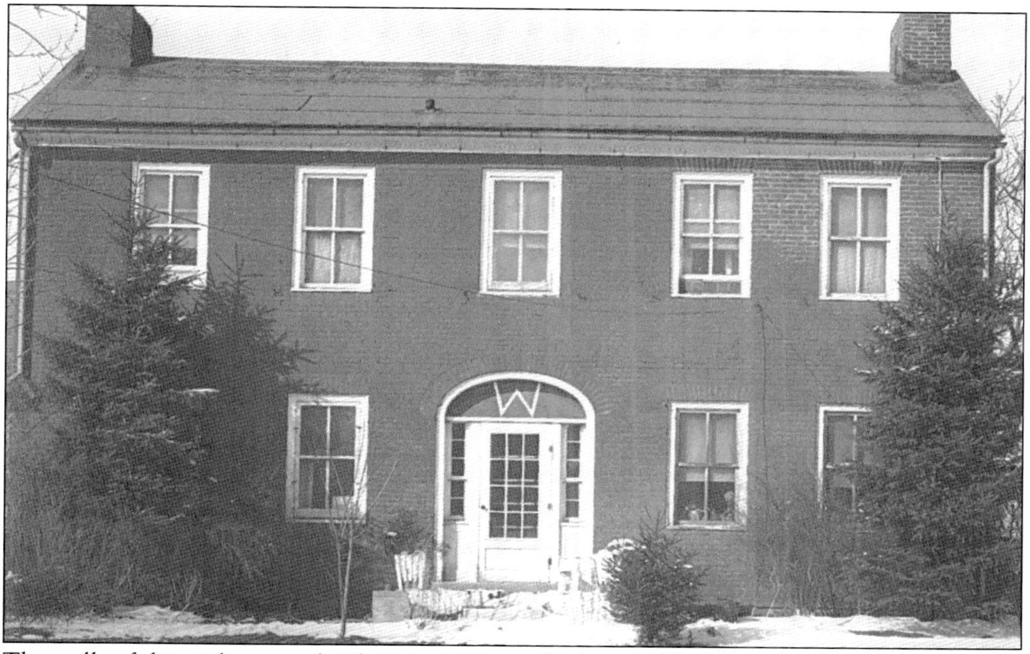

The walls of this eight-room, brick Colonial home built in 1826 were said to be 13 inches thick. The pink-tinged bricks were made on site with clay from the Susquehanna River bank and lime from Little Meadows, Pennsylvania. Surrounded by the Winne sand and gravel operation that often yielded Native American artifacts, it was discovered that the home had apparently been built close to a prehistoric grave site. Constructed originally by John Seymour, the Vestal landmark was demolished in 1954.

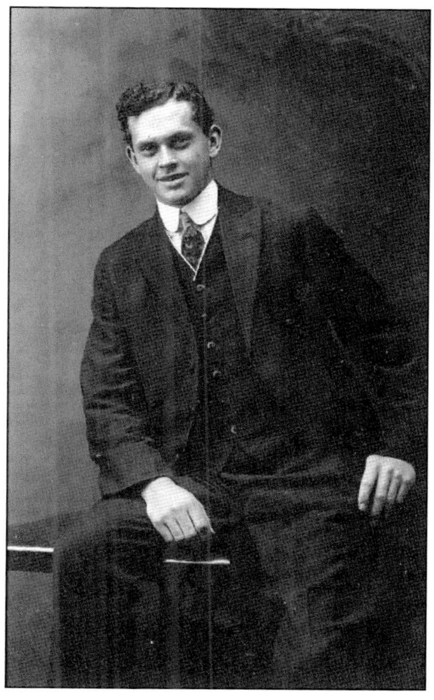

The Seymour house photograph was taken by Ross Corners' Stacey D. Harrington, owner of Harrington's Studio and Engraver and *Endicott Daily Bulletin* photographer. Harrington steps out from behind the camera for this 1916 photograph.

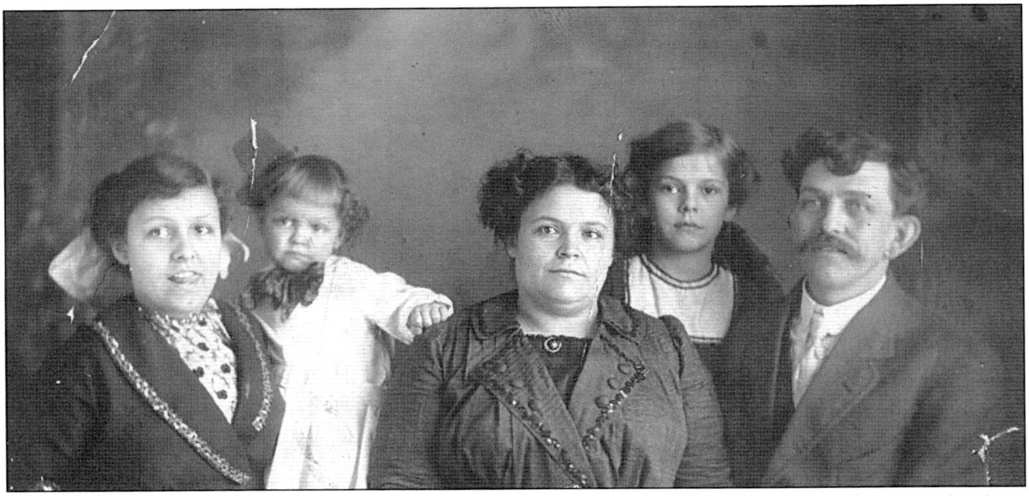

Ross Corners residents Seymour and Belle Newell Harrington are shown here with their three children, Estella, Hazel, and Clyde. Estella would marry Leland Jones, a longtime Vestal supervisor, and Hazel Harrington Steenburg would teach generations of students at the Ross Corners two-room schoolhouse.

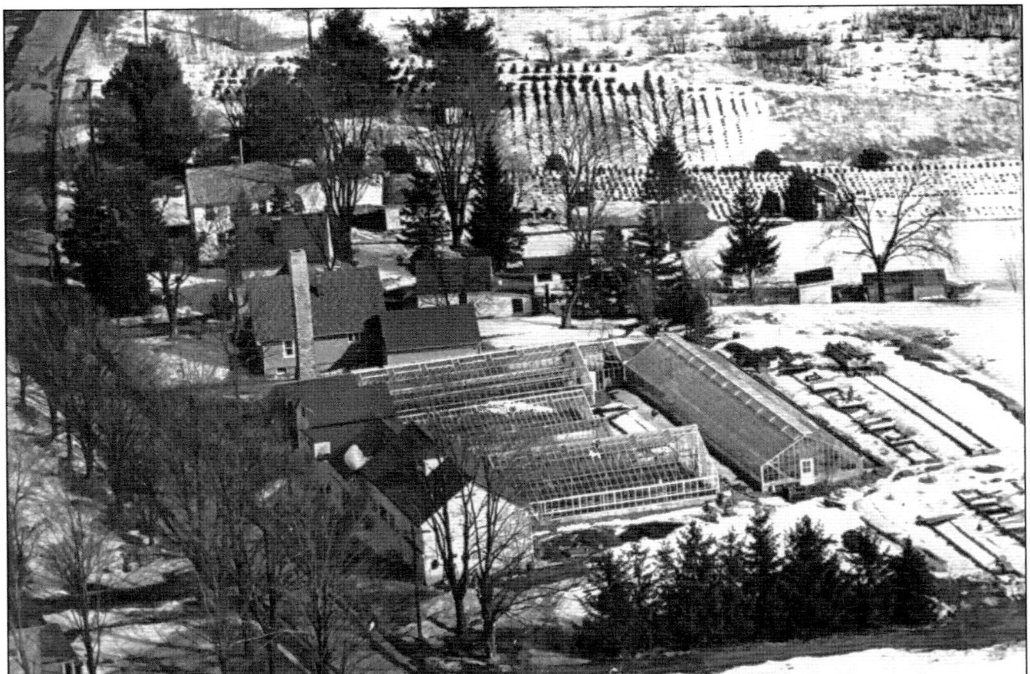

Ward Castle purchased the former Livermore farm in 1918 and moved his family to the old two-family farmhouse on what was then Old Owego Road. Castle farmed and worked a regular job until 1925, when he built the first greenhouse, the beginning of the Castle Gardens farm. The farm closed in 1966, when more than half of the farmland was appropriated for the Route 17 Expressway. The chimney is all that remains of the former Castle farmhouse. Castle Gardens Senior Living and Special Needs Community is located where six greenhouses once stood.

Ward Castle stands in the middle of a field proudly holding two huge Big Bender muskmelons in this 1936 photograph. As young men, sons Bill and Jim raised chickens and sold eggs in addition to growing potatoes on a family-owned 10-acre island in the Susquehanna River.

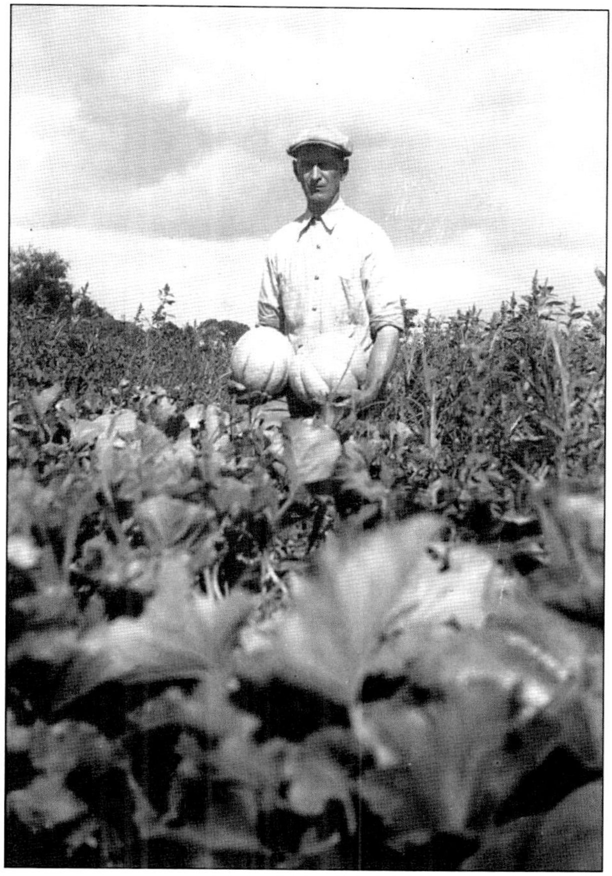

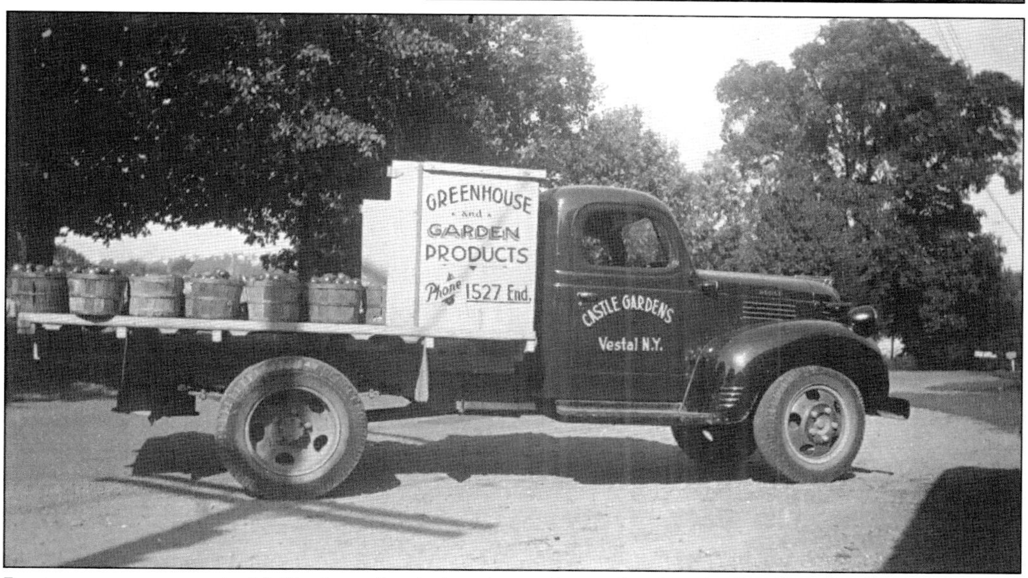

Business was strong in 1947 when, loaded with produce, the Castle Gardens truck was ready to make deliveries throughout the valley. The farm sold plants, produce, and garden supplies.

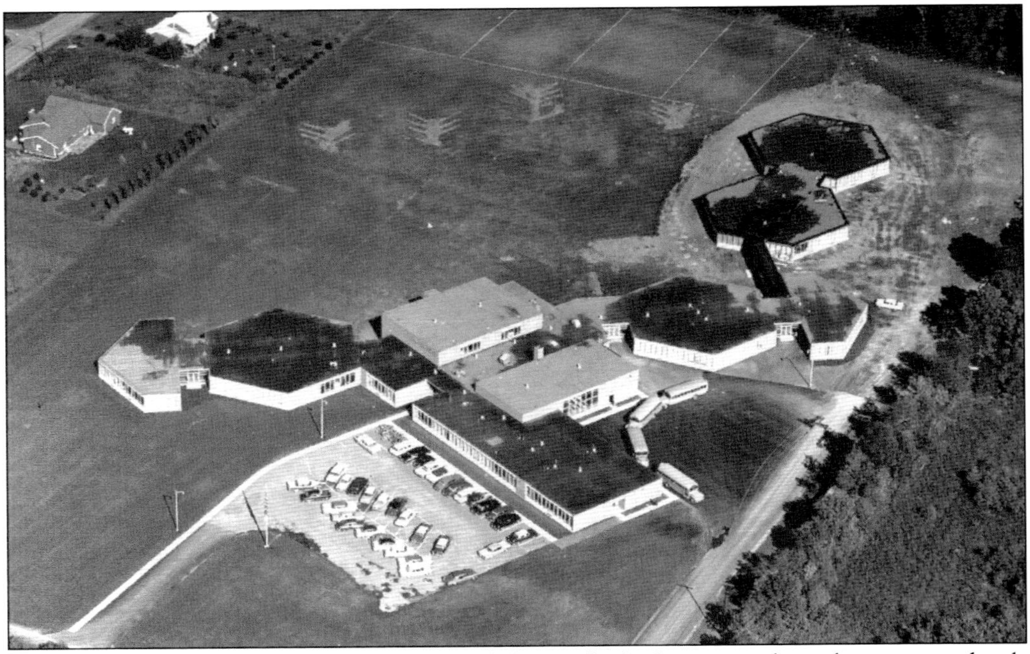

During the 1950s, the Vestal Central School district built three sprawling elementary schools with connecting hexagonal classroom pods. This is the Ross Corners elementary school as it looked in 1958. The aerial photograph was taken by the late Bob Garvin. (Courtesy of Ed Aswad.)

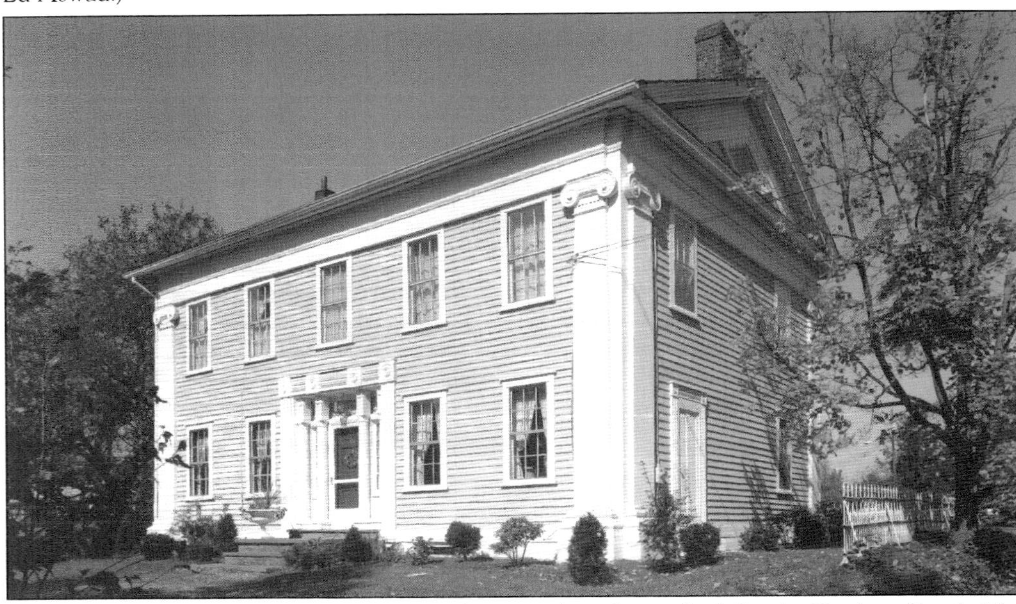

For almost 200 years, Cold Spring Farm has stood at the end of Castle Gardens Road. The Federal-style home is believed to have been built about 1810. Early settler George DuBois owned the home for over 40 years. For a time, the home was divided into three apartments, but recent owners have restored the house to its one-family origins. The current owner was recognized by the Preservation Association of the Southern Tier for his preservation efforts.

Four

TRACY CREEK

Located in the southwest corner of the town of Vestal, Tracy Creek, once known as Hard Scrabble, was named for early settler Thomas Tracy. At age 31, Samuel Campbell built the first house in 1831 along Tracy Creek. Unfortunately, Campbell was drowned the following year while rafting lumber down the Susquehanna River.

Dairy farming and lumbering were Tracy Creek's primary industries. Three brothers, Arnold, Luther, and Abram Goodno, built and operated three of the earliest water-powered mills. Fire claimed the steam mill built by Chauncey Carter in 1851, as well as the mill built by James Noyes to replace it.

Church services were held in the schoolhouse until 1832, when the First Reformed Methodist Church was built at a cost of $1,000. The church, which could seat a congregation of 400, had only 20 members.

The first blacksmith shop was built by Charles Burrows and Peter White, who is believed to be the first blacksmith. Tracy Creek boasted several stores, the first owned by Robert Wheeler in 1870, followed by Richard Baker's store in 1878, Jerry Howard's in 1880, and John Baker's in 1882. In about 1905, Lucius Mason opened a store on Tracy Creek Road. James Lyman Card was the first burial in the Tracy Creek cemetery in 1832.

Students attended either Upper or Lower Tracy Creek School, and residents could choose for their final resting place either Upper or Lower Tracy Creek Cemetery.

A controversy that began in 1873, when a schoolboy found a crudely cut tombstone with the inscription "William Plat, Died Nov. 4th, 1721," continues to this day. Located between Vestal Center and Tracy Creek, historians have investigated and debated the stone's authenticity in an effort to determine whether or not it is a hoax. If the stone is real, Plat could be the first European buried in Broome County. For a time, the thriving hamlet of Tracy Creek was more prominent than central Vestal.

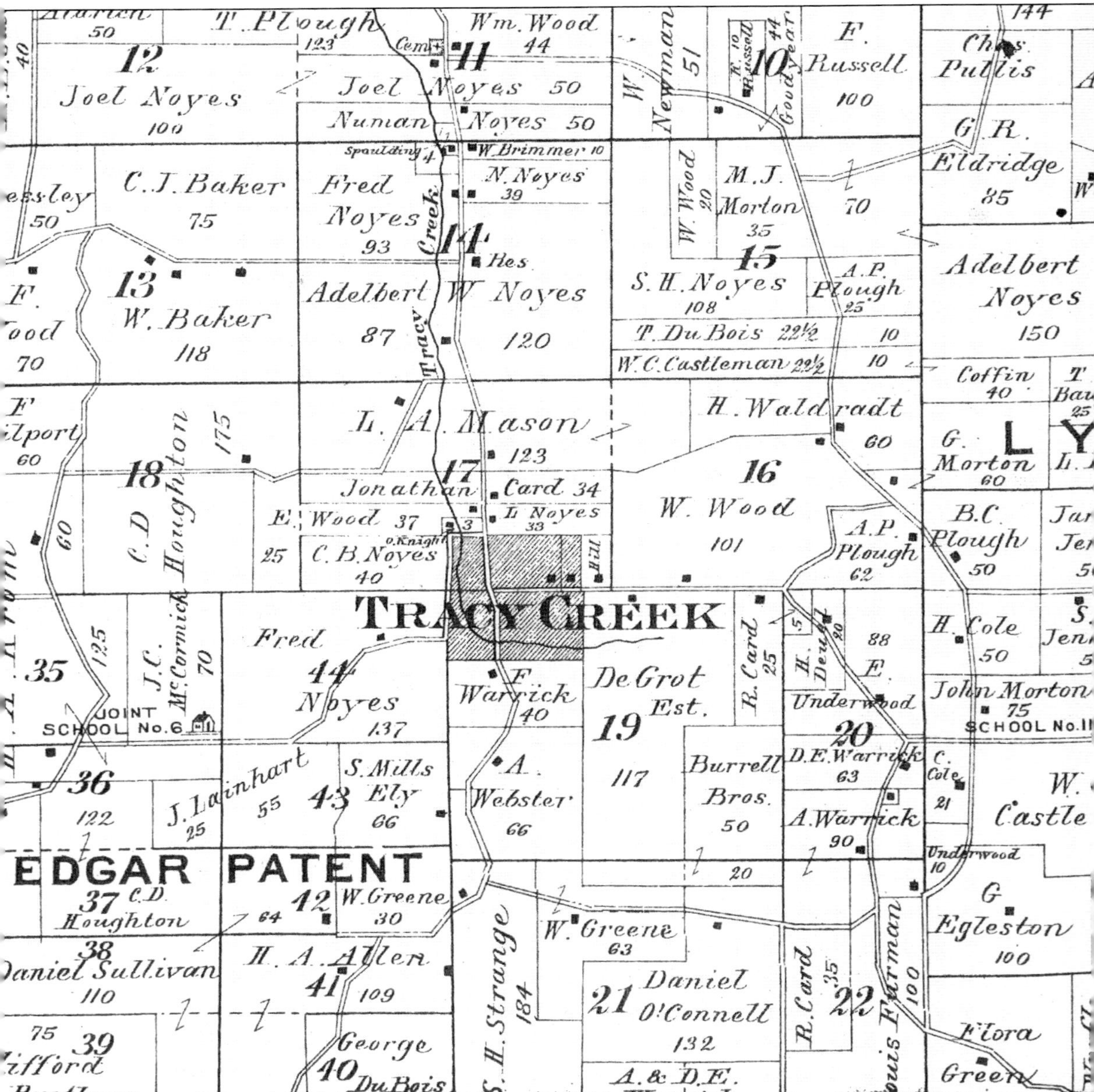

The hamlet of Tracy Creek lies in the southwest corner of the Town of Vestal.

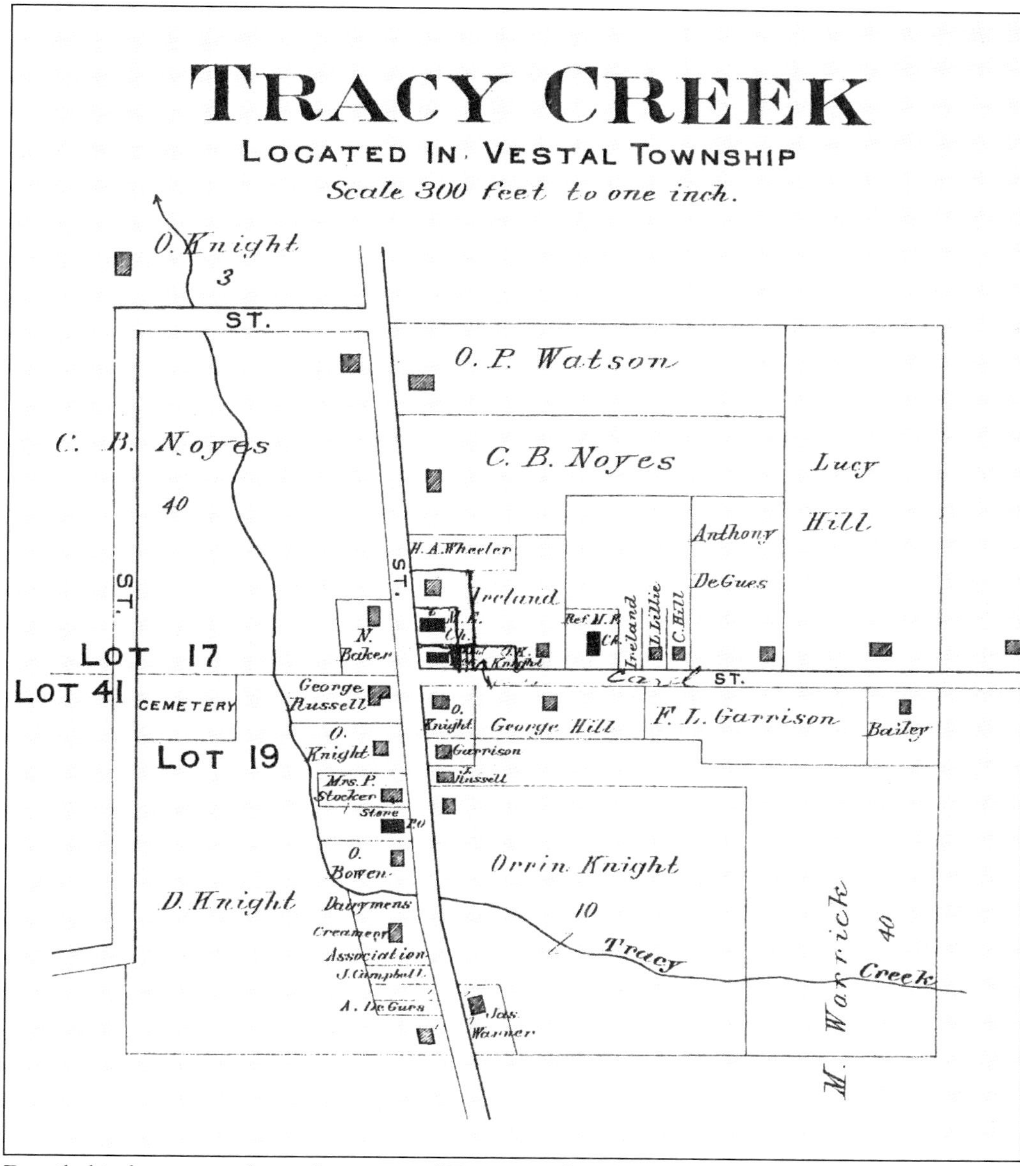

Detailed information about the center of Tracy Creek is found in this 1908 map.

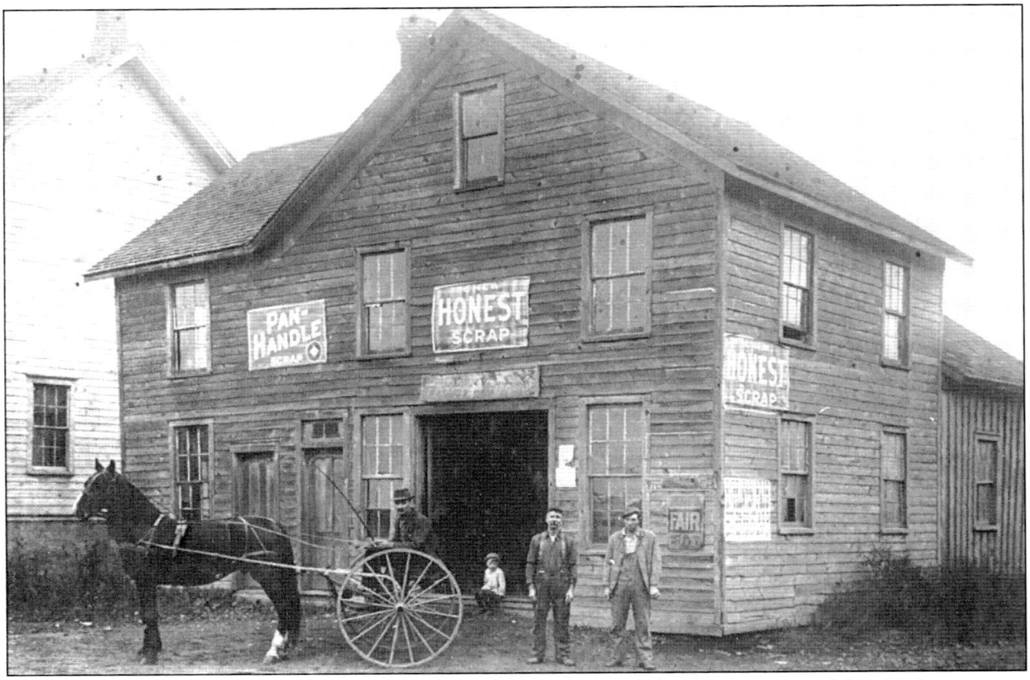

Stephen Plough operated this store in Tracy Creek around the beginning of the 20th century. Old signs announcing a Binghamton Fair can be seen near the entrance, while large "Chew Honest Scrap" and "Pan-Handle Scrap" signs command one's attention.

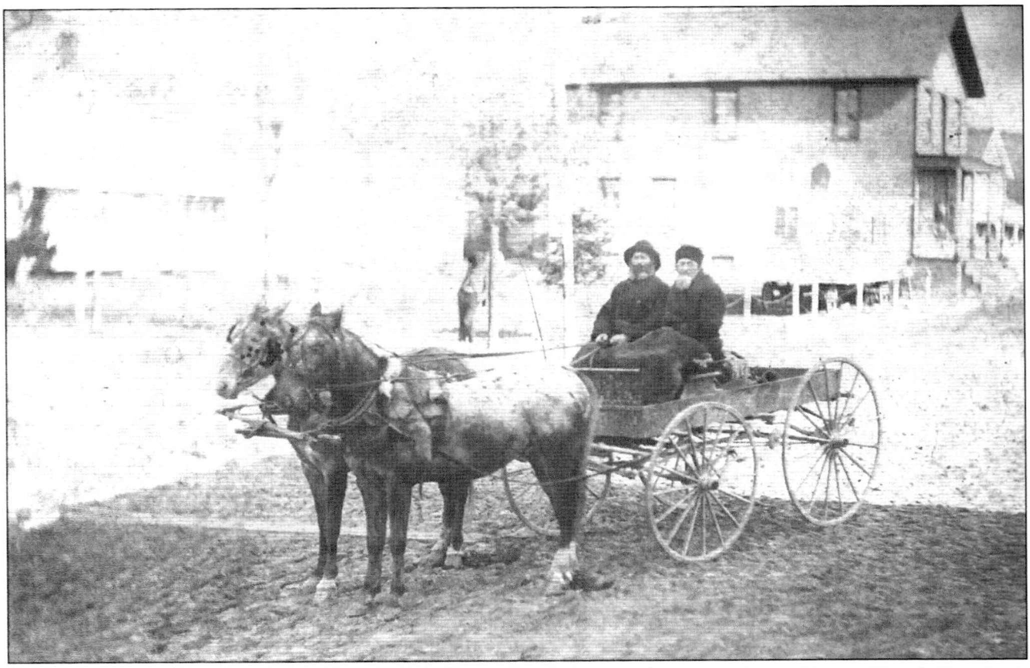

Early Tracy Creek settler Abram Plough drives his horse and wagon down Tracy Creek Road. A farmer, Plough operated a store in the community.

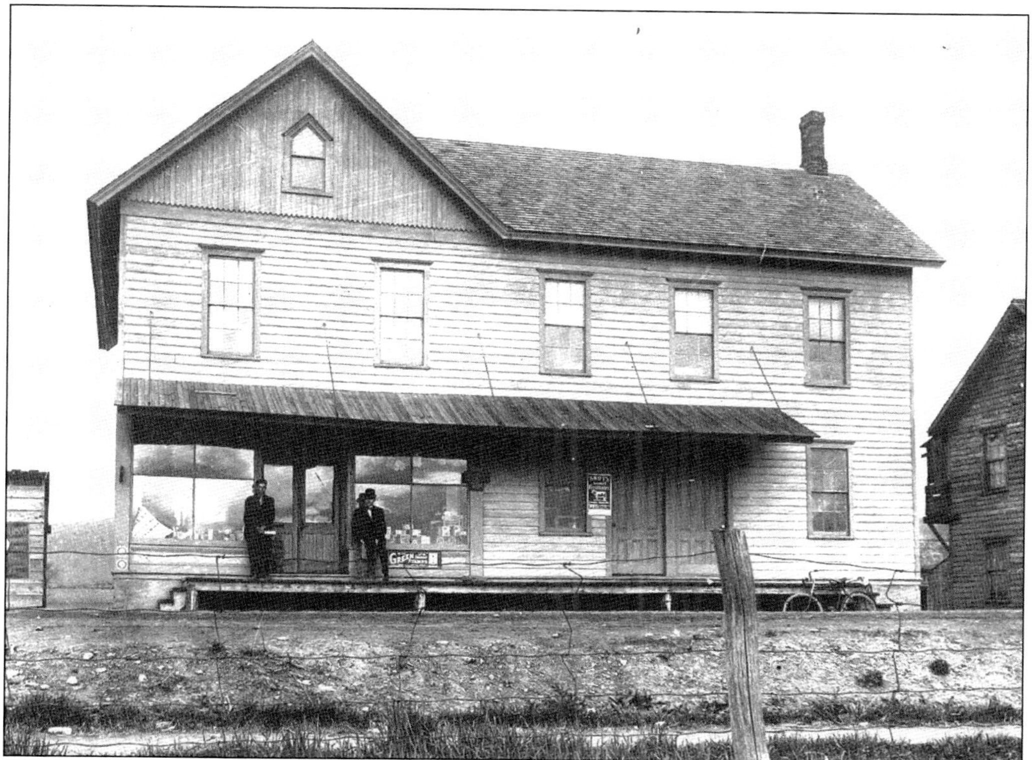

The Mason and Knight and Company store on Tracy Creek Road was owned by Lucius A. Mason according to 1905 receipts found in an old trunk. Mason died in 1907, leaving wife Amelia Russell Mason and young L. A. Mason. It is unknown whether the upstairs was used as a residence or for storage.

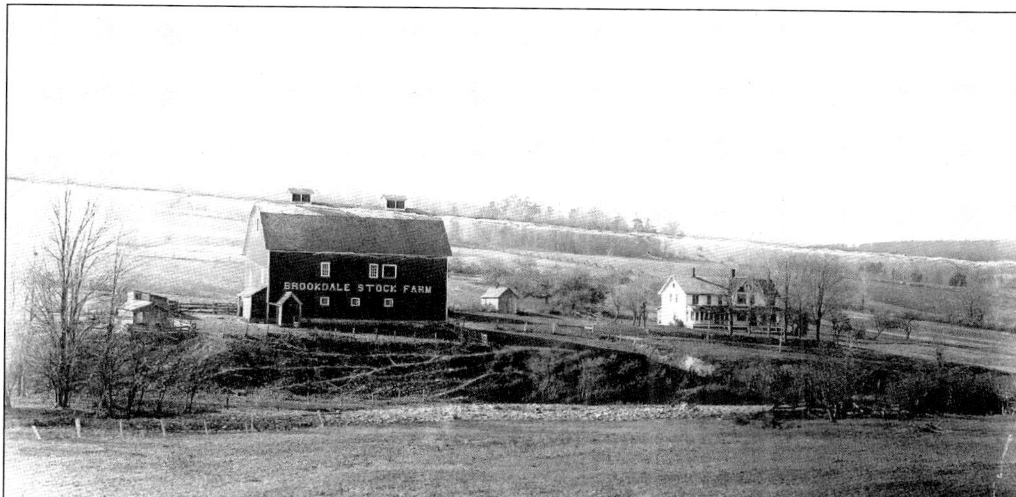

L. A. Mason owned the large Brookdale Stock Farm on Mason Road in the hamlet of Tracy Creek, where he raised registered Holstein cattle. When it was discovered that several animals had acquired tuberculosis, the entire herd had to be put down as a precaution. The herd was later replaced.

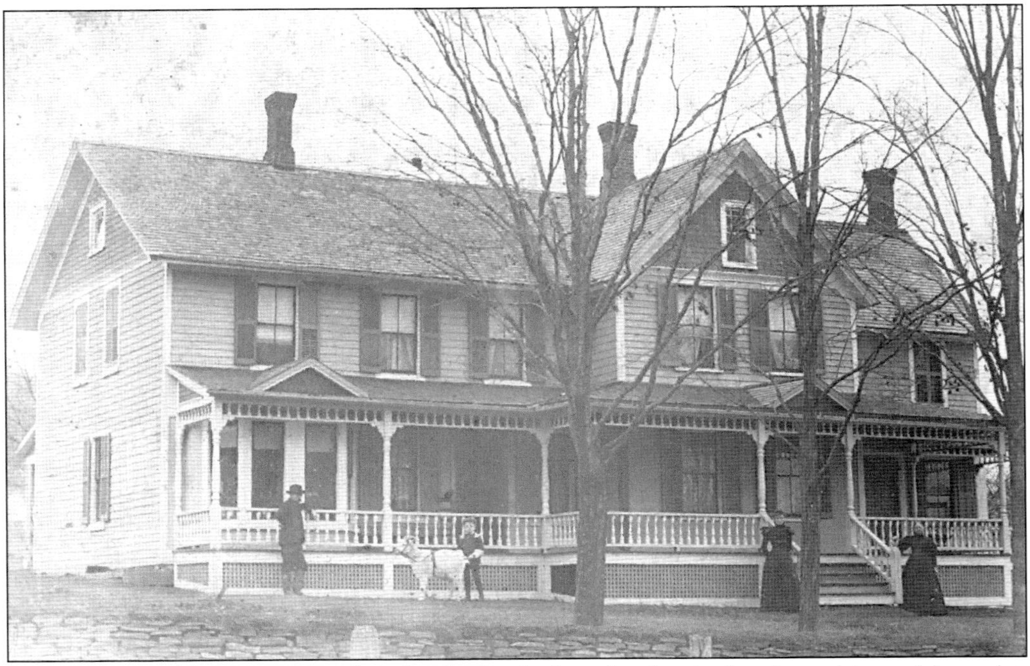

In 1849, Winfield Scott Mason bought the land where he first built a log cabin and later this house. Family members and a goat pose in front of the large two-family Mason residence on Mason Road. It is one of only a few homes to be owned and lived in continuously by the same family. Lucius A. and Amelia Mason's granddaughter currently lives at the residence.

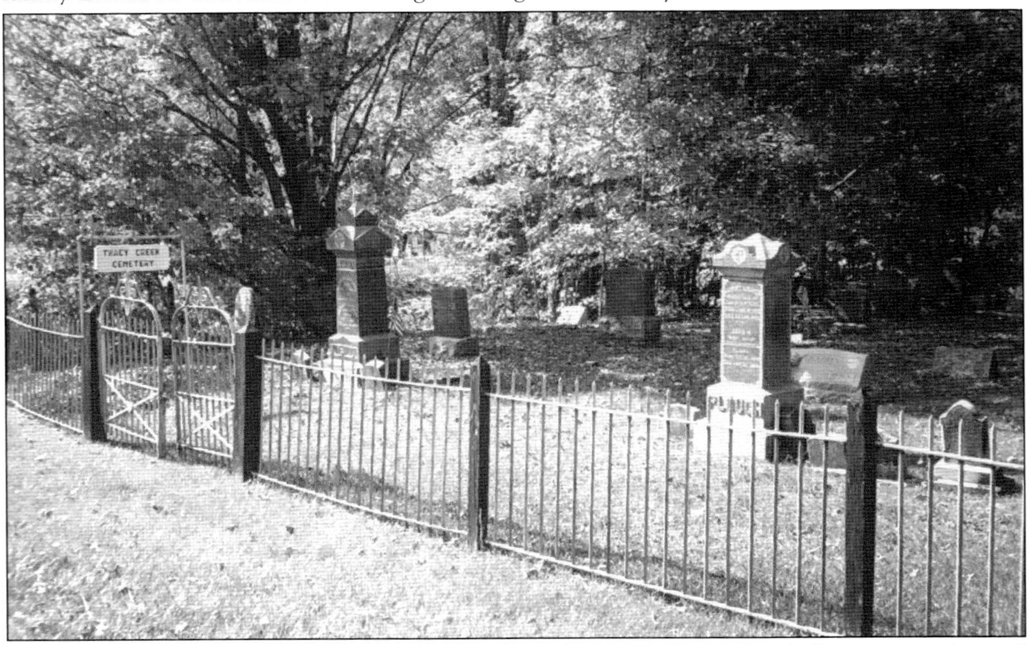

The Tracy Creek cemetery, referred to by locals as the Lower Tracy Creek Cemetery, is located at the intersection of Tracy Creek Road and Ridge Road. Divided by a small stream, the north side of this 1827 cemetery contains the oldest graves. There are no remaining plots.

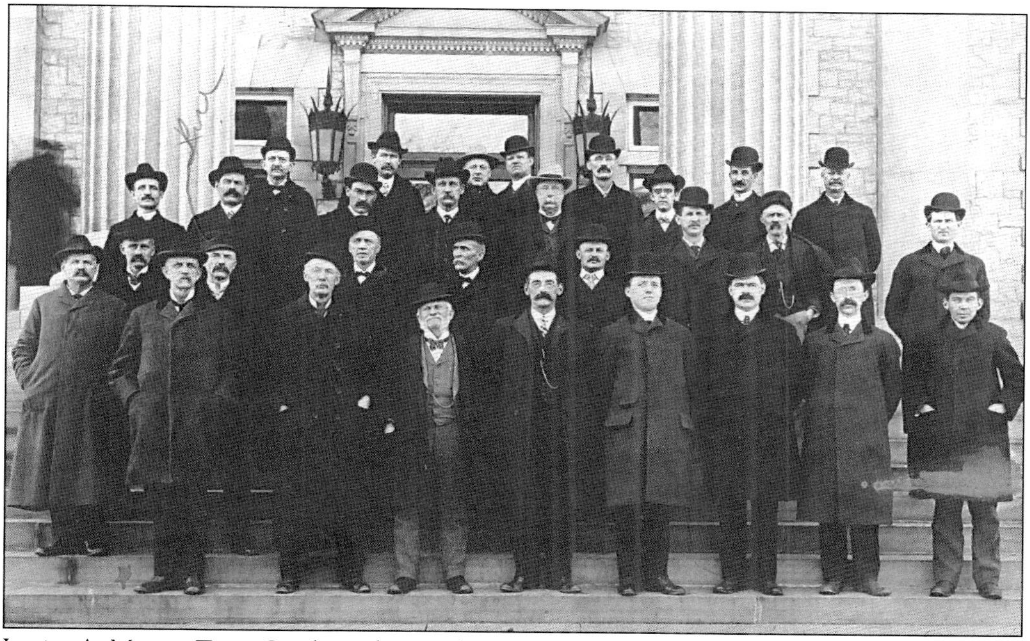

Lucius A. Mason, Tracy Creek resident and Town of Vestal supervisor, stands in the second row, second from the left in this 1902 photograph of the Broome County board of supervisors. A list of the members, not in the order photographed, identified the 13 Binghamton ward members and the 15 town supervisors.

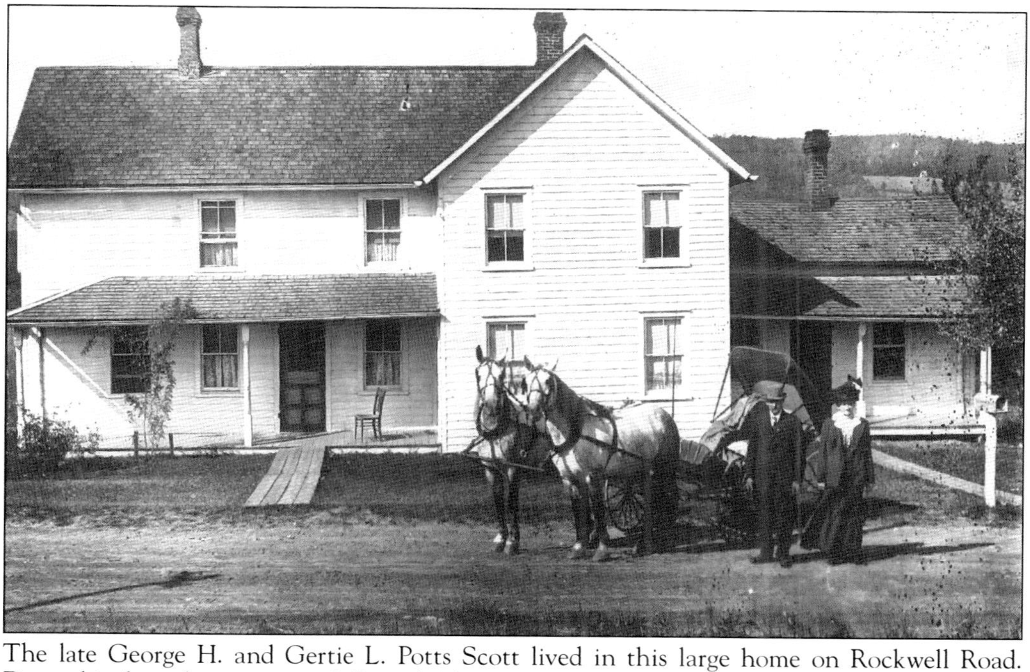

The late George H. and Gertie L. Potts Scott lived in this large home on Rockwell Road. Dressed in formal attire, twins J. D. and Alice Scott stand with horse and buggy in front of their parents' home in this 1920s photograph. Note the wooden sidewalk at the entrance and the mailbox on the right.

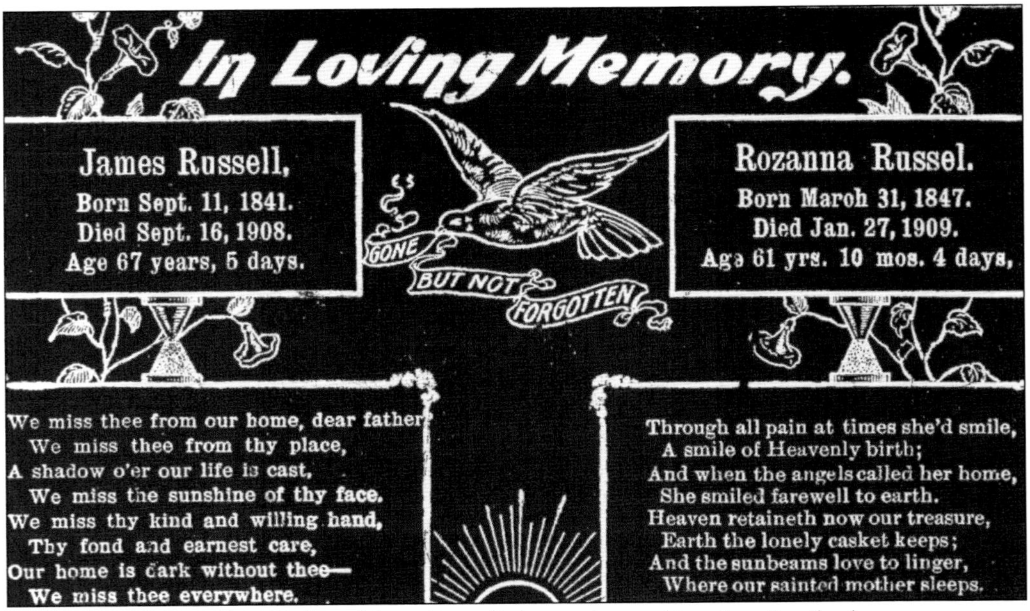

In Loving Memory.

James Russell,
Born Sept. 11, 1841.
Died Sept. 16, 1908.
Age 67 years, 5 days.

GONE BUT NOT FORGOTTEN

Rozanna Russel.
Born Maroh 31, 1847.
Died Jan. 27, 1909.
Aga 61 yrs. 10 mos. 4 days,

We miss thee from our home, dear father
We miss thee from thy place,
A shadow o'er our life is cast,
We miss the sunshine of thy face.
We miss thy kind and willing hand,
Thy fond and earnest care,
Our home is dark without thee—
We miss thee everywhere.

Through all pain at times she'd smile,
A smile of Heavenly birth;
And when the angels called her home,
She smiled farewell to earth.
Heaven retaineth now our treasure,
Earth the lonely casket keeps;
And the sunbeams love to linger,
Where our sainted mother sleeps.

This black memorial card, found by a Russell descendant with other family documents in an old trunk, memorializes husband and wife James and Rozanna Russell. Notice that Rozanna's surname is spelled with only one L.

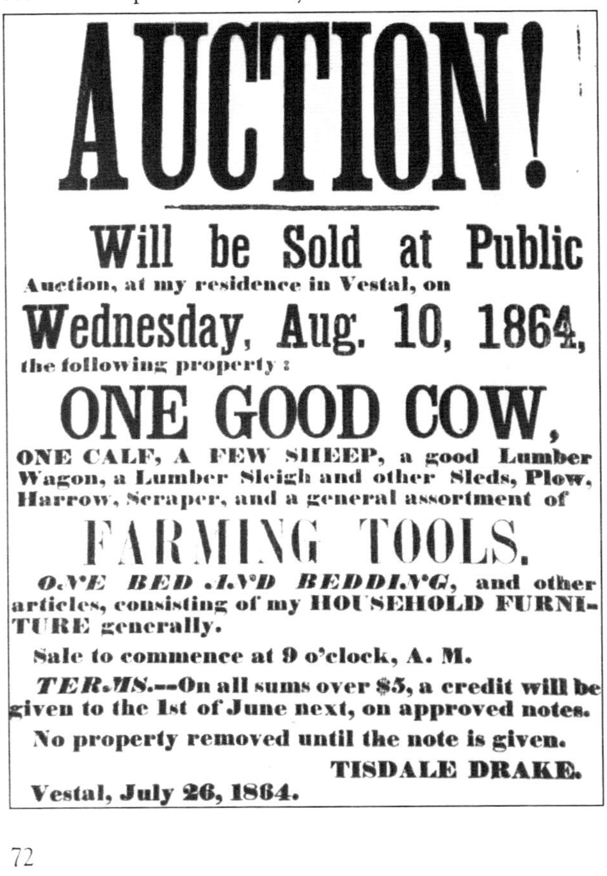

AUCTION!

Will be Sold at Public
Auction, at my residence in Vestal, on
Wednesday, Aug. 10, 1864,
the following property:
ONE GOOD COW,
ONE CALF, A FEW SHEEP, a good Lumber Wagon, a Lumber Sleigh and other Sleds, Plow, Harrow, Scraper, and a general assortment of
FARMING TOOLS.
ONE BED AND BEDDING, and other articles, consisting of my HOUSEHOLD FURNITURE generally.
Sale to commence at 9 o'clock, A. M.
TERMS.—On all sums over $5, a credit will be given to the 1st of June next, on approved notes.
No property removed until the note is given.
TISDALE DRAKE.
Vestal, July 26, 1864.

Farmer Tisdale Drake came to Vestal before 1820. He and his wife, Belinda, lived on a farm near Knight Road until 1864, when he hung these posters advertising a public auction of "One Good Cow," other farm animals, and household furnishings. A widower until his death in 1872, Tisdale would share eternity with his wife at the Vestal park Cemetery.

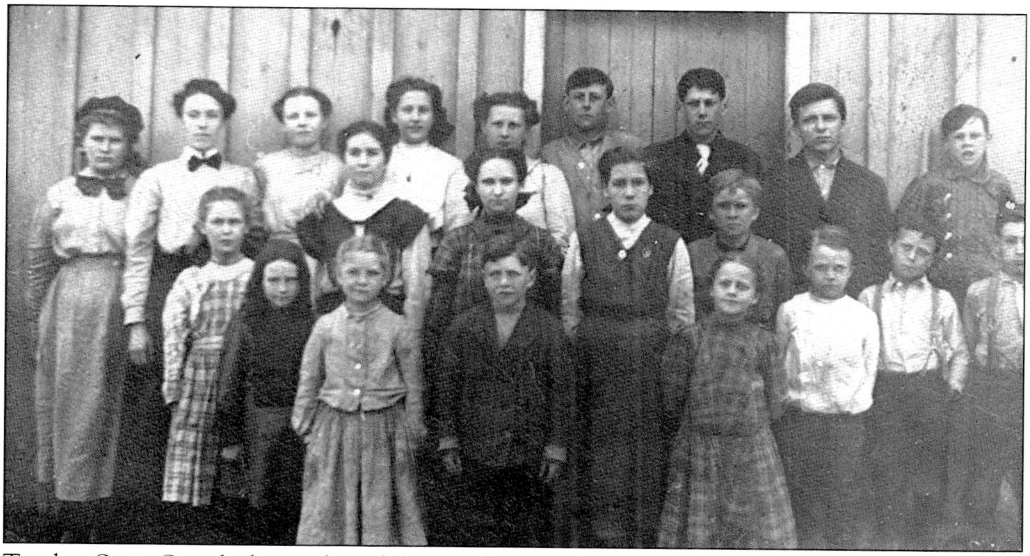

Teacher Susie Gunglach stands with her students at the lower Tracy Creek one-room school in 1909 at top and below on October 22, 1913. Although the photographs do not list the students names, Gunglach compiled a list of students dated 1909 and 1913 with the following names: Pearl Russell, Olga Brimmer, Lena Gibbs, Minnie Brimmer, Charles Potts, Edwin West, Claude Noyes, Arthur Brimmer, Dora Potts, Leola Brimmer, Hazel Roger, Flossie McCormick, Earl Brimmer, Alice Scott, Marion Potts, J. D. Scott, Arvilla Bailey, Olin Noyes, Everett Russell, Tom McCormick, Florence Potts, Claude Noyes, Mamie Wood, Ruby Wood, Sadie Wood, Della Wood, Bessie Russell, Pearl McCormick, Thelma Brimmer, Bernice Wood, Cecil Noyes, and Lula McCormick.

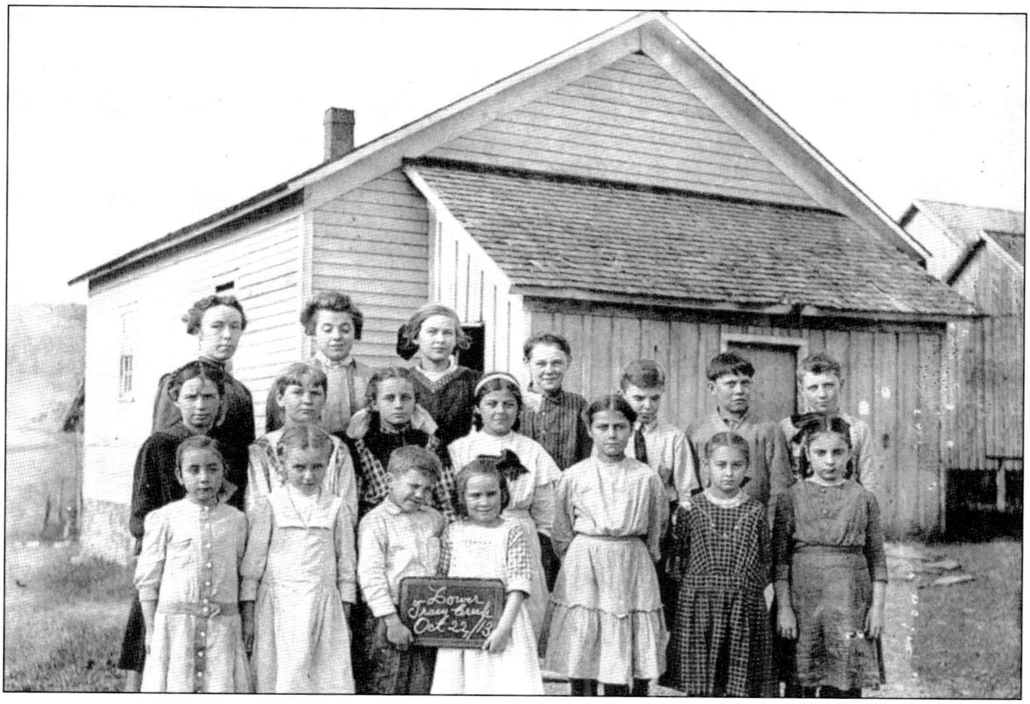

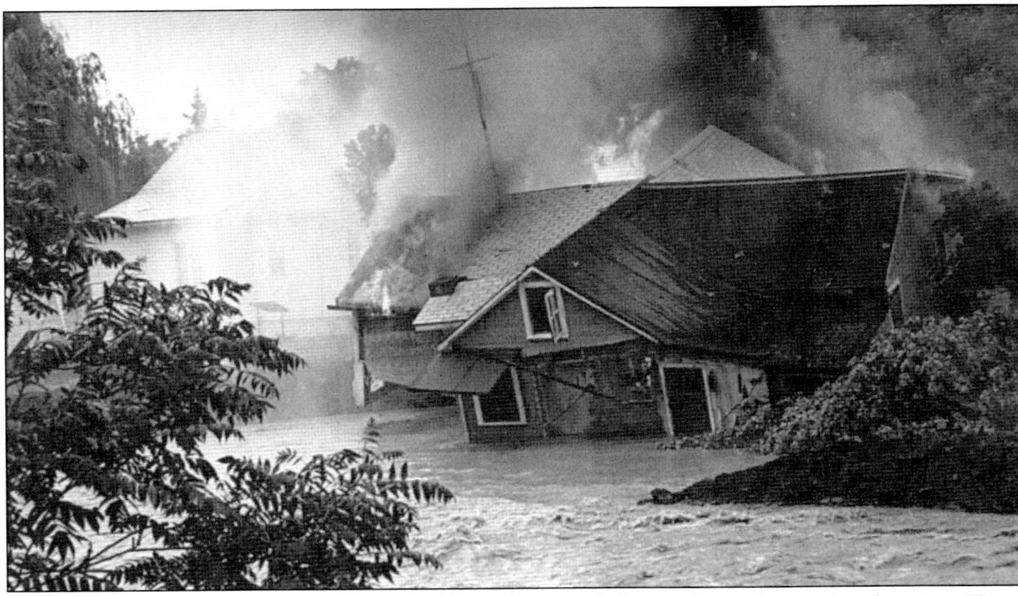

During Hurricane Agnes in June 1972, Albert Crandall's house slipped into the churning Tracy Creek when the bank eroded. The house was set on fire to prevent it from floating downstream and jamming the Ross Corners Bridge. The tactic worked.

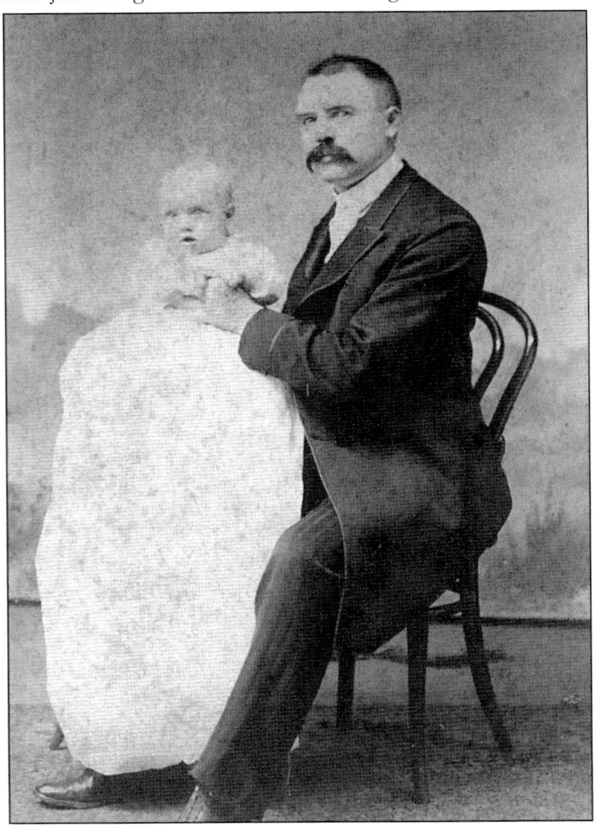

Four-month-old L. A. Mason is held by his father Lucius A. Mason in this 1891 picture. The initials L. A. were listed as the child's given name. Lucius was Town of Vestal supervisor from 1879 to 1880 and son L. A. was supervisor in 1902 and again from 1905 to 1906.

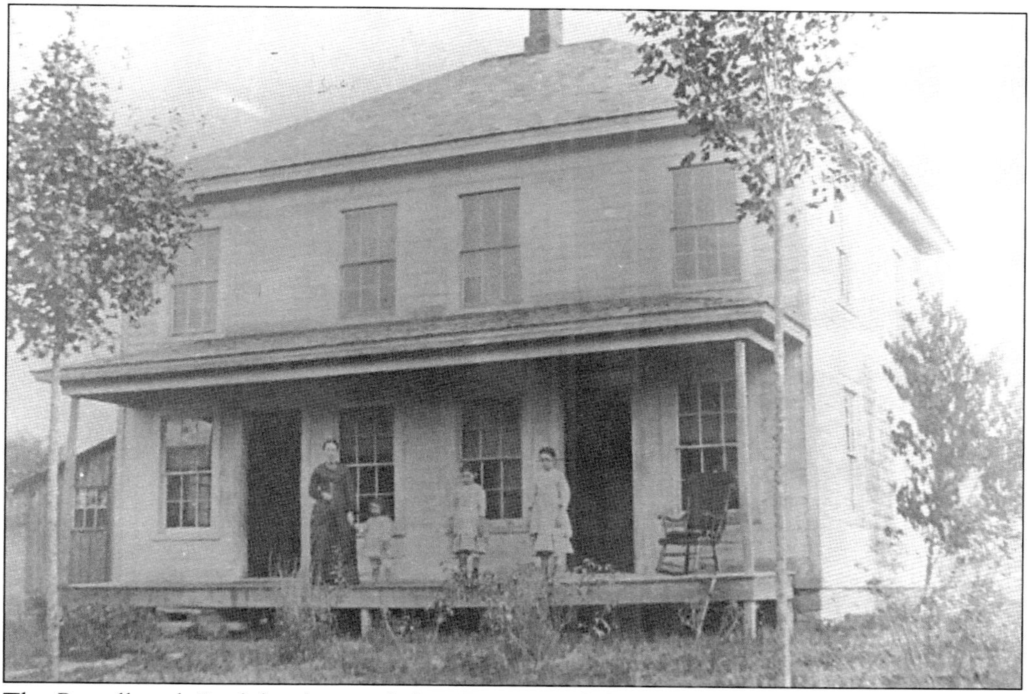

The Russell and Card families settled in Tracy Creek before 1866. Adelia, Clara, Dora, and Edith Card stand on the wide front porch of the Card farmhouse. Family members in this portrait are, from left to right, (first row) Adelia Card, Estelle Card, and Romanzo Card; (second row) Herman Card; (third row) Dora Card Russell, Clara Card Jenks, and Edith Card Munson.

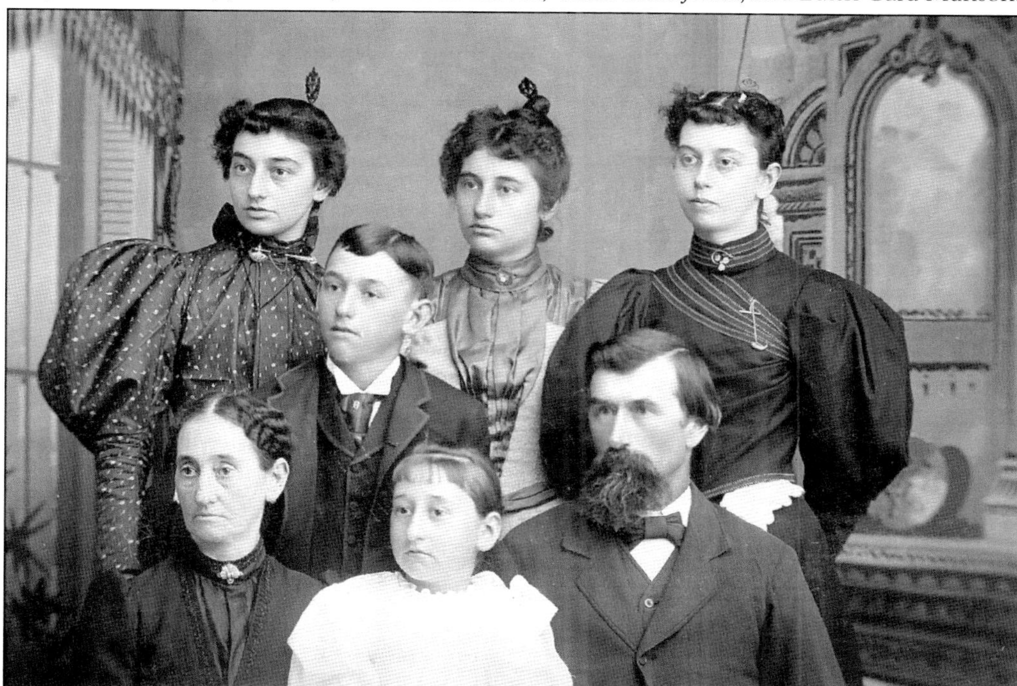

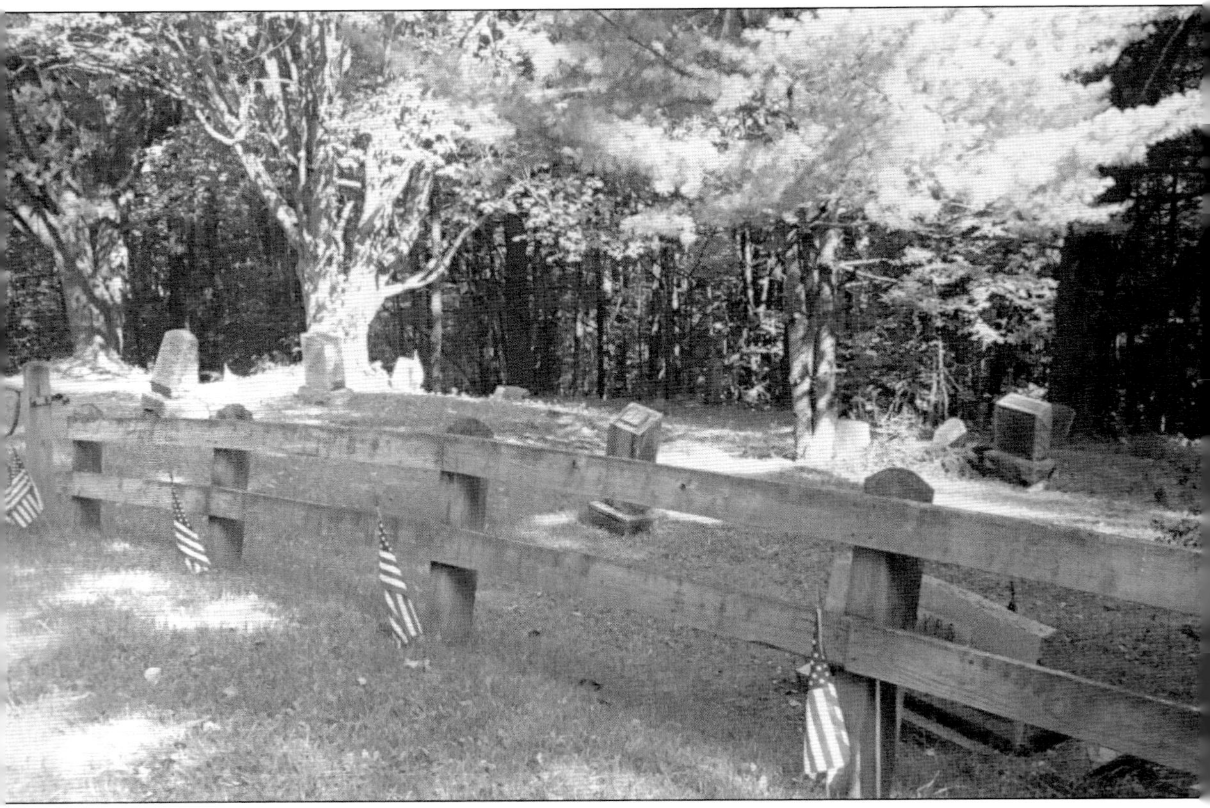

Located on a down slope along Crumm Road where it climbs the steep hillside, the Crumm Road cemetery is easy to miss. Displaying names of early Tracy Creek pioneers, some of the gravestones at the road's edge are barely behind the fence. Crumm Road Cemetery is also known as Upper Tracy Creek Cemetery.

Five

Twin Orchards

Twin Orchards is one of Vestal's smaller hamlets. Composed primarily of two large farms formerly owned by Washington I. Weed and John Mersereau, the land was acquired by William Rood in 1890. The name Twin Orchards was derived from the apple orchards on both sides of what was known as the Vestal-Binghamton concrete highway, today Vestal Road, and to some stubborn former residents, Old Vestal Road.

Before there was a Twin Orchards there was William Rood's Maples Stock Farm. Rood acquired three farms totaling 587 acres, where he raised world-famous herds of Holstein-Friesian cattle, a breed developed in the Netherlands. Industrialist George F. Johnson rented the former Rood home in 1930 to use as a training camp for German boxer Max Schmeling to prepare for his title bout with world champion and Binghamton-born Jack Sharkey. A sign in front of the home read, "En-Joie Health Camp – Max Schmeling's Home." Jack Sharkey won the fight.

In 1926, Johnson told his shoe workers, "There isn't going to be any business boom this year. Don't look for it. Your work will be fair. You will have plenty of time to make garden. You will have plenty of time to be sorry for the money you fooled away, but you still have all your life ahead of you. Learn from mistakes, apply the knowledge that comes from age."

The Troy Chemical Company, a fertilizer developer that bought the Rood farm in 1923 and subdivided it into building lots, capitalized on Johnson's statement by advertising in a full-page advertisement on May 20, 1926, that "Twin Orchards offers you big fertile lots, ideal for gardening. Twin Orchards lots are so rich that they raise wonderful produce without top dressing." True enough, spring floods regularly deposited a new layer of silt and drainage was good. The advertisements also proclaimed "high ground, no fear of water," but homeowners in 1936 quickly learned the price of deceptive advertising.

Although Twin Orchards had two small grocery stores and the Twin Orchards Baptist Church, it remained a residential community whose children were bused to schools in Willow Point and Vestal.

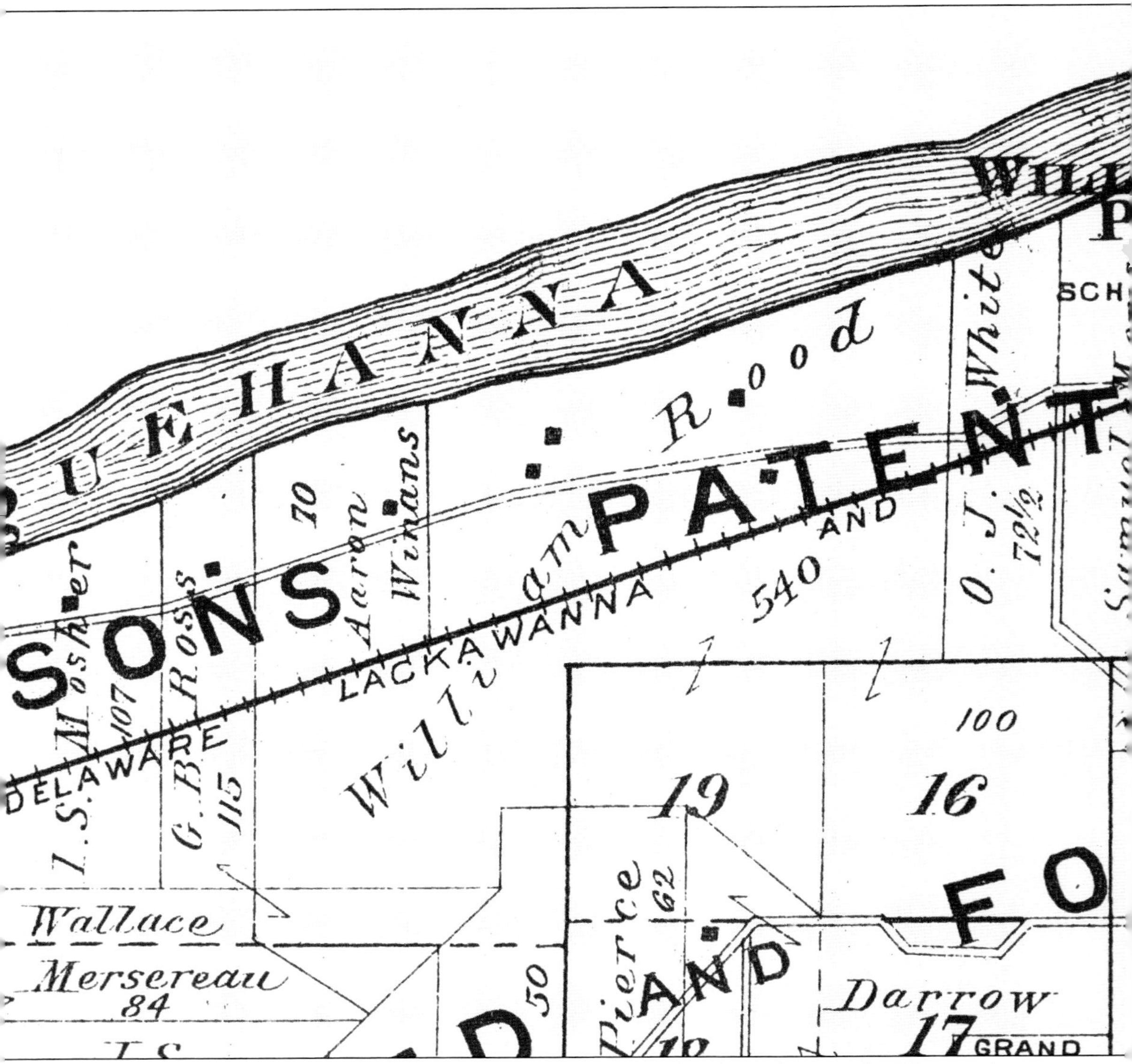

The residential community of Twin Orchards was bordered on the west by Winans Avenue, African Road on the east, old Route 17 on the south, and the Susquehanna River on the north, as shown in this 1908 map.

Seen here is all that remains of the large 1878 Victorian home of William Rood, owner of Maples Stock Farm. Once part of the large 587-acre farm, the home at the end of a locust-lined driveway sat abandoned for years before being demolished in preparation for the construction of the Route 17 Expressway in 1968. When fully operating, the well-kept farm consisted of several huge barns, a large creamery, a granary, and outbuildings. Visitors of the time described a scene of cattle grazing in pastures as far as the eye could see. A 1901 fire destroyed the main barn and several other buildings. By 1923 a large section of the farm had been sold to developer Troy Chemical Company.

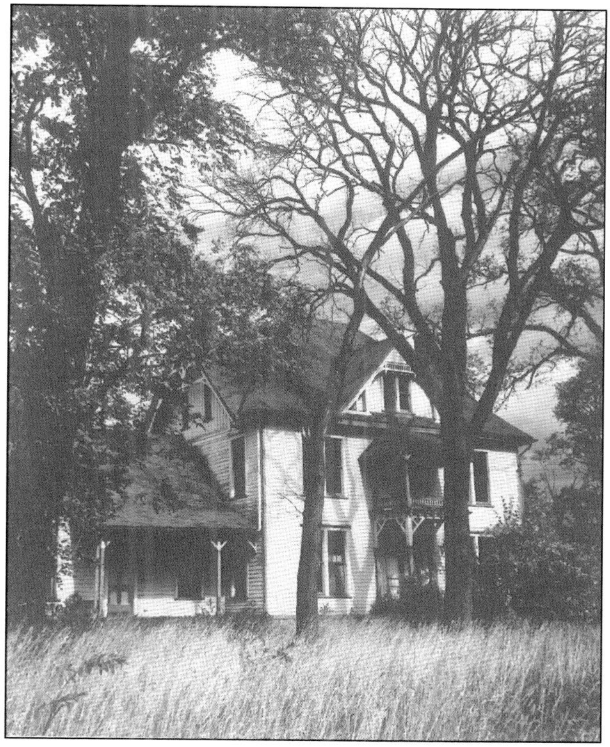

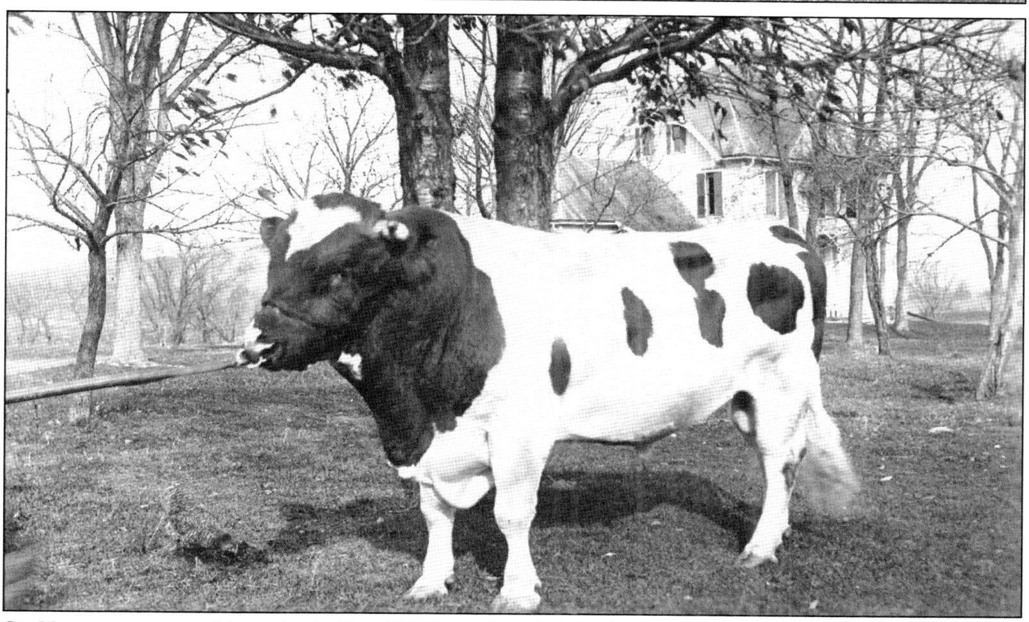

Sir Henry was one of the prize bulls of William Rood's Maples Stock Farm. Ribbons and certificates record the first prizes won at fairs throughout New York State and New England. Several times a year, circulars and other printed material bearing photographs of these prize-winning cattle with names such as Sir Netherland of Vestal and Sir Jewel of Maples were mailed around the world. (Courtesy of the Broome County Historical Society.)

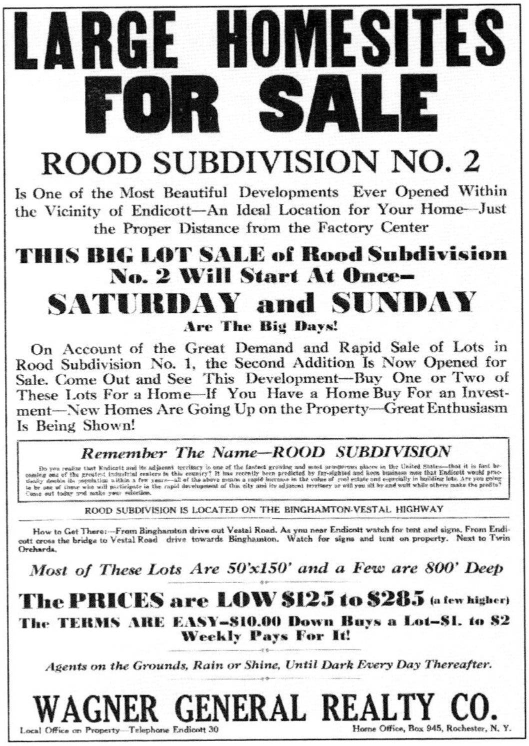

A poster from 1935 advertised the sale of large home sites in Rood Subdivision No. 2. It promised "Agents on the Grounds, Rain or Shine, Until Dark Every Day Thereafter." The reverse side of the poster diagramed the site plan and told potential buyers, "If You Have No Way of Coming to Lot Sale Call Endicott 30 and Our Car Will Call for You."

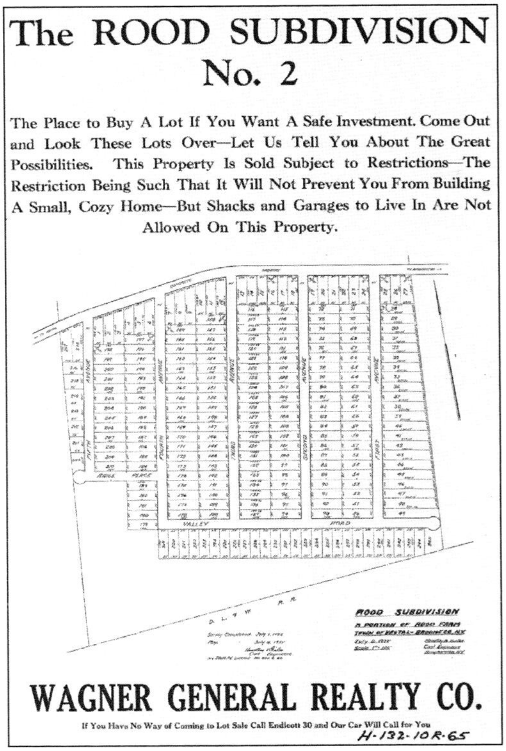

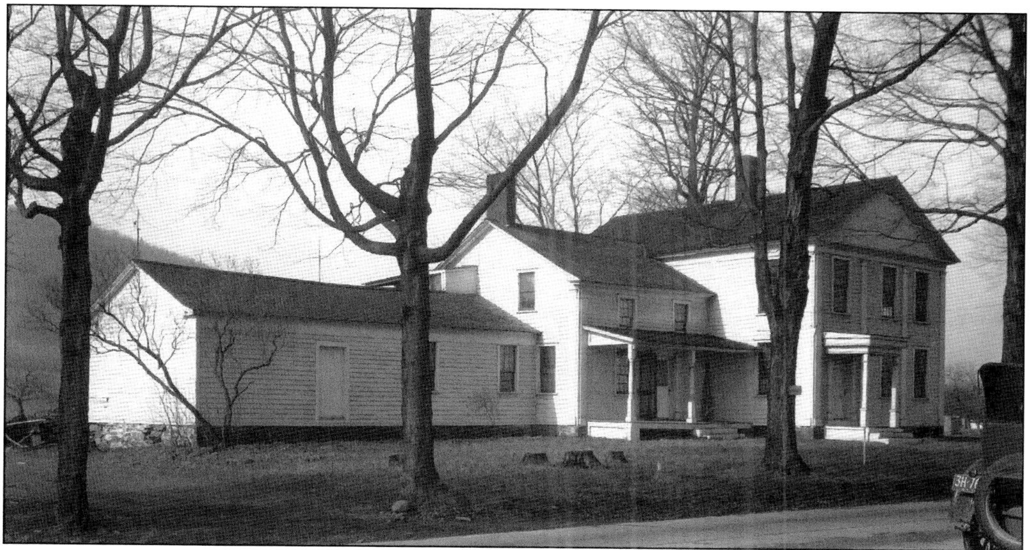

This 1835 home was advertised for sale in 1926 as a fine picturesque farmhouse offering an exceptional opportunity to establish a paying tearoom or antique shop. The advertisement continued, "Directly on the superb concrete highway over which now flows most of the Southern New York through motor traffic, it is 15 minutes from Binghamton, five minutes to Endicott." In need of restoration and 172 years old, the home retains a commanding presence in "the Orchard."

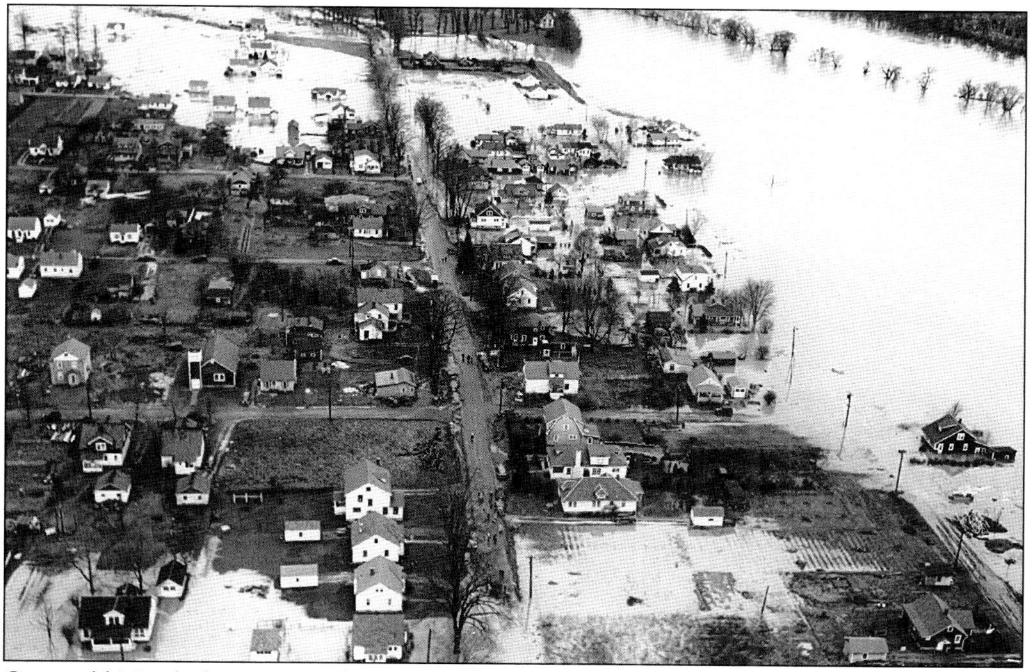

On a cold March day in 1948, the water of the Susquehanna River overflowed its banks to slip quietly into the Twin Orchards neighborhood. While some homes had water on the first floor, many suffered only wet basements and others remained dry. The Rood home can be seen at the very top edge of the photograph, at the end of a long driveway off Vestal Road.

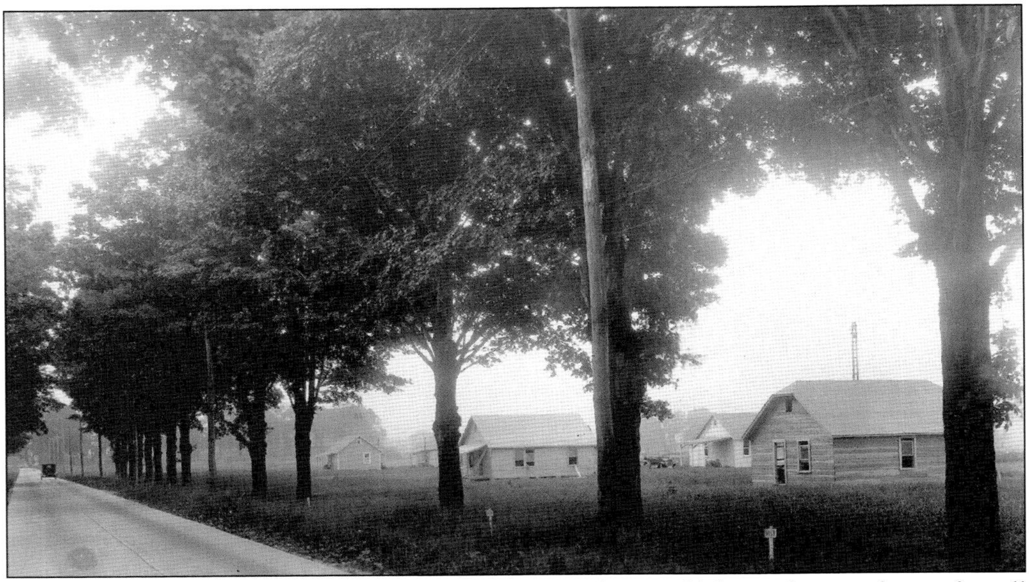

A scene along maple-lined Vestal Road about 1930 shows sold lot makers in front of small bungalows. Both the house and lot could be purchased for "a few dollars down and as little as $4.00 a week." Lots were 50 feet wide, and the developer would allow individuals to purchase a lot and build their own home.

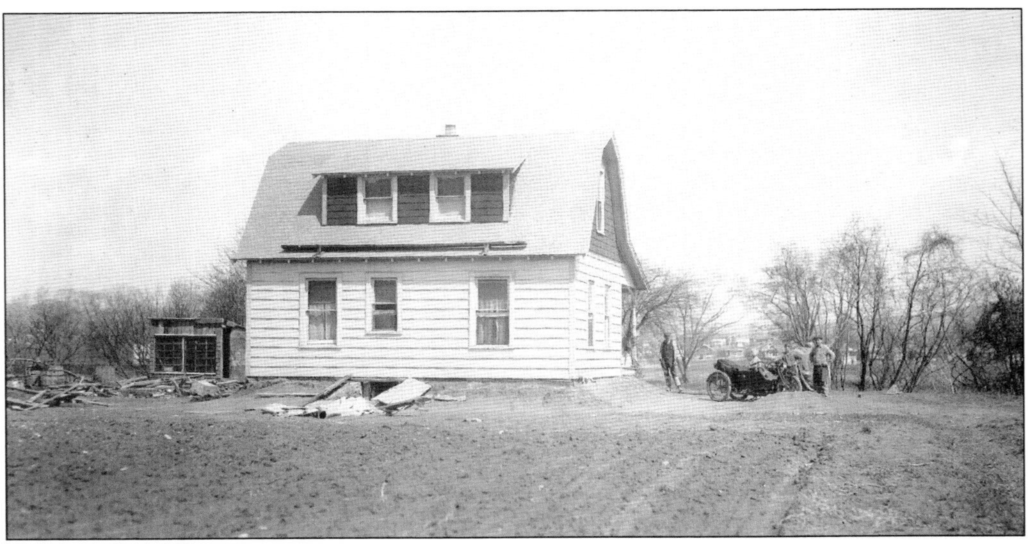

Larger homes were also built, as shown in this two-story home with a gambrel roof and exterior entrance to a cellar. Porches and extra rooms were added to smaller homes soon after they were purchased.

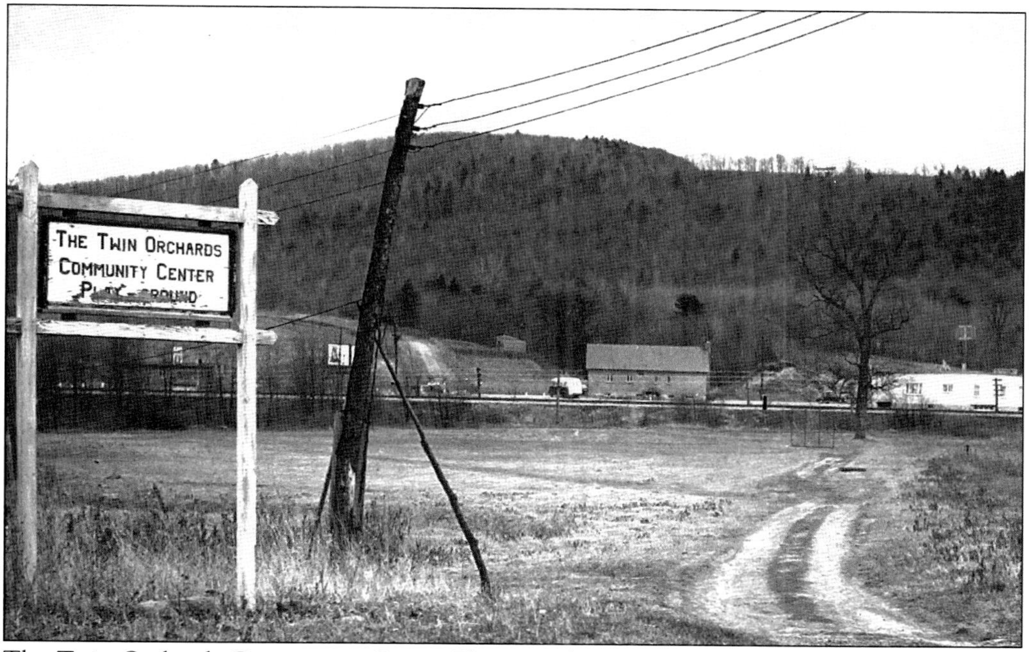

The Twin Orchards Community Center Playground started as an open field with a backstop for summer softball games. Not seen in the photograph is the community center building that could be used for all types of social activities. The park, complete with play equipment, is one of 20 parks in the town today.

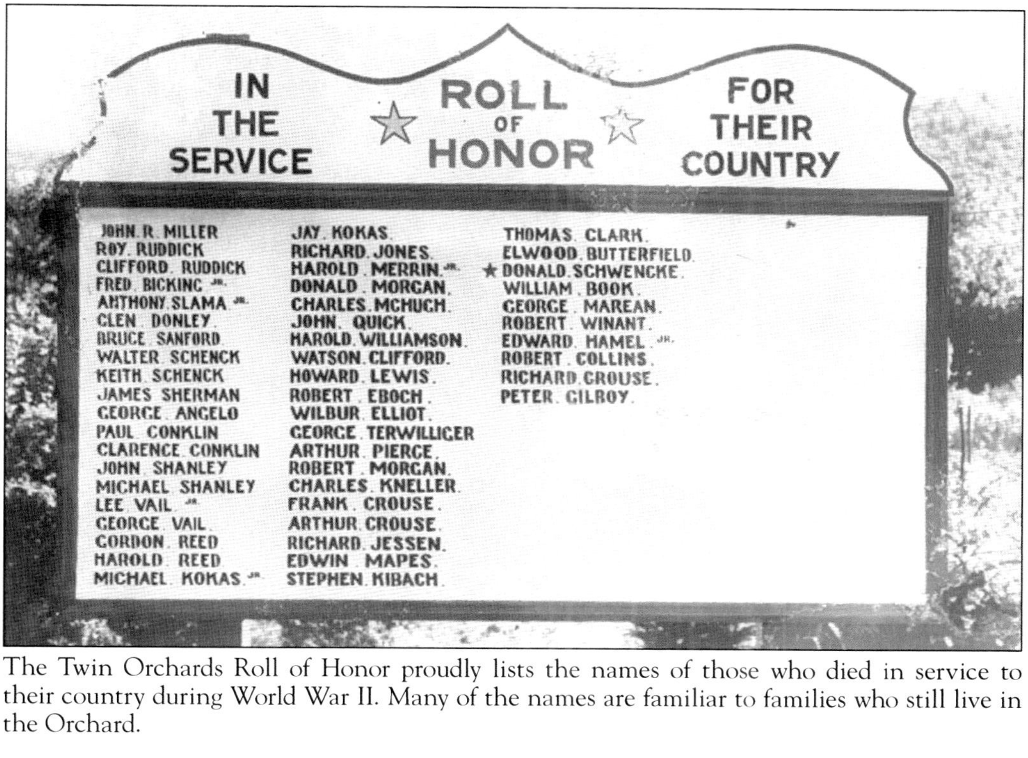

The Twin Orchards Roll of Honor proudly lists the names of those who died in service to their country during World War II. Many of the names are familiar to families who still live in the Orchard.

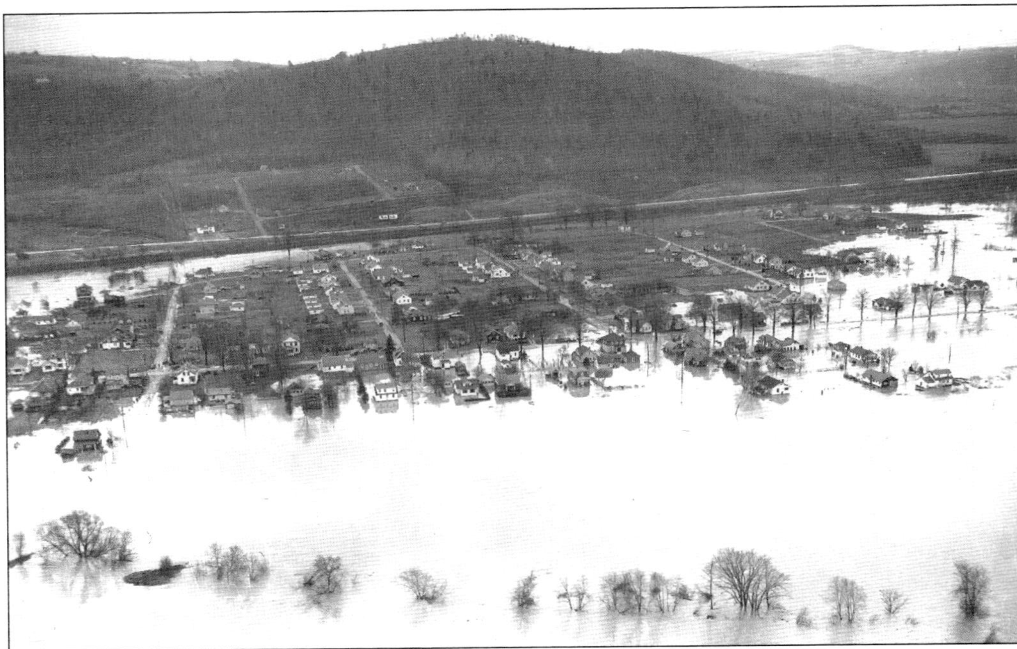

Another aerial scene of the March 1948 flood in Twin Orchards shows the riverbank tree line near the bottom, Vestal Road running horizontally near the midpoint, and the Vestal Parkway, formerly Route 17, running horizontally at the foot of the hill. In its infancy, the parkway had billboards but few buildings. (Courtesy of Ed Aswad.)

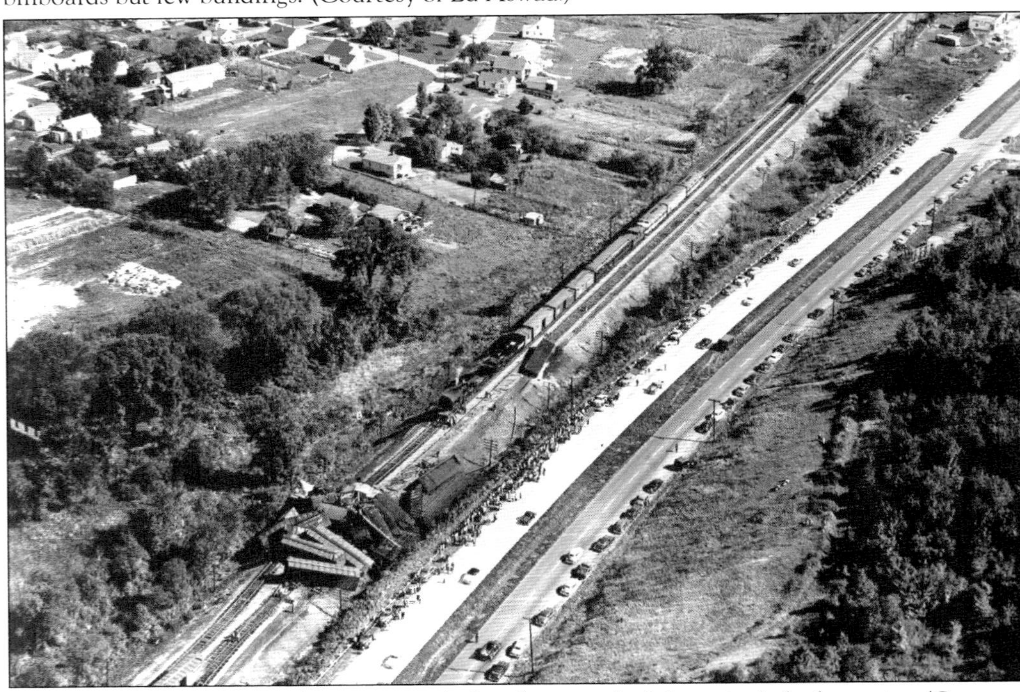

Twin Orchards experienced a train wreck that fortunately did not include dynamite. (Courtesy of the Broome County Historical Society.)

Six

Vestal Center

The hamlet of Vestal Center is situated on the Big Choconut Creek, east of Tracy Creek. An early settler, Jabish Truesdell, one of George Washington's bodyguards, arrived from Connecticut about 1804. A bustling community, Vestal Centre, as it was spelled until 1893, had an undertaker, a blacksmith shop, a wagon maker, gristmills, sawmills, and planning mills, a post office, a creamery, three one-room schools, a tannery, two churches, a hotel, a boardinghouse, and stores. William and Jennie Hillis moved to Vestal Center in 1884, where they started one of the three boardinghouses used by lumbermen and bark peelers working in the French Tract.

The Friendsville Stage, a large open stagecoach, ran from Friendsville, Pennsylvania, through Vestal Center to Binghamton, providing mail and passenger service. Vestal Center residents gathered at Batcher's Inn in 1912 when ex-president Theodore Roosevelt came to town to campaign as the Bull Moose candidate.

The descendants of early Vestal Center settlers remained in the hamlet to become land and business owners, as well as government leaders. They included Charles Russell, Daniel Price, Jacob Maricle, John Fairbrother, Henry Osincup, N. Grippen, Daniel DePew, and Charles Swan, to name a few.

Because road names changed over the years, Chocount Creek Road is now Route 26, Sugar Creek Road is now Powderhouse Road, the current West Hill Road began after it crossed Glenwood, and the small section from Chocount Creek Road to Glenwood Road was known as Center Hill Road. Glenwood Road was known as "the back road to Vestal Center." Vestal Center today is primarily a residential community.

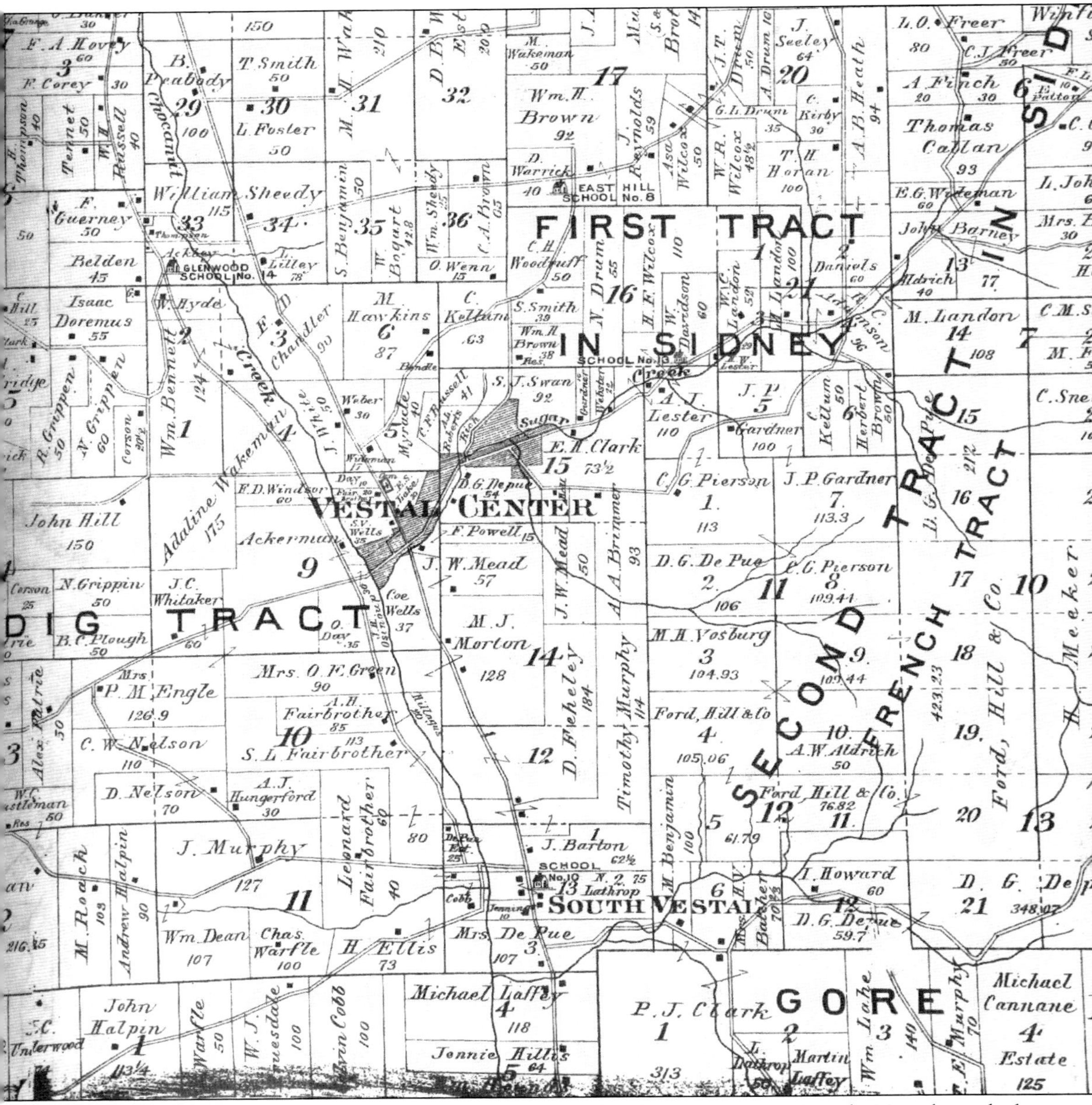

The southeast portion of the township includes Vestal Center, South Vestal, and the French Tract.

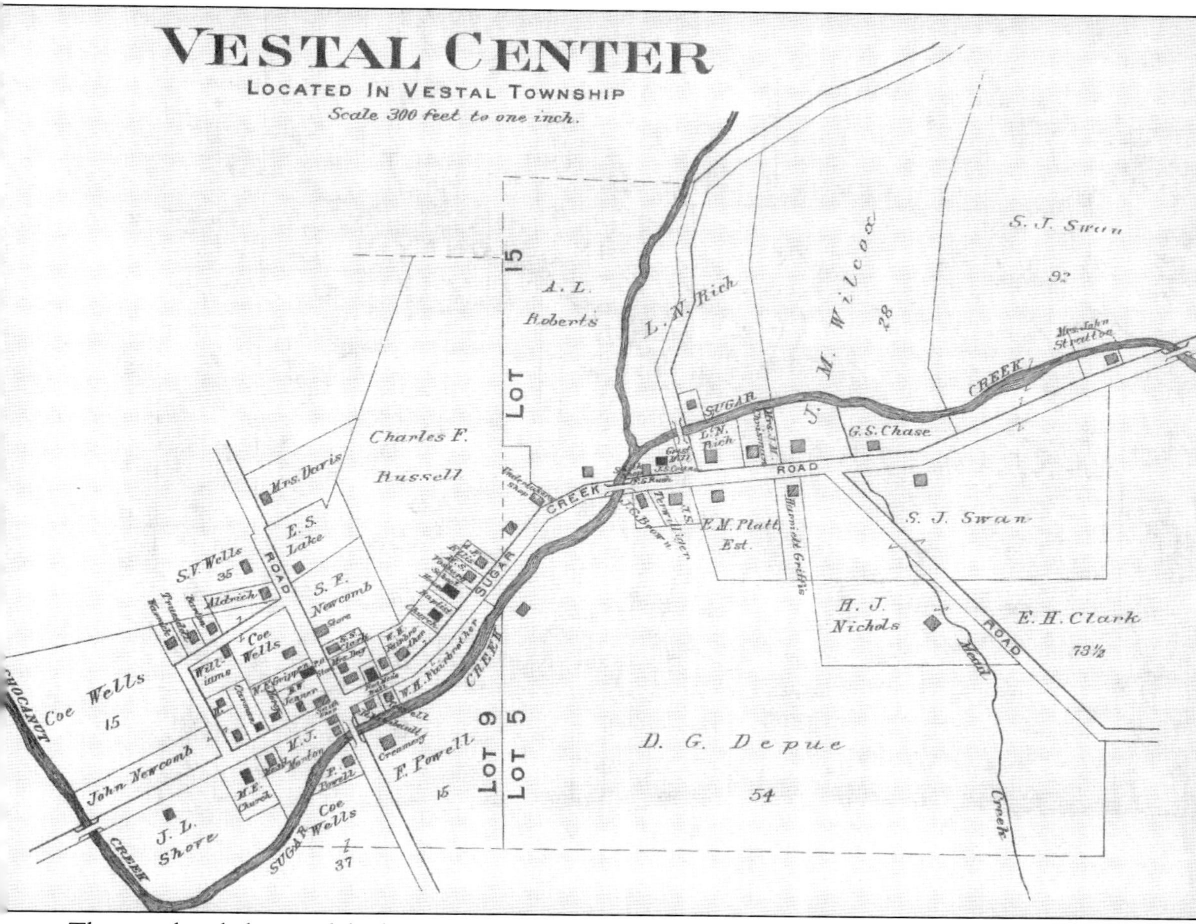

This is a detailed map of the business section of Vestal Center in 1908.

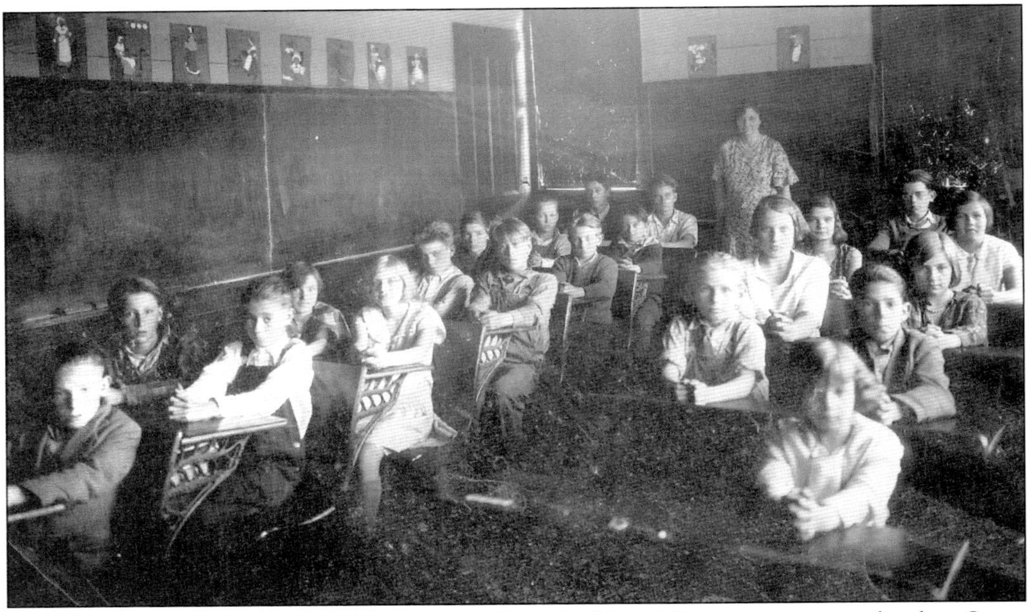

There are few smiles in this 1931 class picture from the Vestal Center two-room school on Sugar Creek Road. Some of the students have been identified; they are from front to back beginning with the row along the chalkboard: Doug Ellis, Ethel Wilcox, Earl Benjamin, Philip Wilcox, Clyde Pierce, and Ed Tucker; (second row) Curtis Cargill, ? Clark, Charlotte Harvey, Beverly Ellis, unidentified, unidentified, unidentified, and teacher; (on the right side of the room, row closest to the aisle) ? Hickling, Goldie May Warrik, Charlotte Tucker, ? Clark; (row on the right) Dorothy Warner, Melvin Cargill, Ruth Striley, and Darleen Warner.

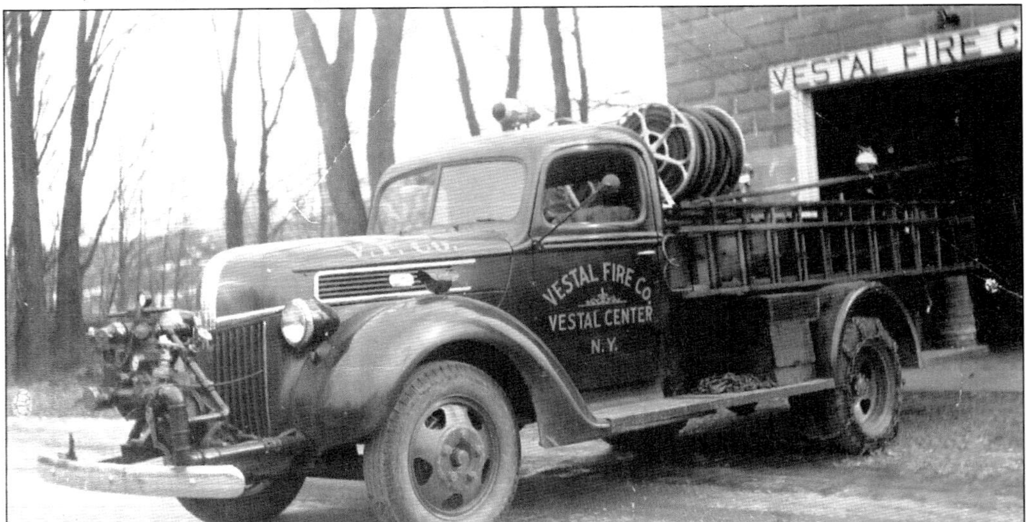

The Vestal Center Volunteer Fire Station No. 2 was incorporated in June 1938 with 65 charter members. The first building, located on Sugar Creek Road, was erected the same year with only one bay. This 1941 Ford pumper was designated E2, a code indicating that it was an engine belonging to Company No. 2. By 1950, more space was needed and a second truck bay was added to the building.

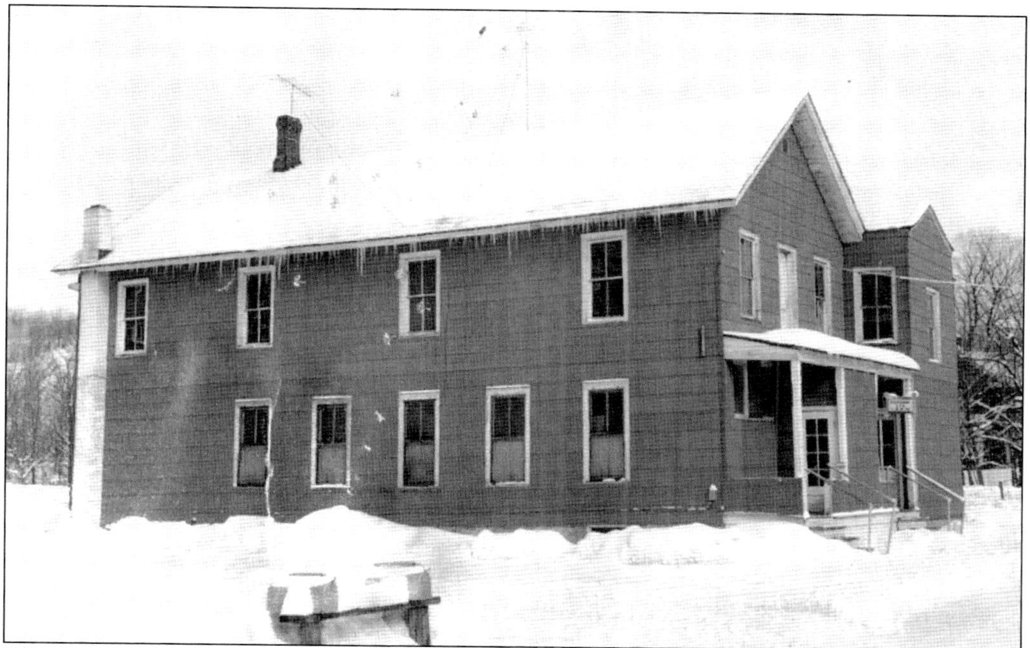

The first Redmen's Lodge was located on Sugar Creek Road across from the fire station. The building had previously been a grocery store and a cigar factory. Although this building was demolished, a new Redmen's Lodge was built less than a block from the original location.

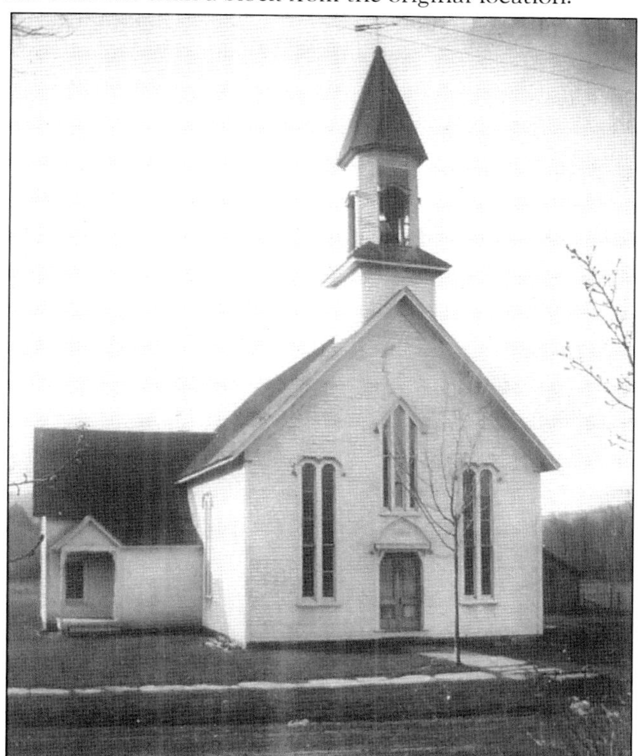

The Vestal Center Methodist Church on Center Hill Road was built in 1875. A small prayer room was added to the large clapboard church in about 1896. Until 1915, there were horse sheds on the west side of the church. More recently, a larger addition, consisting of a fellowship hall and Sunday school classrooms, replaced the prayer room. This well-cared-for historic church remains the center of community activity in the hamlet.

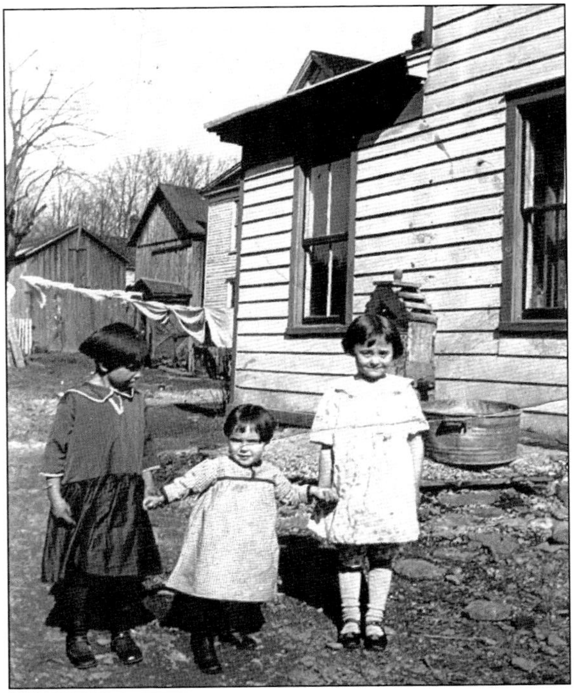

Vestal Center had two community wells, complete with hand pump and drinking dipper. One was located between George Sumner's store and the Batcher Hotel. The other was on the east side of Choconut Creek Road, near the corner of Sugar Creek Road, now Powderhouse Road. The three girls holding hands in front of the community well in this 1928 photograph are, from left to right, Maxine Clapper, Dorothy Cargill, and Ruth Cargill.

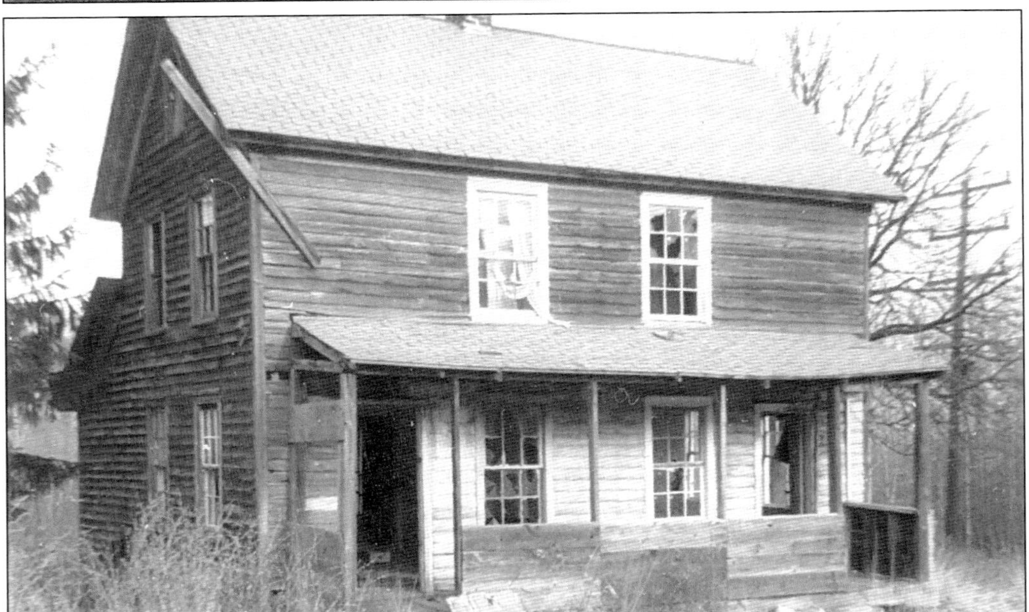

By January 1960, the Anna Stone house located near Stone and Powderhouse Roads was abandoned. The Stone farm, also called Hawthorne Heights, was the location of four brick magazines where black powder, dynamite, and fireworks were stored first by the Schaghticoke Powder Company and later by Callahan and Douglass. When the 1901 train wreck occurred, some residents thought the powder houses had exploded. These powder magazines influenced the renaming of Sugar Creek Road to Powderhouse Road.

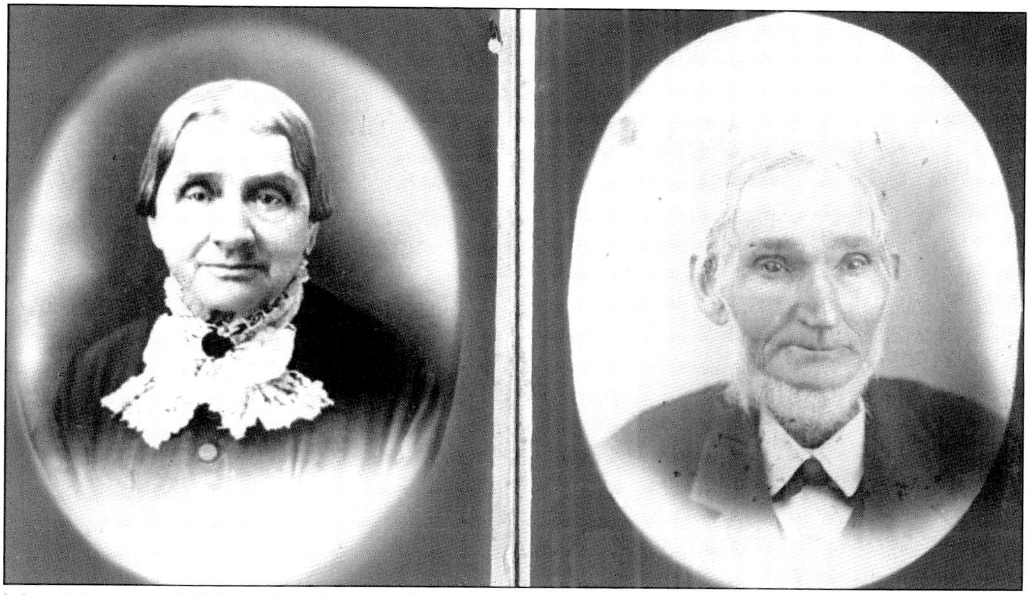

Meet Hiram and Selina Gardner. A farmer, Hiram was also a clergyman, while Selina tended the house. Son Lyman Gardner, who lived with them, was listed as a peddler in the 1880 census. Gardner Road bears their name.

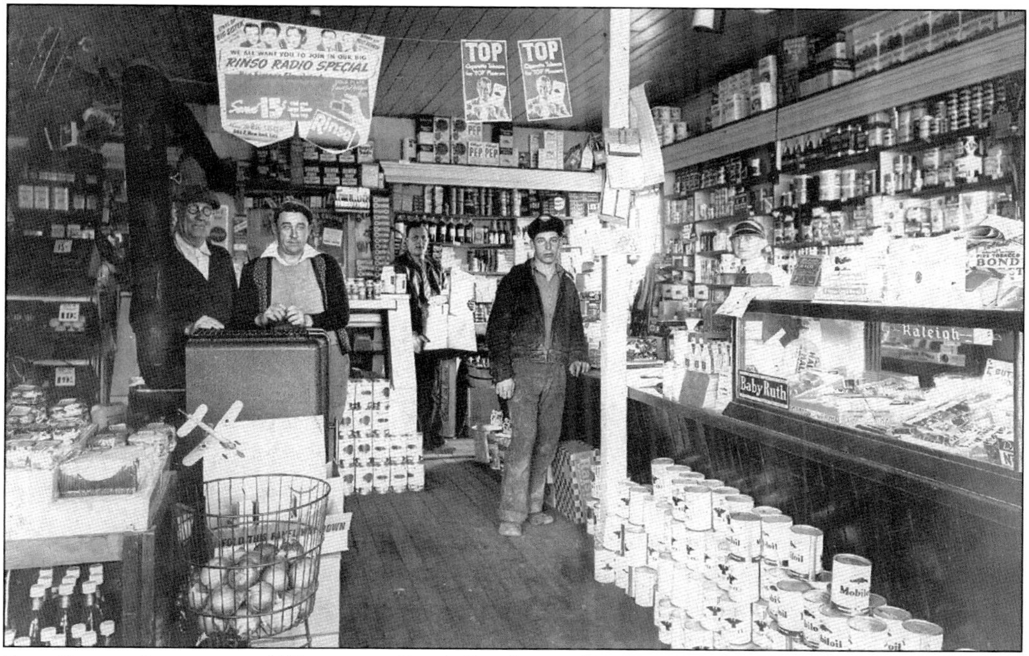

Standing at the corner of Choconut Creek Road, now Route 26, and Center Hill Road, which is now West Hill Road, was George Sumner's general store. Built before 1870, the building is now an apartment house. This photograph shows the well-stocked shelves of Sumner's store, which carried everything from candy to motor oil. The customers in this 1930s picture are, from left to right, George Bond, Seymour Jenkins, and Curtis Cargill. Sumner stands behind the counter at the right.

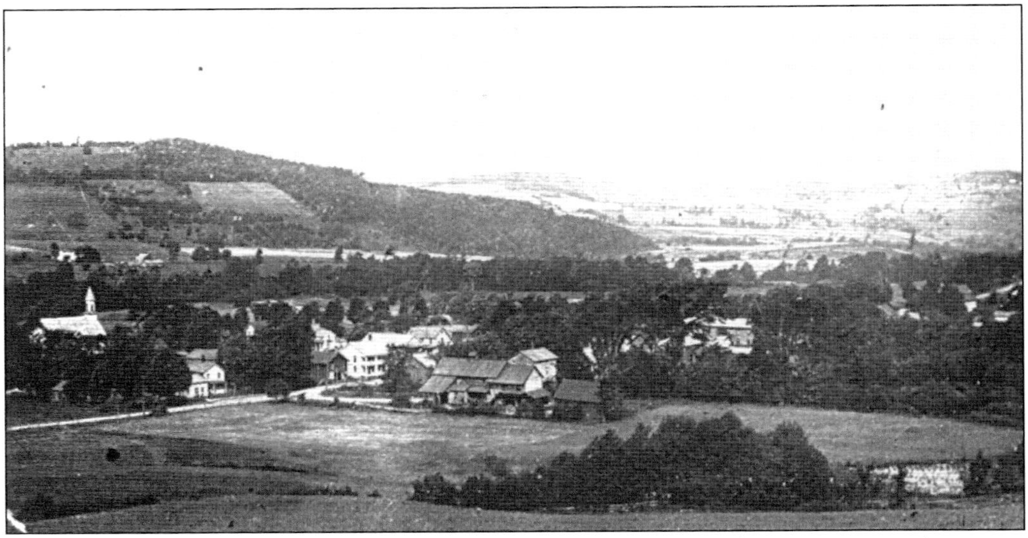

This 1909 aerial view of Vestal Center looking northwest shows the creamery in the center foreground, the steeple of the Methodist church at the left, the blacksmith's shop across the road from the creamery, and Batcher's Hotel to the right of the blacksmith's shop. Today's wooded hillsides were open fields in 1909.

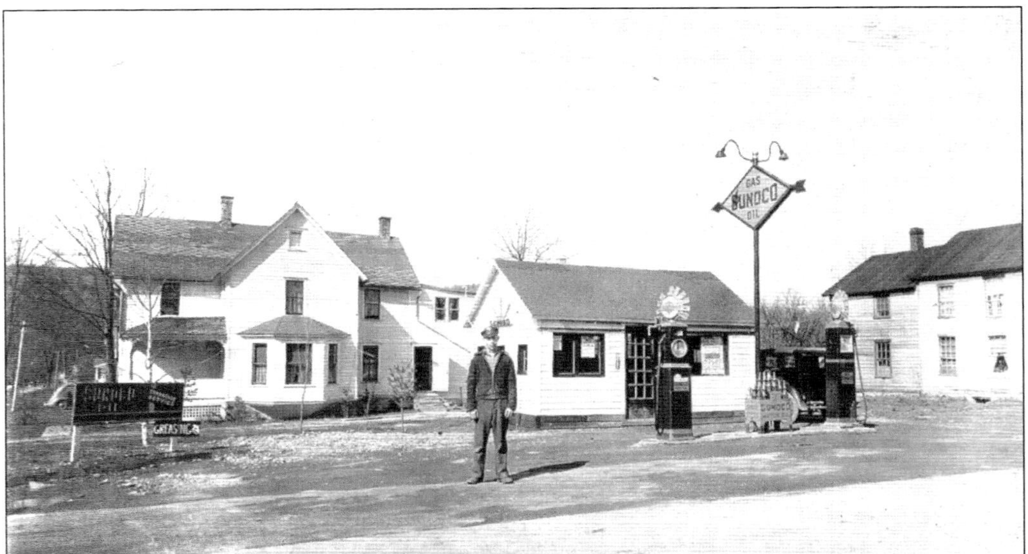

By the late 1930s, Choconut Creek Road had been paved, and the blacksmith's shop, no longer needed, had been replaced with a small Sunoco gas station.

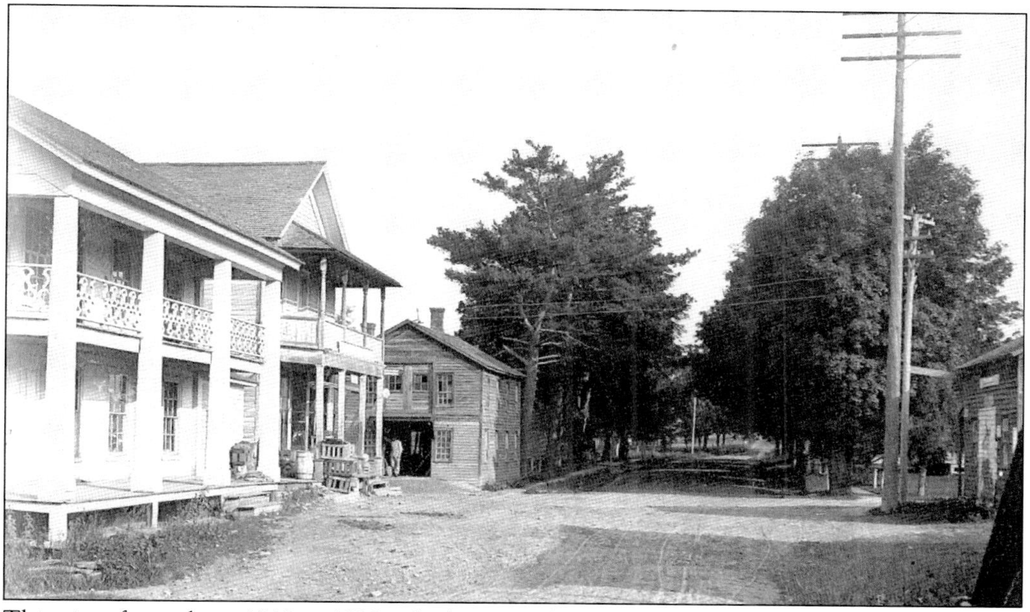

This view from about 1910 to 1920 is looking north on Choconut Creek Road through Vestal Center's main intersection. Center Hill Road is to the left, and Sugar Creek Road is to the right. The buildings on the left are the Batcher Hotel, George Sumner's store, and the blacksmith's shop with the open door. The photographer is standing on the bridge that crosses Sugar Creek as it winds its way to the Big Choconut Creek.

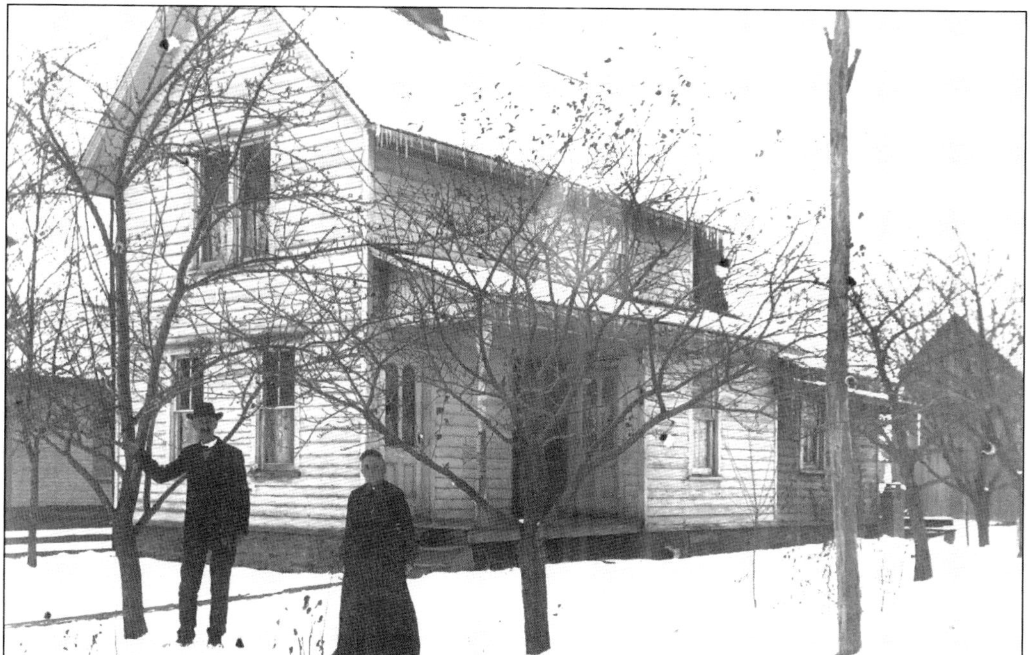

David and Mary Nichols pose in front of their Sugar Creek Road home in approximately 1907. Although homes and businesses around them changed or are no longer, the house and the barn remain much the same today as in this picture.

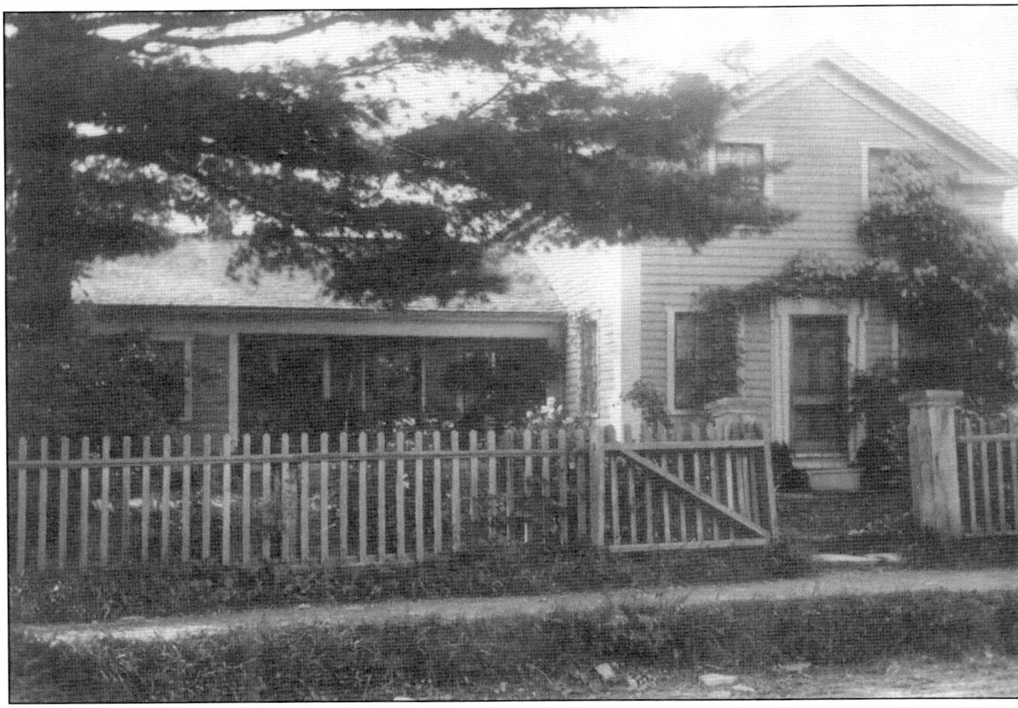

Just east of the Vestal Center Baptist Church and the two-room schoolhouse on Sugar Creek Road was the Charles F. Russell Funeral Home. Charles Russell was born on Glenwood Road and was the son of early settler Aaron Russell. Charles's granddaughter lives on a parcel of land adjoining the original Glenwood Road farmhouse. This house has been remodeled into a private residence, and the fence no longer defines the edge of the front lawn.

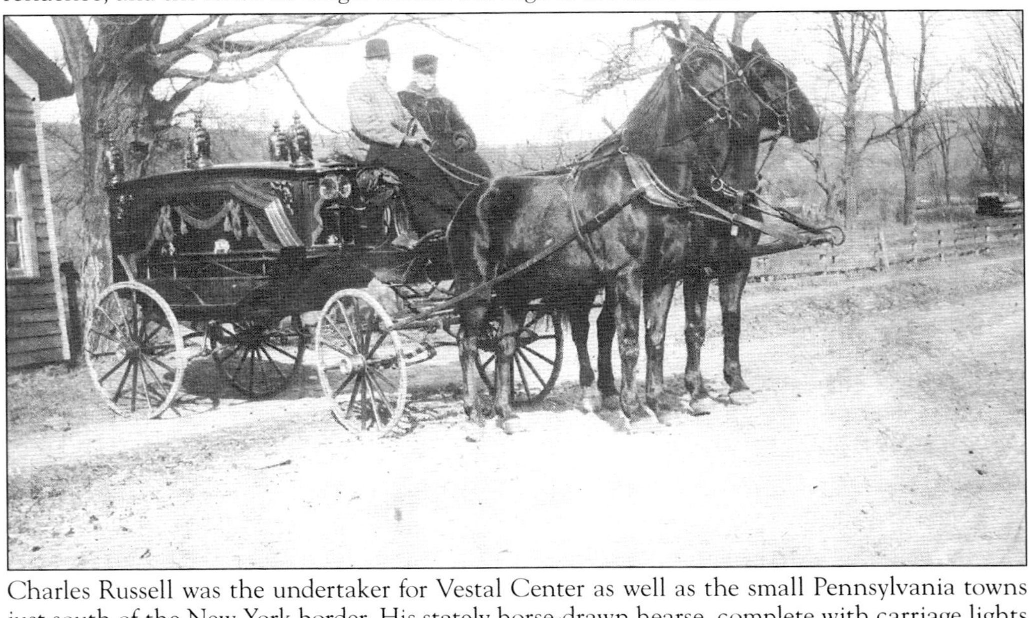

Charles Russell was the undertaker for Vestal Center as well as the small Pennsylvania towns just south of the New York border. His stately horse-drawn hearse, complete with carriage lights and elegant drapes, carried many residents to their final resting place.

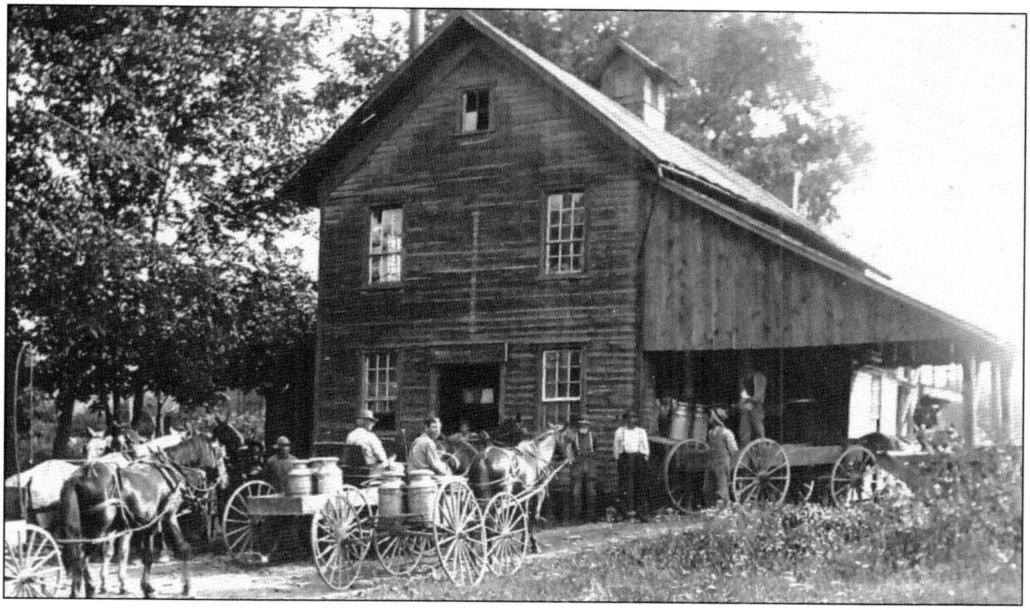

Dairy farmers line up to unload their wagons at the creamery in this photograph from around 1900. The creamery was located just south of Sugar Creek Road, near the site of the current fire station. Established as a corporation in February 1898, the Vestal Center Creamery Company was set up for a 25-year duration. There were five directors, Sylvenus Fairbrother, David Feheley, Marvin Morton, John Osincup, and William Fairbrother, and 17 subscribers.

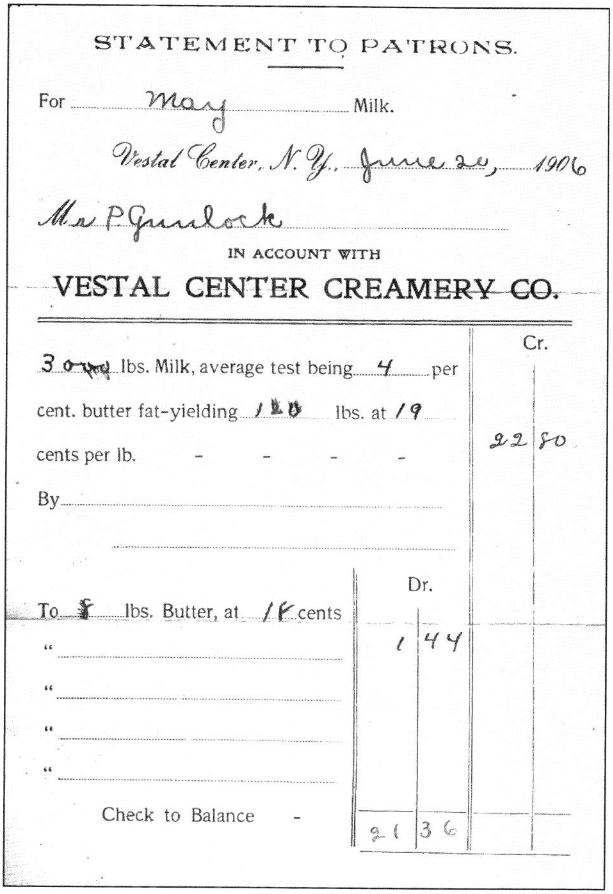

STATEMENT TO PATRONS.

For May Milk.

Vestal Center, N. Y., June 20, 1906

Mr P. Gunlock

IN ACCOUNT WITH

VESTAL CENTER CREAMERY CO.

		Cr.
3000 lbs. Milk, average test being 4 per cent. butter fat-yielding 120 lbs. at 19 cents per lb. - - - -		22 80
By		
	Dr.	
To 8 lbs. Butter, at 18 cents	1 44	
"		
"		
"		
"		
Check to Balance -	21 36	

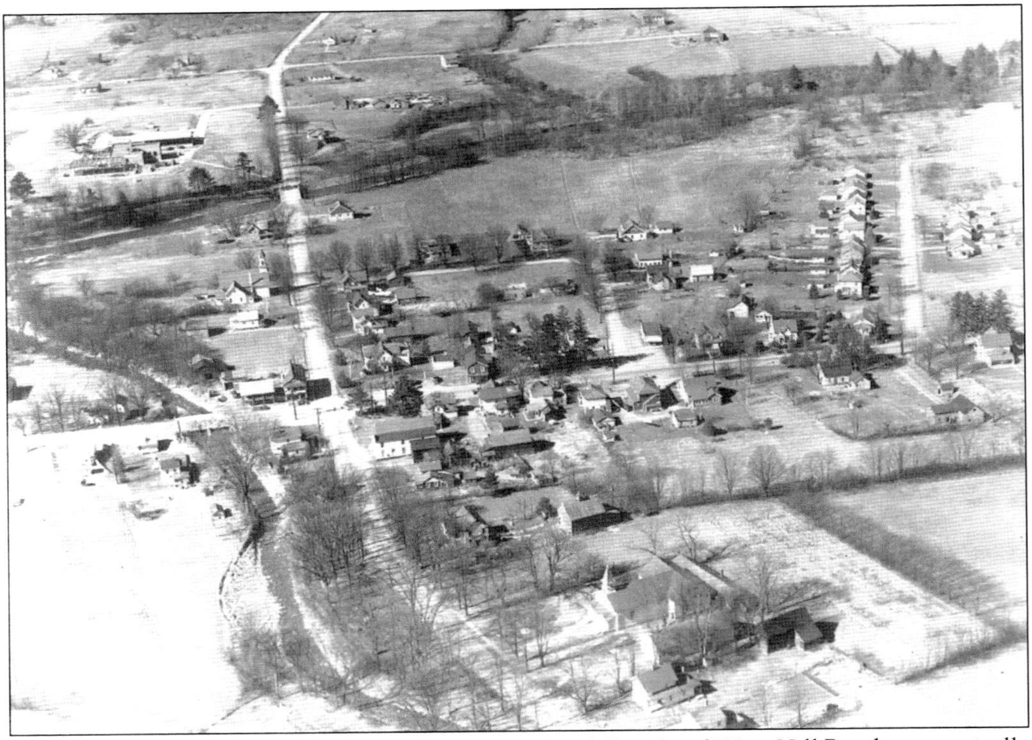

An aerial photograph shows Vestal Center. Sugar Creek Road and West Hill Road run vertically near the left. Choconut Creek Road, now Route 26, runs horizontally near the center, and Glenwood Road appears horizontally near the top. The Vestal Center Baptist Church, the first church in the hamlet, is at the bottom near the middle. Batcher's Inn and Sumner's Store are at the intersection. The Vestal Center School built in 1939 is near the top left corner.

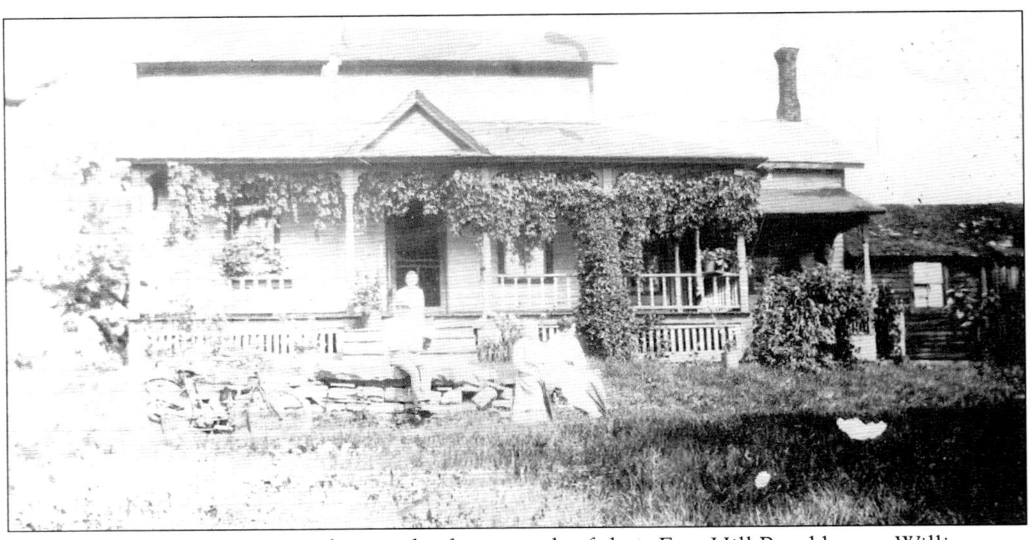

William and Eva McManus relax on the front porch of their East Hill Road home. William was a farmer who took eggs and honey to market in a red and green wagon. A 1927 fire destroyed the home, leaving only the chimney standing.

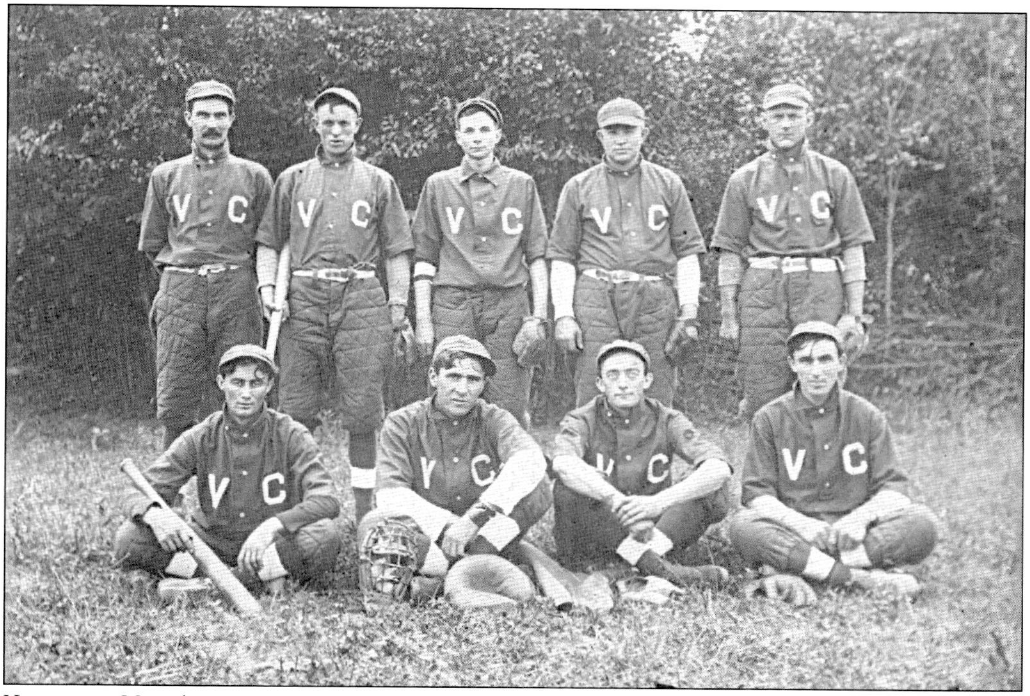

Known as Vestal Center's "Champion Nine," they were the hamlet's ball club of 1906. They are, from left to right, (first row) George Landon, Richard Day, Floyd Ball, and L. Haskell; (second row) Fred Clark, Earl Hillis, supervising principal Frank E. Brimmer, Ray Landon, and Coe Wells.

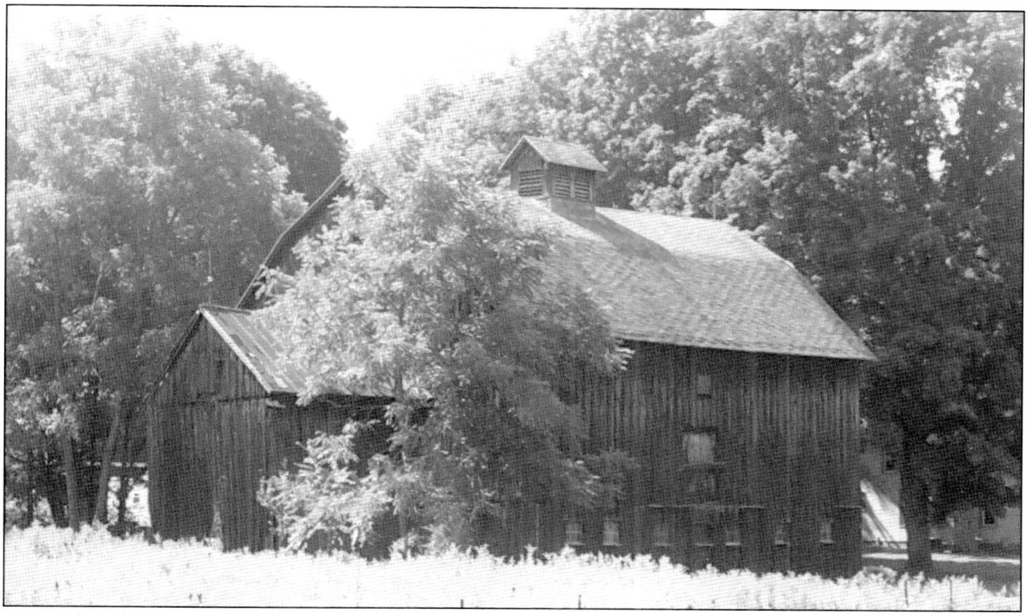

Samuel and Alma Swan lived in a farmhouse on Sugar Creek Road at the western end of Gardner Road. They built this handsome barn in 1880 for a herd of cows, all with names and specific milking times, according to a note on the barn wall.

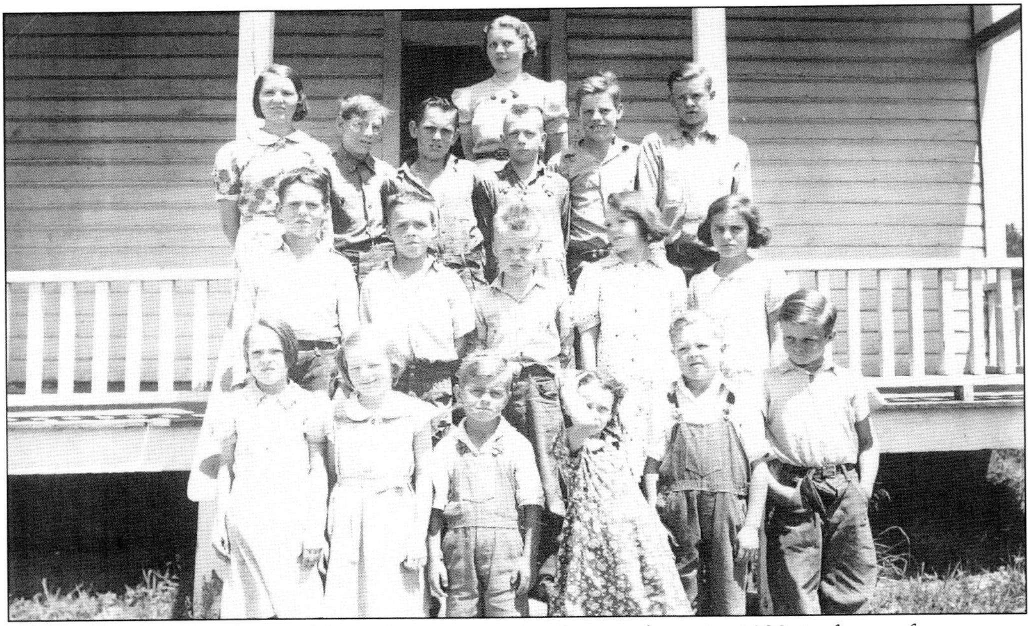

Leah Whitman, a 21-year-old teacher, poses with her students in 1938 in front of one-room Sschool No. 11 on Castleman Road. From the names, it is easy to see that brothers and sisters grew up attending class together. Seen here are, from left to right, (first row) Barbara Nelson, Edith Samson, Elmer Stanton, Helen Davis, Bruce Palmer, and Paul Walters; (second row) Richard Nelson, Douglas Nelson, Richard Samson, Barbara Nelson, and Shirley Stanton. (third row) Carolyn Nelson, Leland Wood, Bernard Stanton, Kenneth Underwood, Russell Stanton, and Herbert Walters.

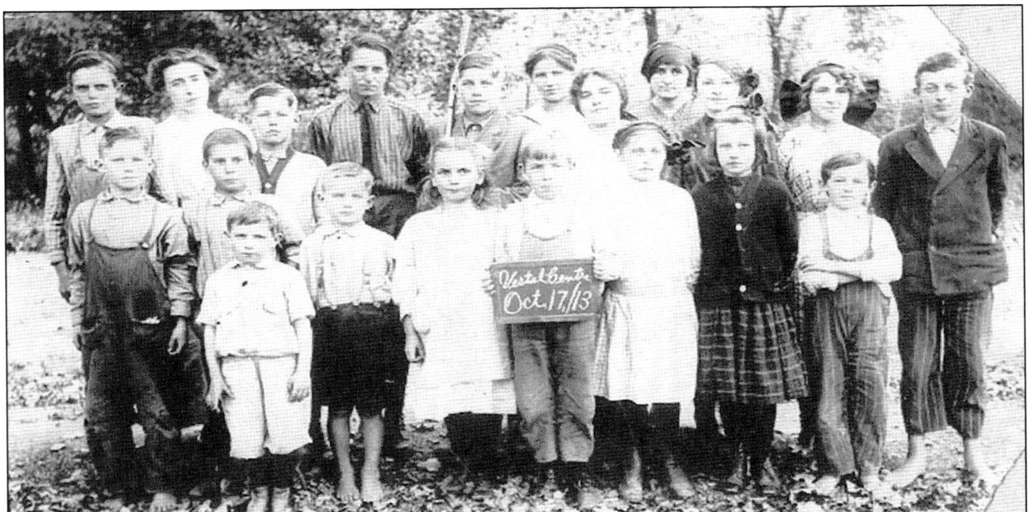

Students from the two-room Vestal Center School pose with a placard bearing the date of October 17, 1913. Only a few of the students have been identified. They are Mildred Landon, standing to the right of the boy with the sign; to the right of Landon is Belle Fairbrother; and behind Belle is Ruth Fairbrother. The barefooted boy on the far right is Herman Fairbrother. The Fairbrothers were among the earliest residents of Vestal Center and were active in town government.

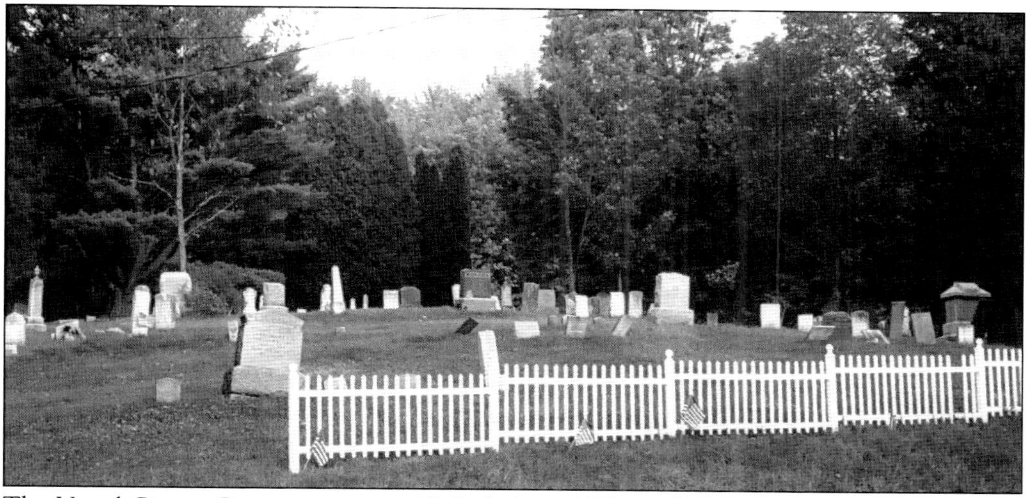

The Vestal Center Cemetery was established about 1813 on the east side of Chocount Creek Road, just north of Vestal Center. The grave of Revolutionary War hero Jabish Truesdell is found in the front row. The Vestal Center Cemetery Association, which was formed in 1909, is no longer active, and although the cemetery has burials, there are no remaining plots.

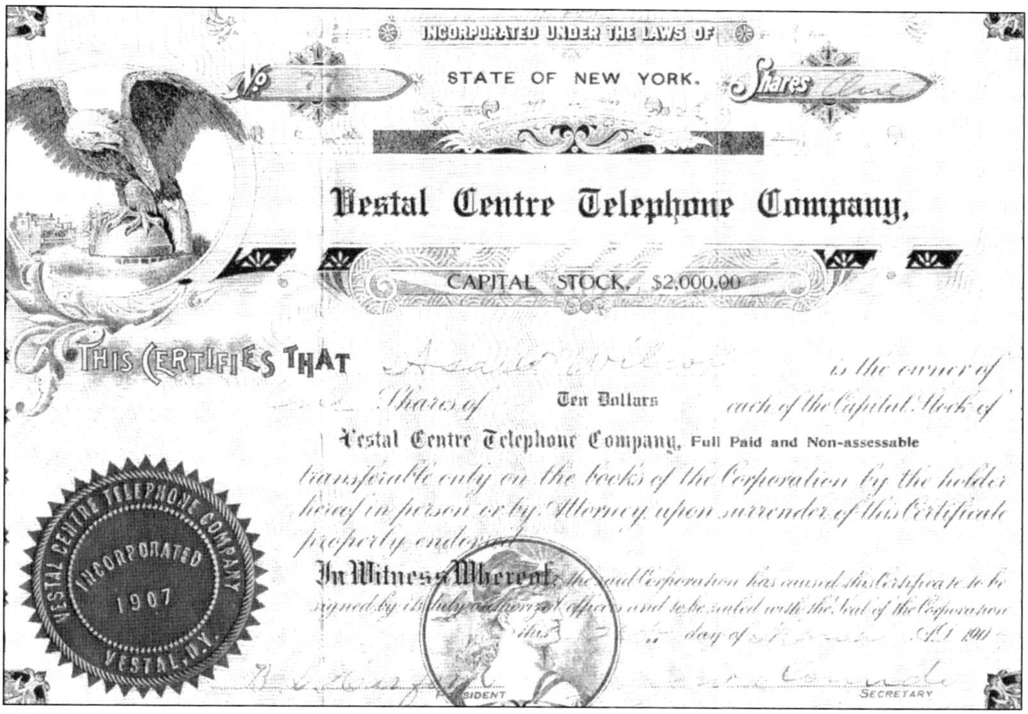

INCORPORATED UNDER THE LAWS OF
STATE OF NEW YORK.
No. 77 Shares One

Vestal Centre Telephone Company,

CAPITAL STOCK, $2,000.00

THIS CERTIFIES THAT Asa Wilson is the owner of One Shares of Ten Dollars each of the Capital Stock of Vestal Centre Telephone Company, Full Paid and Non-assessable transferable only on the books of the Corporation by the holder hereof in person or by Attorney upon surrender of this Certificate properly endorsed.

In Witness Whereof, the said Corporation has caused this Certificate to be signed by its duly authorized officers and to be sealed with the Seal of the Corporation this day of A.D. 1911

VESTAL CENTRE TELEPHONE COMPANY INCORPORATED 1907 VESTAL, N.Y.

PRESIDENT   SECRETARY

The Vestal Center Phone Company was started by Capt. Jim Brown and Edward Lake in 1906. Members purchased shares in the company, which operated until about 1947. Several households shared a party line, with each having a different number of rings to indicate who should answer the call. When they were courting, Jessie Lake and Ray Landon solved the problem of others listening to their conversations by setting a time when both would pick up the telephone to talk without ringing.

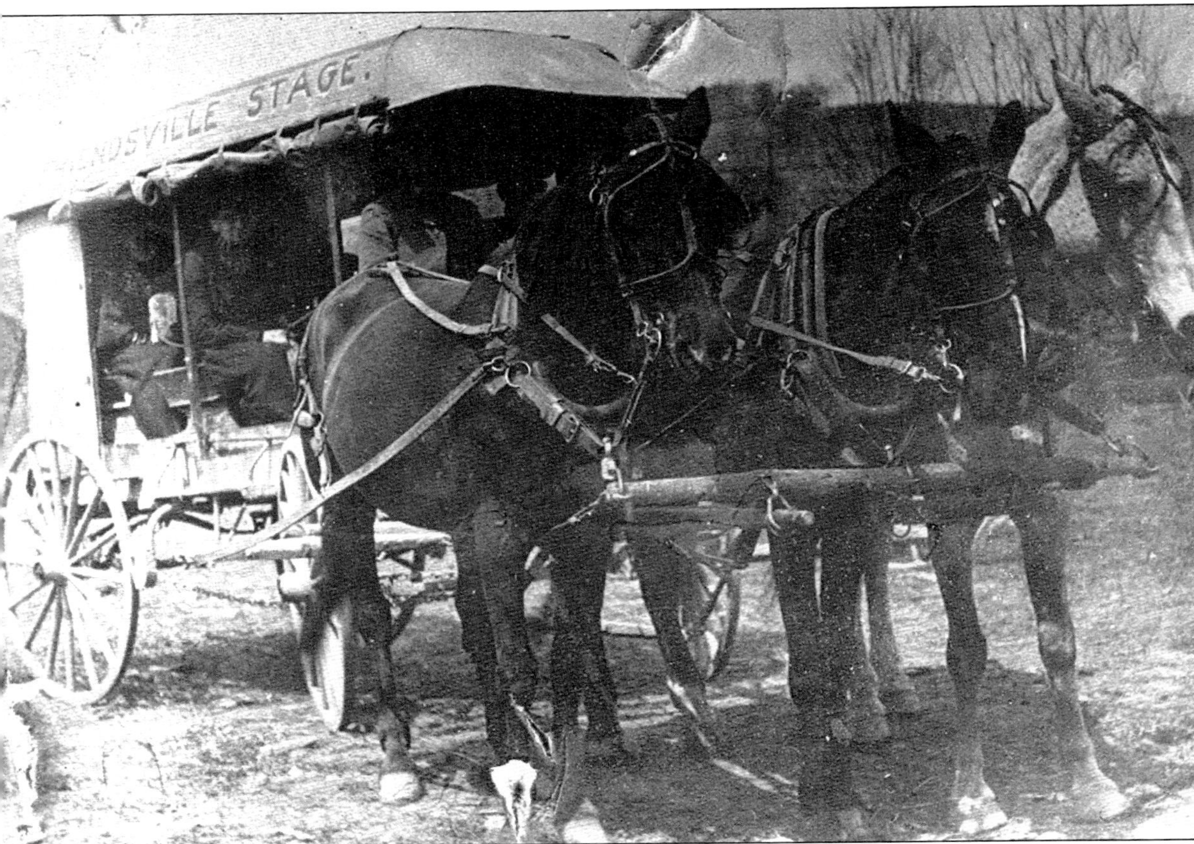

The Friendsville Stage transported passengers, mail, and sometimes freight from Friendsville, Pennsylvania, to Vestal Center and on to Binghamton along the Binghamton-Vestal Center Road, now Powderhouse Road. In bad weather, the steep Ingraham Hill Road in the town of Binghamton required the use of three horses. Extra horses were kept at Vestal Center. Although the route was still active in 1982, passengers and mail were carried by car. A second stage, the "Connie Mack," ran between Friendsville, Pennsylvania, and Apalachin, New York.

Seven

Willow Point

The area of Vestal from approximately African Road east to the city of Binghamton line and south to Bunn Hill is part of the hamlet of Willow Point. Named for the willow trees growing on the point of land jutting into the Susquehanna River, Willow Point was the location of a Native American encampment.

Willow Point had a number of large farms and businesses. In addition to the O'Hara Willow Point Stock Farm, I. A. Martin Dairy Farm, Gates farm, and Hazard Lewis Dairy Farm, there was a chicken farm, general store, and creamery. Like Tracy Creek, students attended Upper or Lower Willow Point Schools based on their proximity to the school.

Construction of the Chenango Canal Extension, a 40-mile extension of the Chenango Canal between Binghamton and Athens, Pennsylvania, began in 1868 with the first 15 miles completed in 1869. The canal bed and towpath skirted the river before turning south as it headed west toward central Vestal. Although property was appropriated and the bed was dug, the future of the canal was in jeopardy when the railroad began surveying for a line through Vestal.

The DL&W stopped in Willow Point, the only stop other than the Vestal depot. Noosbickle's Store also served as the Willow Point Post Office. The small cemetery along the Vestal-Binghamton Highway belonged to the Willis family.

Many of the photographs in this section are from the Walter P. Gates collection of glass plate negatives donated to the Vestal Museum. Because of this young man's interest in photography, the rich history of the Willow Point hamlet has survived even though the buildings have not. The 1908 map clearly documents exactly where Gates traveled to record the history of the hamlet. Descendants of the families and friends in his pictures have continued to live in Vestal.

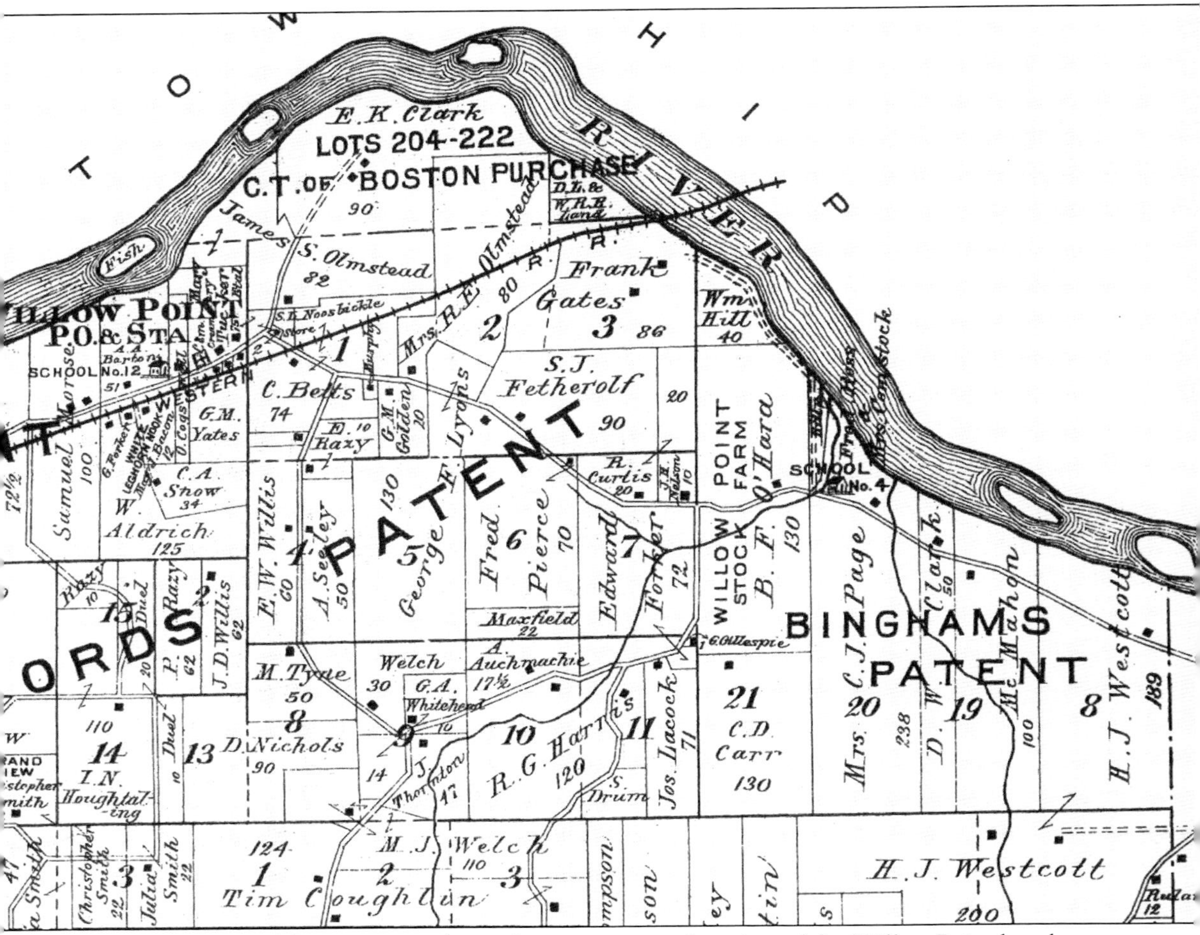

This portion of the 1908 map shows the approximate location of the Willow Point hamlet.

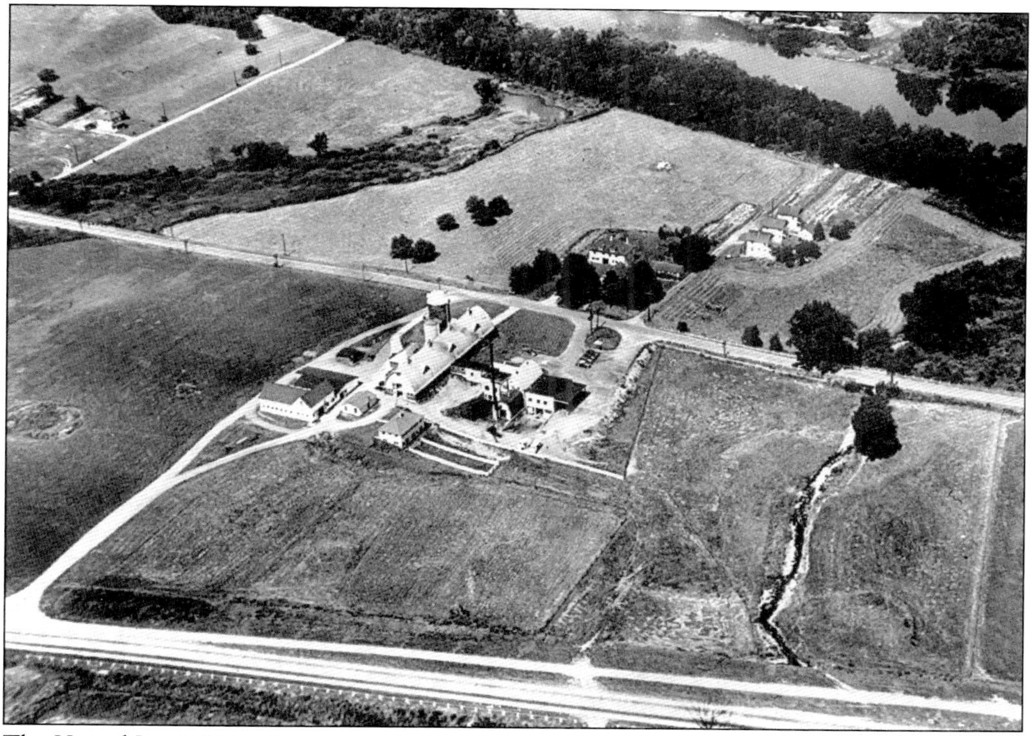

The Hazard Lewis Dairy Farm lands began in the north at the Susquehanna River and extended south across the present-day Vestal Parkway up the slopes of Bunn Hill. With 40 employees, an annual payroll of $120,000, and $750,000 in annual business, the farm was one of the largest in the area. In 1956, the MacArthur Development Corporation purchased the farm and later sold its grazing fields south of the parkway for the new Harpur College campus, now Binghamton University.

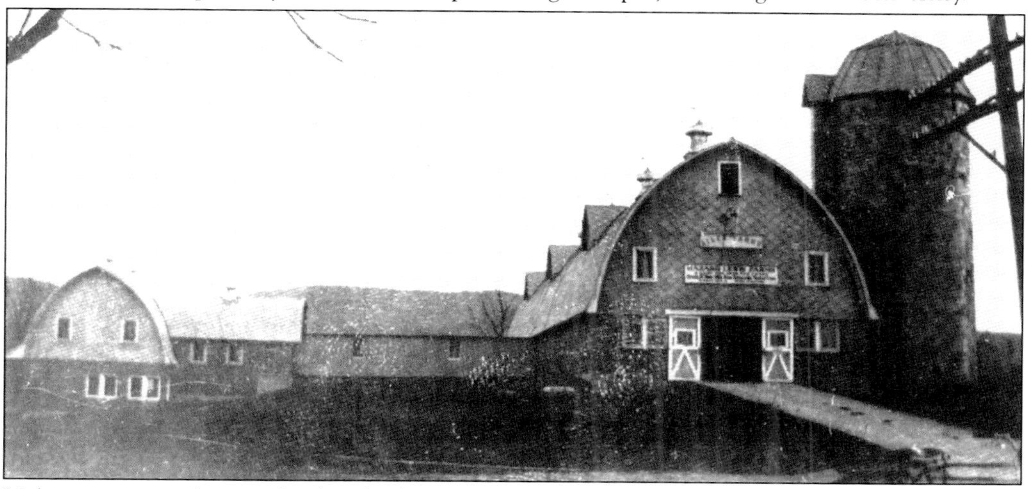

Holstein cows are known for their high milk production, and the Hazard Lewis Dairy Farm's barn held a herd that produced the milk on many kitchen tables between 1829 and 1950. The clink of glass bottles could be heard as the delivery truck drove throughout neighborhoods delivering the morning milk. Deliveries were so early that during the extreme cold of a January day the paper bottle cap would be lifted on a frozen column of milk or cream before it could be brought indoors.

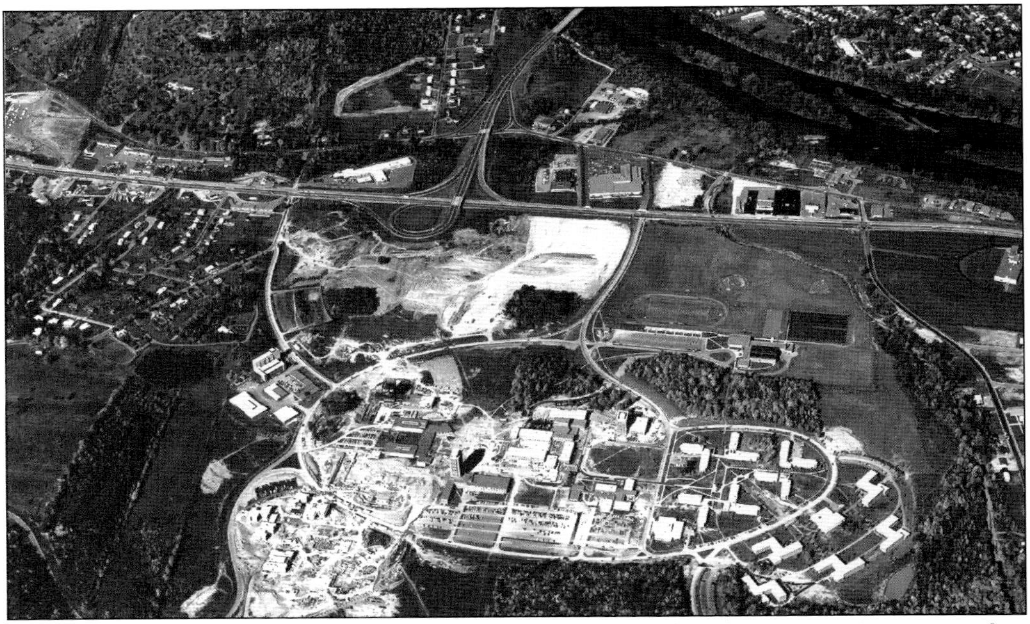

Triple Cities College, a branch of Syracuse University, opened its doors in 1946 as an overflow campus offering liberal arts courses to returning GIs. In September 1950, the college was renamed Harpur College in honor of leading Colonial educator, statesman, and county pioneer Robert Harpur. The campus, under construction in this photograph, is now Binghamton University, with an enrollment of more than 15,000 students.

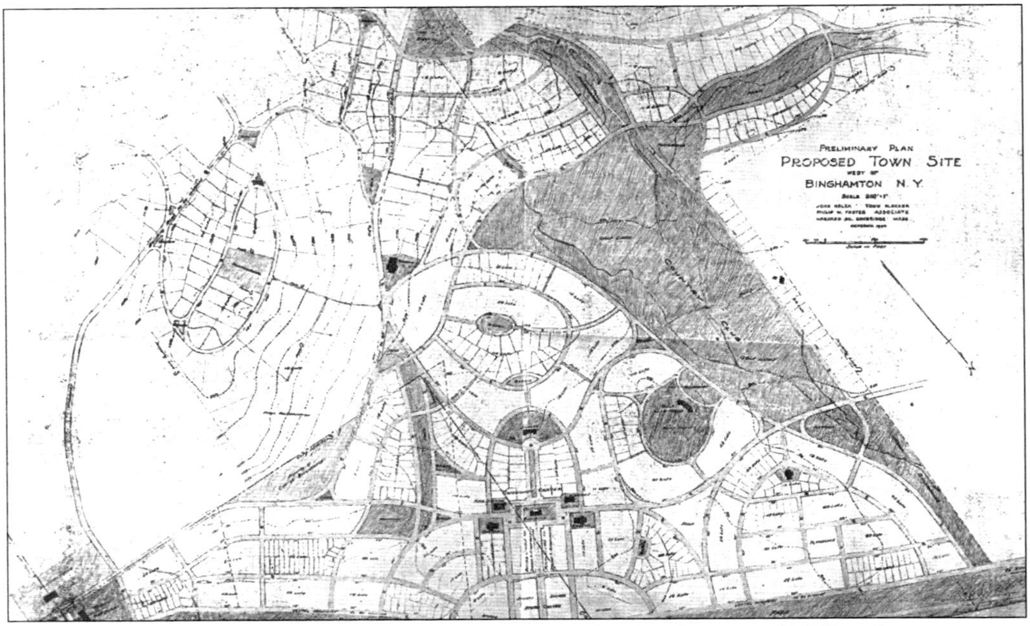

Town planner John Nolen presented this preliminary plan for the area of Willow Point just west of the Binghamton city line. Although not built as shown, some of Nolen's ideas were reflected in the development of roads in the area. (Courtesy of the Division of Rare and Manuscript collections, Carl A. Kroch Library, Cornell University.)

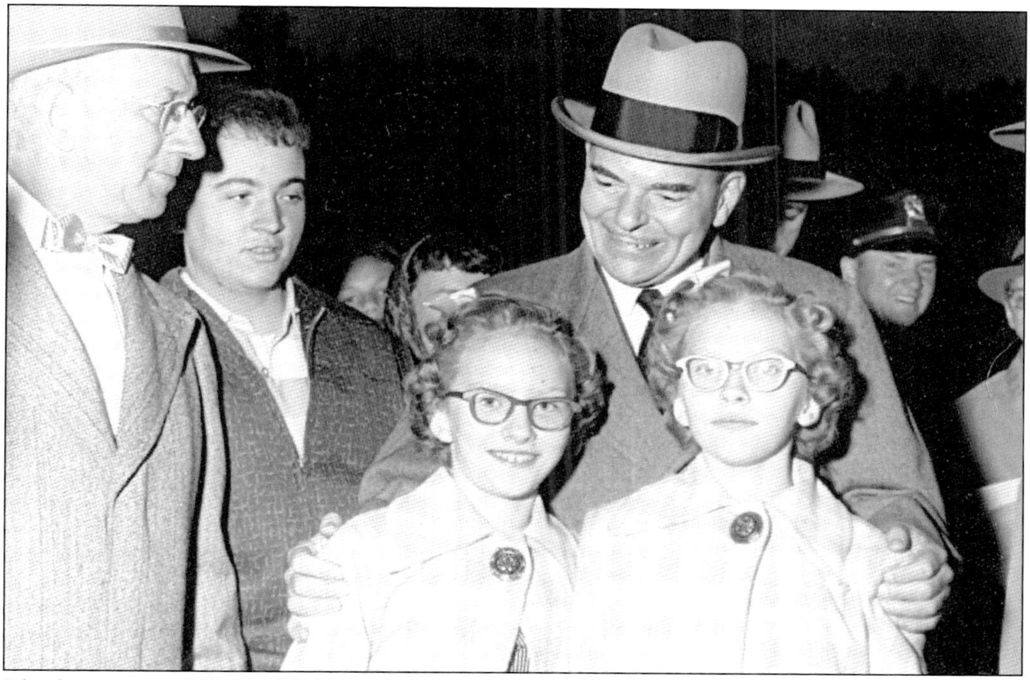

The long-awaited C. Fred Johnson Memorial Bridge between Willow Point and Johnson City expanded access to the eastern portion of Vestal, which included the new Harpur College campus east of Bunn Hill Road. New York governor Thomas Dewey attended the opening of the span on October 6, 1954. In the photograph, town supervisor Leland Jones is at the far left and Dewey is at the center, with Dorinda and Diana Loveless in front of him.

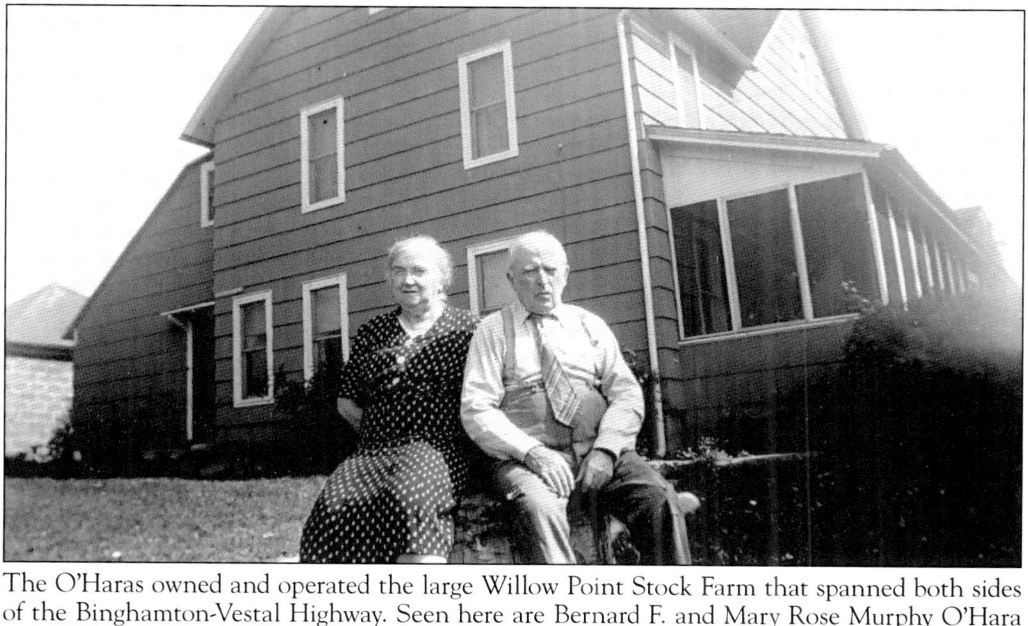

The O'Haras owned and operated the large Willow Point Stock Farm that spanned both sides of the Binghamton-Vestal Highway. Seen here are Bernard F. and Mary Rose Murphy O'Hara outside their farmhouse. To accommodate construction of the Route 201 C. Fred Johnson Bridge, their home was moved from the Vestal Road near Old Lane Road to O'Hara Drive.

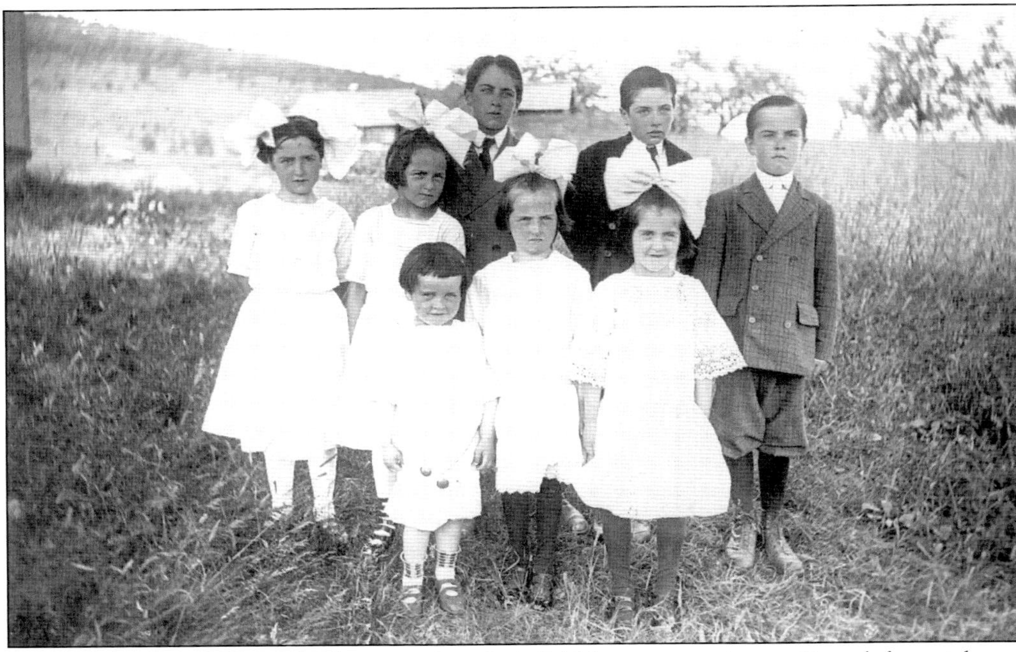

Eight of the nine O'Hara children stand in their field for a group picture. From left to right are (first row) Thomas, the small boy in the front; (second row) Julia, Mary, Margaret, and Mildred; (third row) Vincent, Joseph, and Bernard.

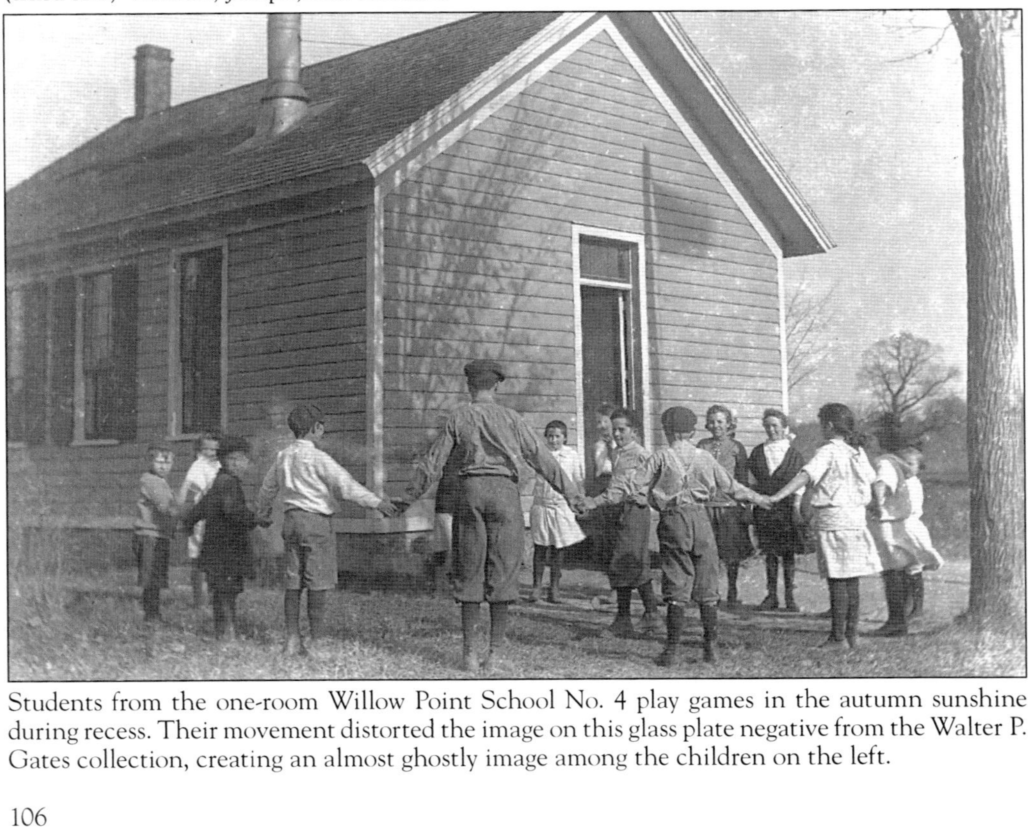

Students from the one-room Willow Point School No. 4 play games in the autumn sunshine during recess. Their movement distorted the image on this glass plate negative from the Walter P. Gates collection, creating an almost ghostly image among the children on the left.

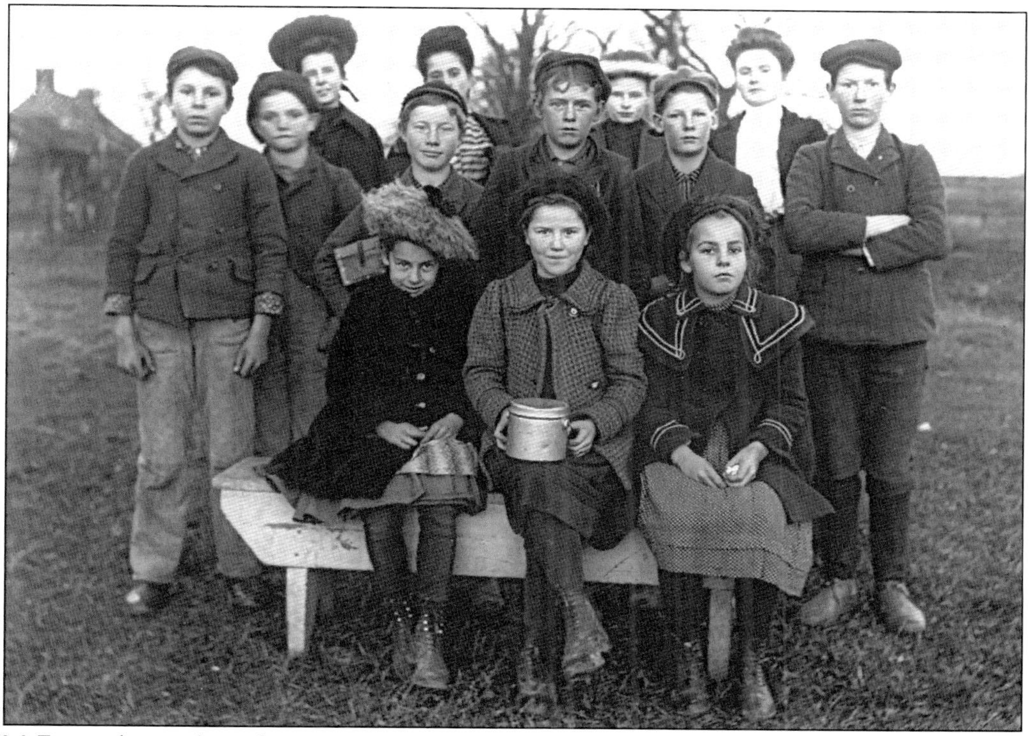

M. Estes, who taught at the Lower Willow Point School, assembled her students for this November 1904 picture. The girls sitting on the bench are wearing quality clothing and footwear, probably in anticipation of the "picture day." Notice the tin lunch pail held by the girl in the center.

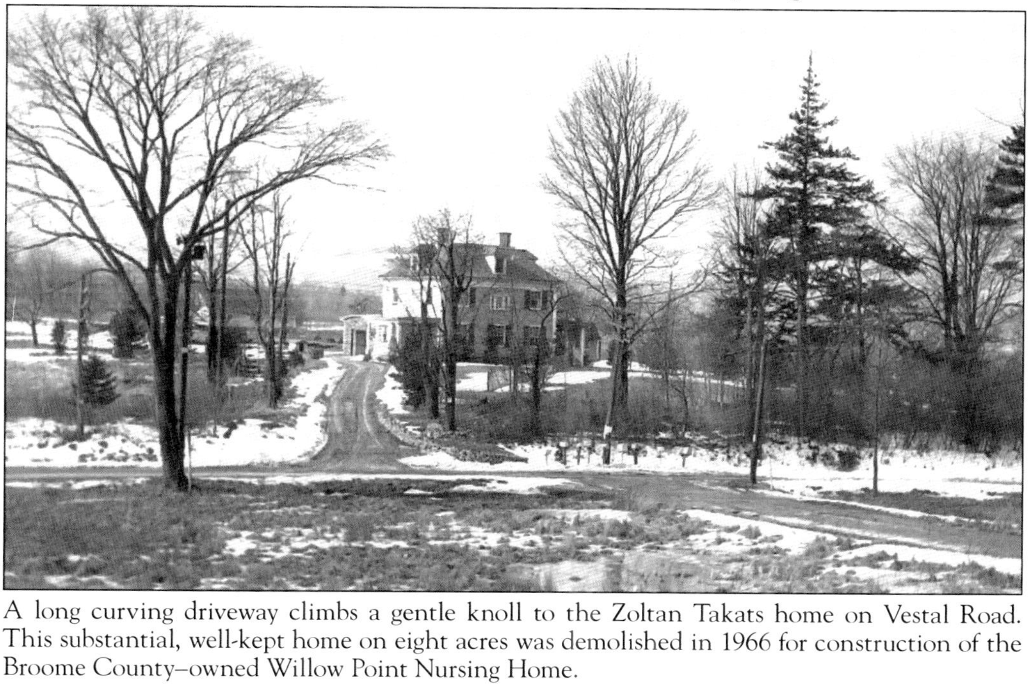

A long curving driveway climbs a gentle knoll to the Zoltan Takats home on Vestal Road. This substantial, well-kept home on eight acres was demolished in 1966 for construction of the Broome County–owned Willow Point Nursing Home.

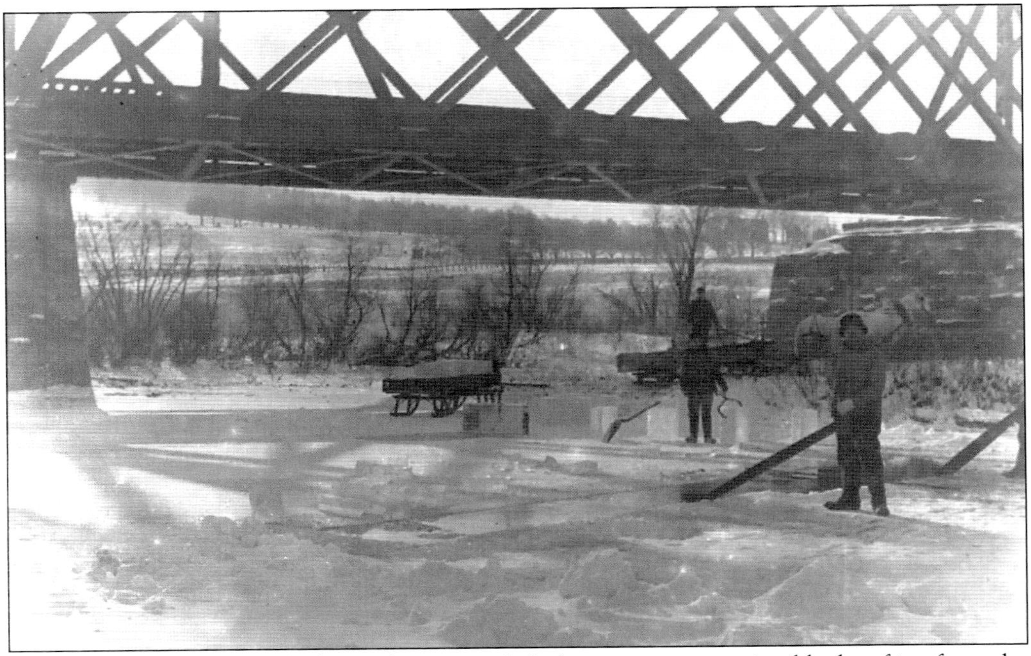

Using ice saws, tongs, and a horse-drawn ice sled, these men are cutting blocks of ice from the Susquehanna River under the DL&W bridge at Willow Point in 1898. Not only was the work cold, the width of the river under the bridge made it dangerous for the inexperienced.

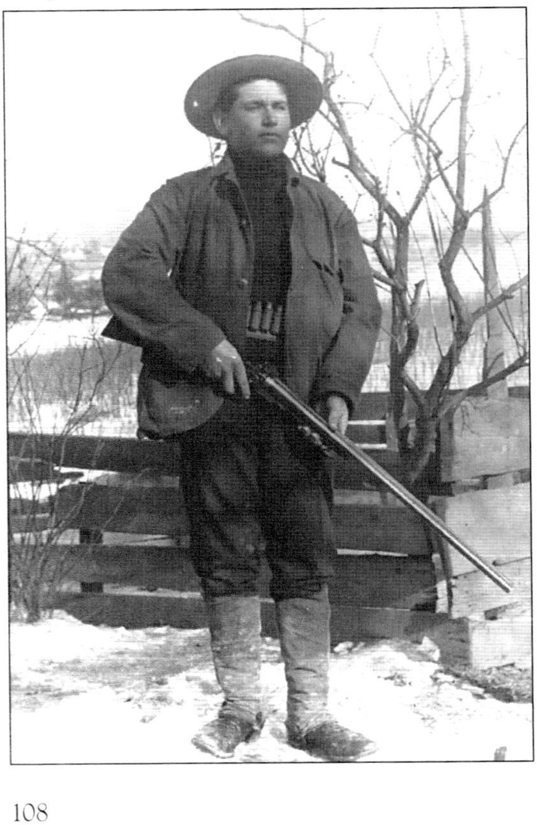

Amateur photographer Walter P. Gates strikes a pose in hunting attire. During the period from approximately 1904 to 1917, Gates photographed the everyday lives of family, friends, and neighbors in the Willow Point area. His collection of more than 500 glass plate negatives was donated to the Vestal Museum. Not only are the negatives in excellent condition, the photographer had labeled them with names and often dates.

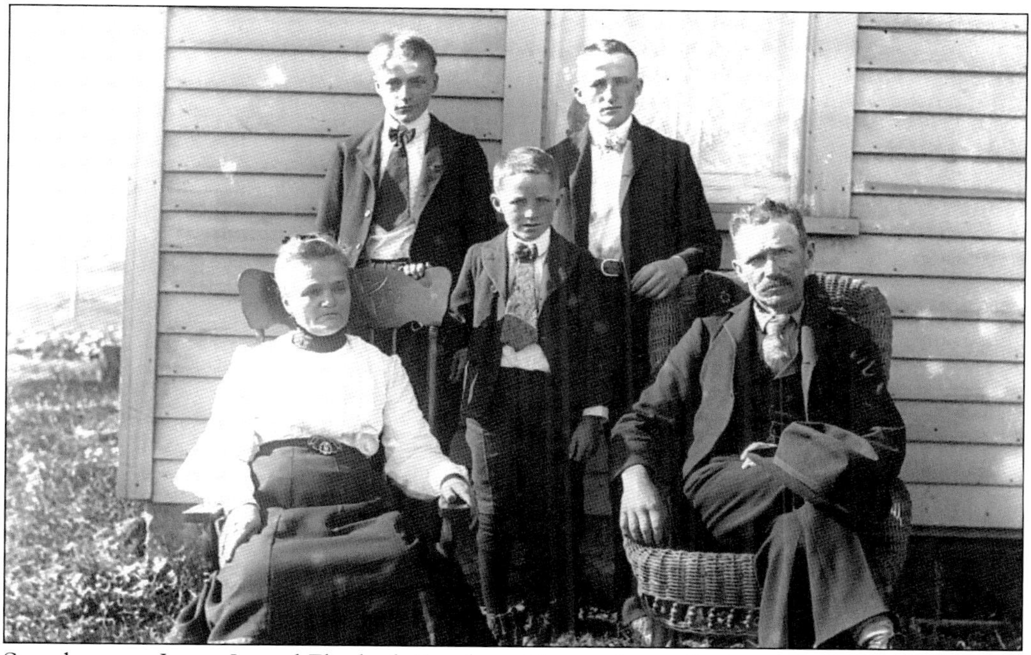

Seen here are Jasper L. and Elizabeth Stanley with sons Leon, Fred, and Earl outside the Page farmhouse on Coughlin Road where they resided in the fall of 1904.

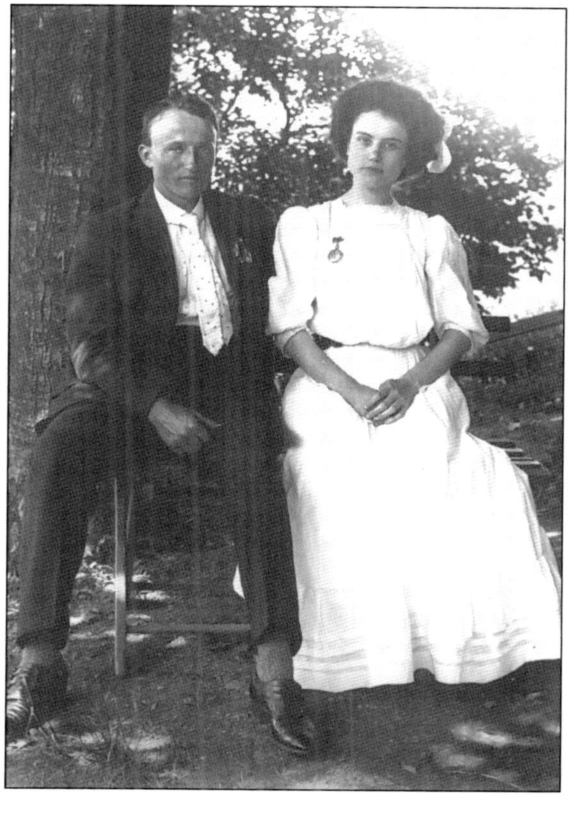

Earl Stanley and Agnes Connis, both in their early 20s, were courting when this photograph was taken at the Stanley home. Records show they were married in 1912 and had two children by the 1920 census.

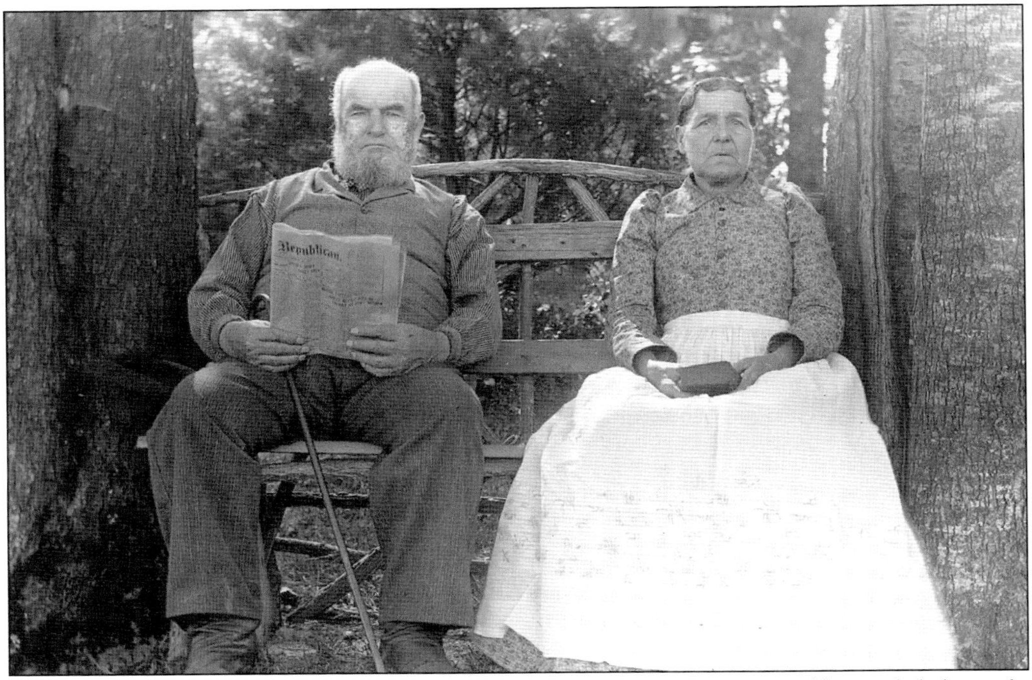

Still formidable at age 83, patriarch William P. Gates reads the *Broome Republican* while his wife, Elizabeth, relaxes with her Bible, as 19-year-old grandson Walter captures their images more than 100 years ago.

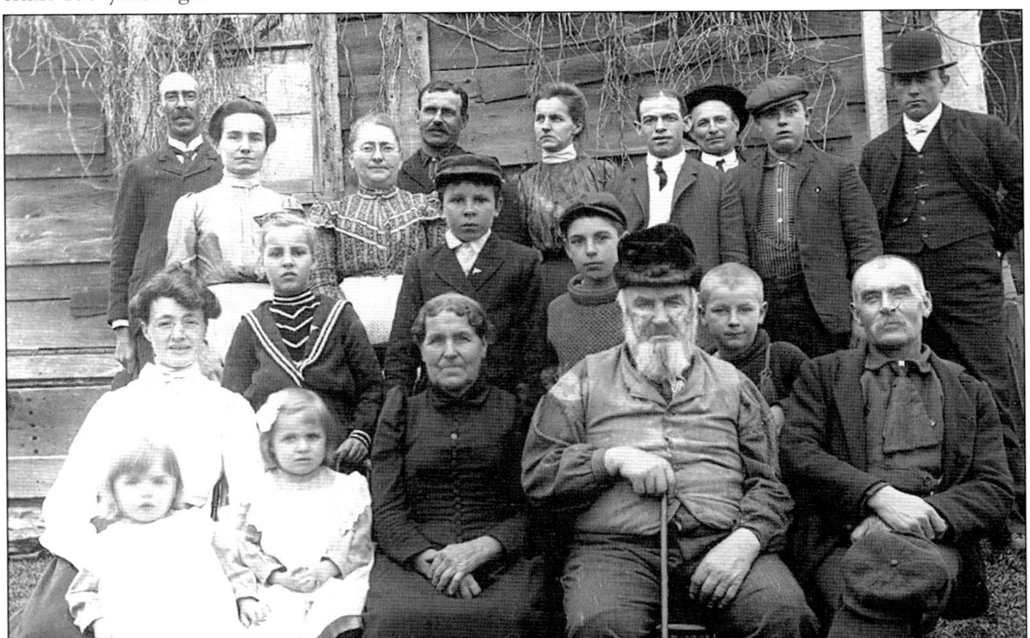

In about 1904, 19 members of the Gates family gather for this multigeneration family photograph by family photographer Walter.

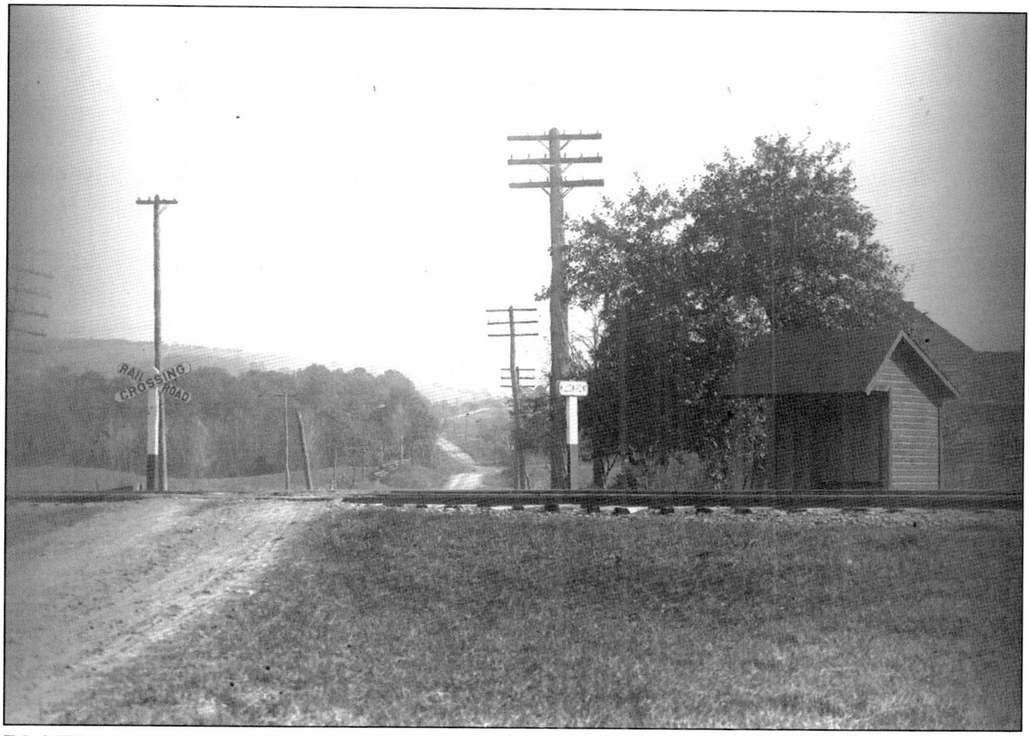

DL&W passengers could board or disembark the train at the tiny Willow Point shelter station rather than traveling to the depot in central Vestal. Crumpled like a piece of paper, it is evident that this automobile was no match for a large locomotive on a September day in 1917, when a man and woman lost their lives as the car they were driving was hit by the 8:30 passenger train at the Willow Point crossing.

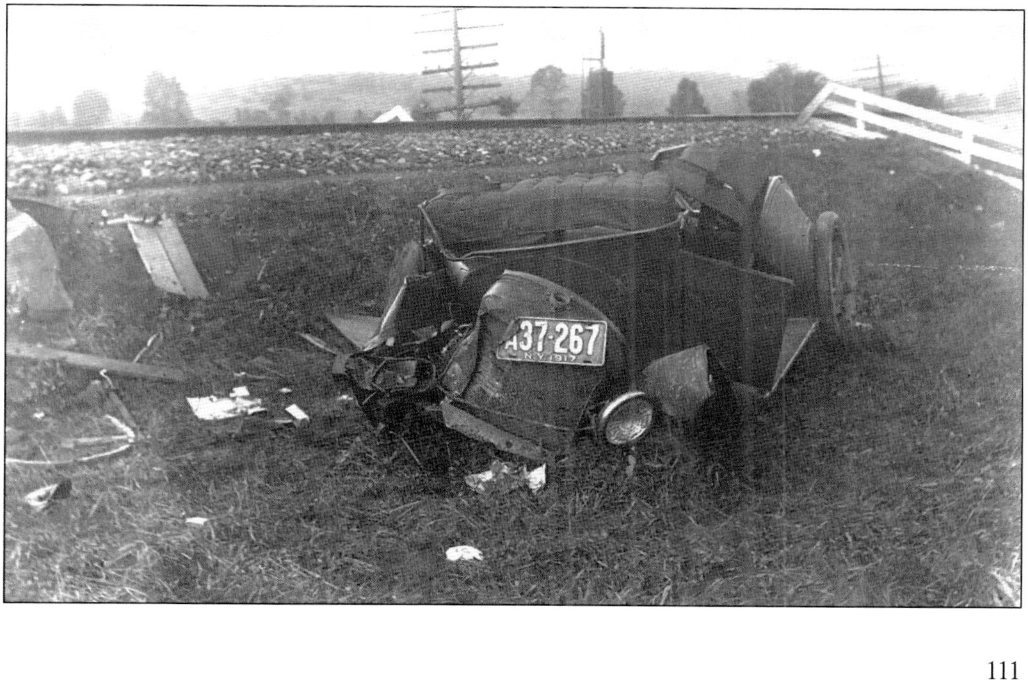

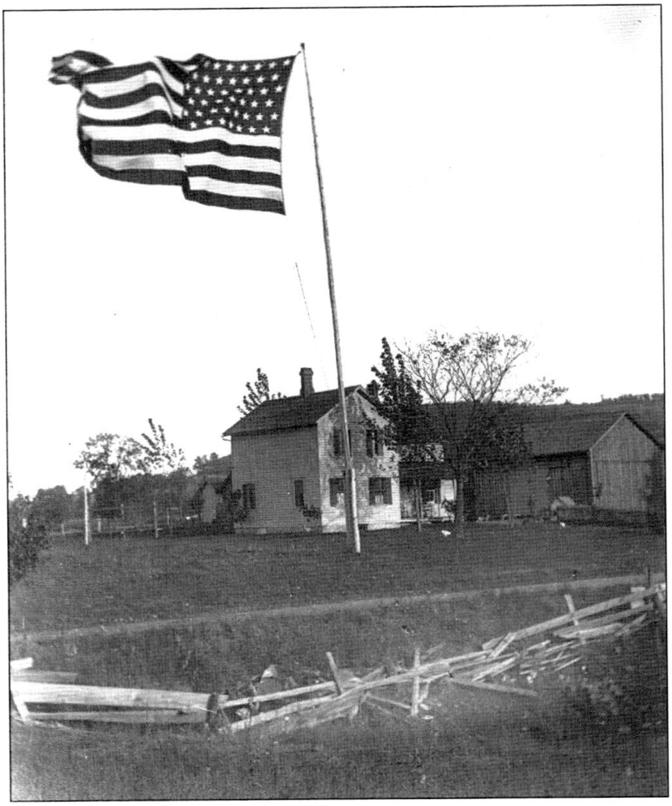

A large, 45-star flag flies atop a tall flagpole on the Willow Point poultry farm of Charles A. Snow. The label "White Leghorn Nook" appears on the 1908 map near the Snow farm. Eugene Palmer and Charles Winans were two other nearby poultry farmers.

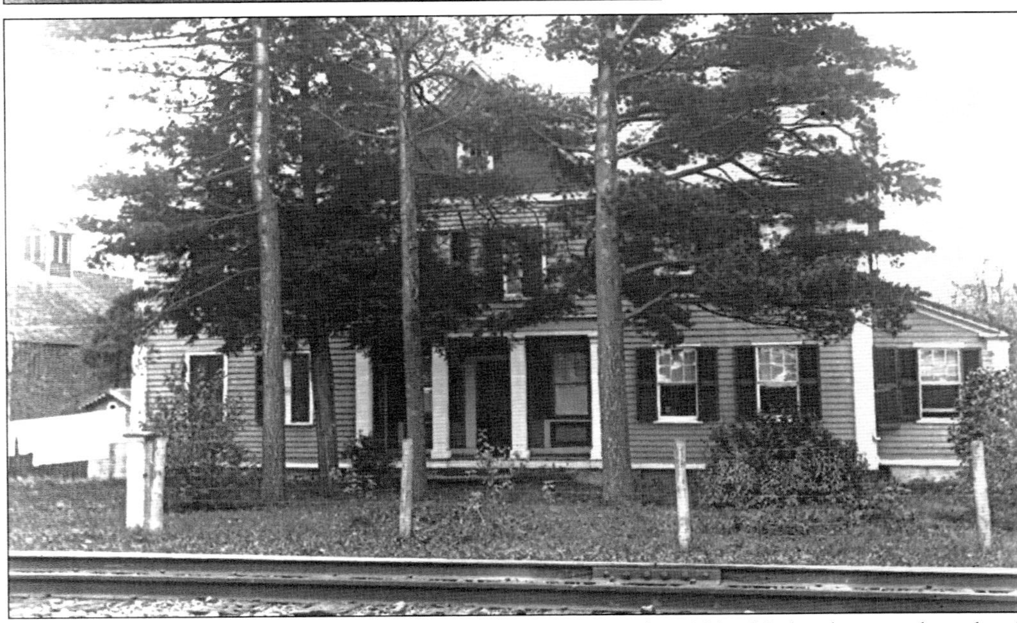

Every passing train must have rattled the dishes in Orcelia Aldrich's kitchen cupboards. A simple barbed-wire fence is the only thing separating the DL&W tracks and the front of porch of the William Aldrich home.

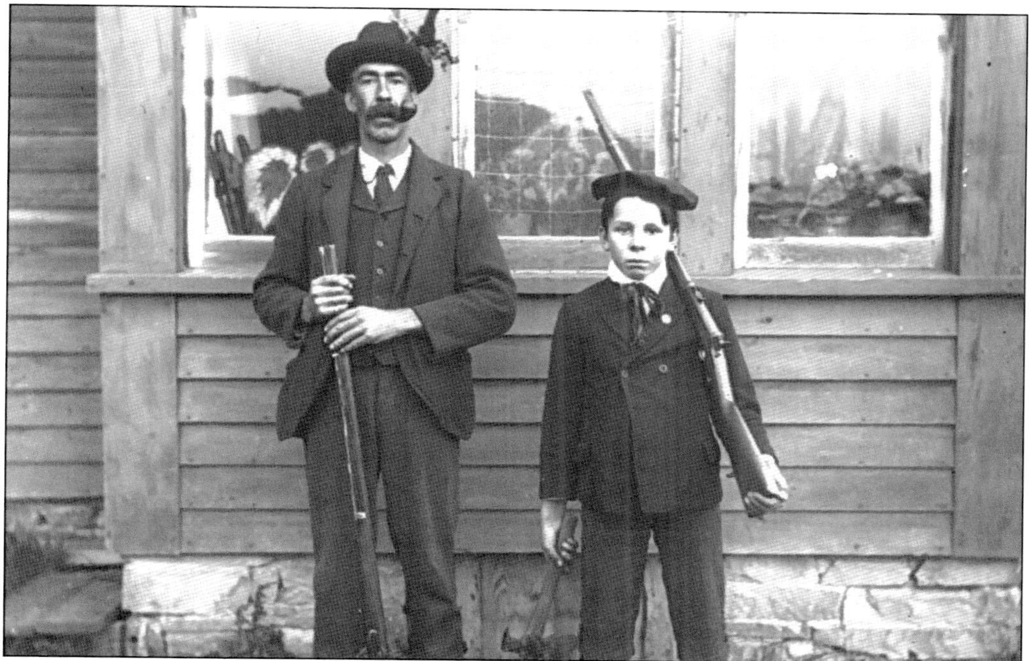

John D. Willis and son Glenn stand outside their home just to the west of Jensen Road. Dressed in their Sunday best, father and son appear to have chosen favorite objects for the photograph; in addition to their guns, John smokes a pipe and Glenn carries a hatchet.

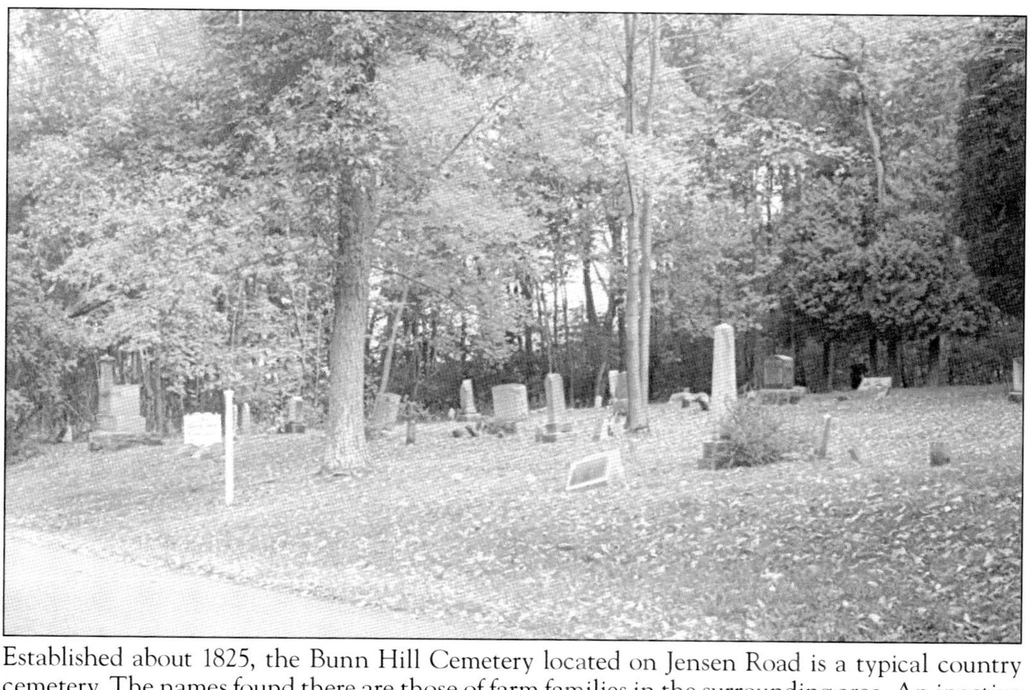

Established about 1825, the Bunn Hill Cemetery located on Jensen Road is a typical country cemetery. The names found there are those of farm families in the surrounding area. An inactive cemetery, it is now being maintained by the Town of Vestal.

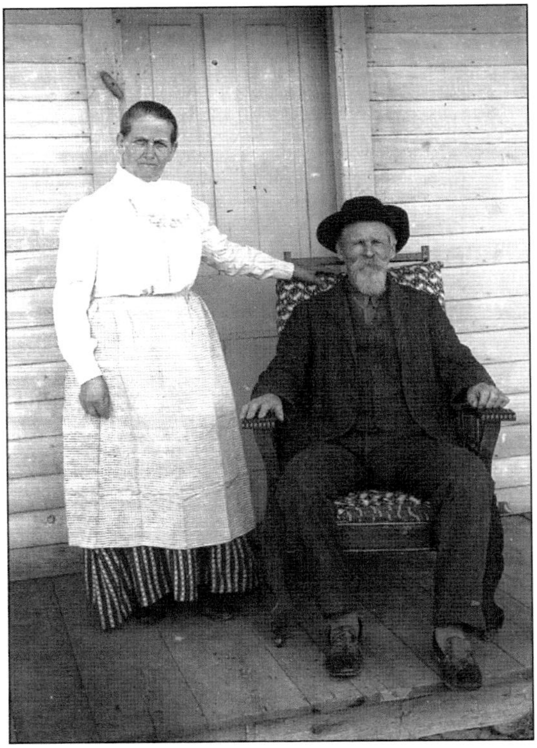

By 1900, William Drum was a 60-year-old retired farmer living with his wife, Mary, on Drum Road. Their presence on the road grew as sons married and started families of their own. Drum Road was later renamed Bunn Hill Road.

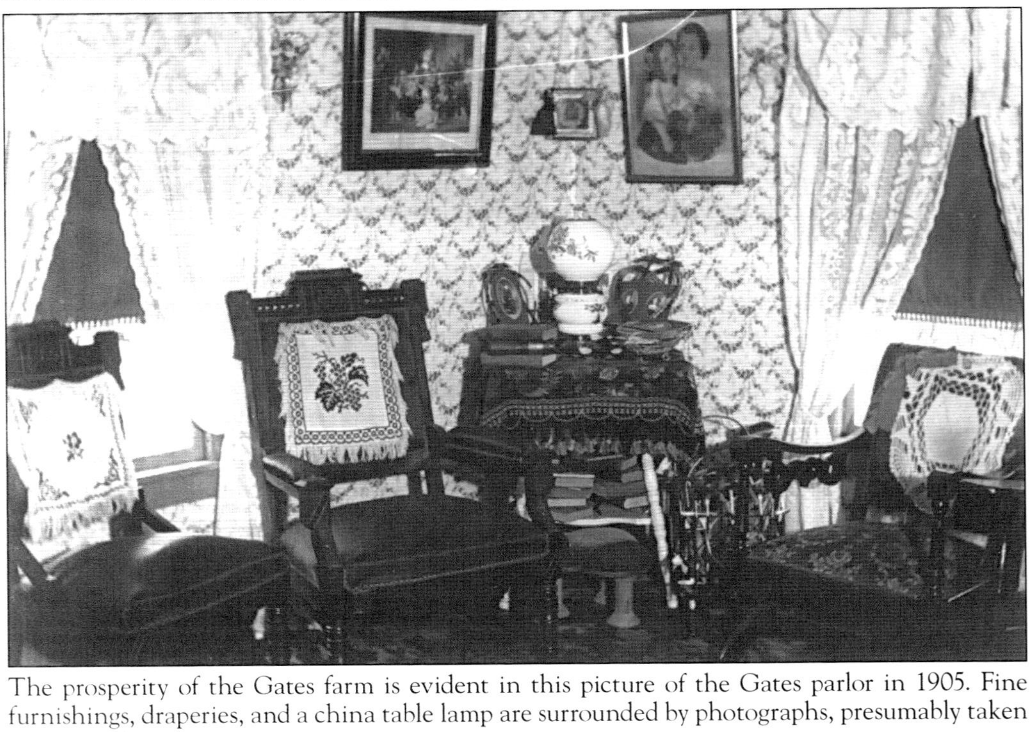

The prosperity of the Gates farm is evident in this picture of the Gates parlor in 1905. Fine furnishings, draperies, and a china table lamp are surrounded by photographs, presumably taken by son Walter.

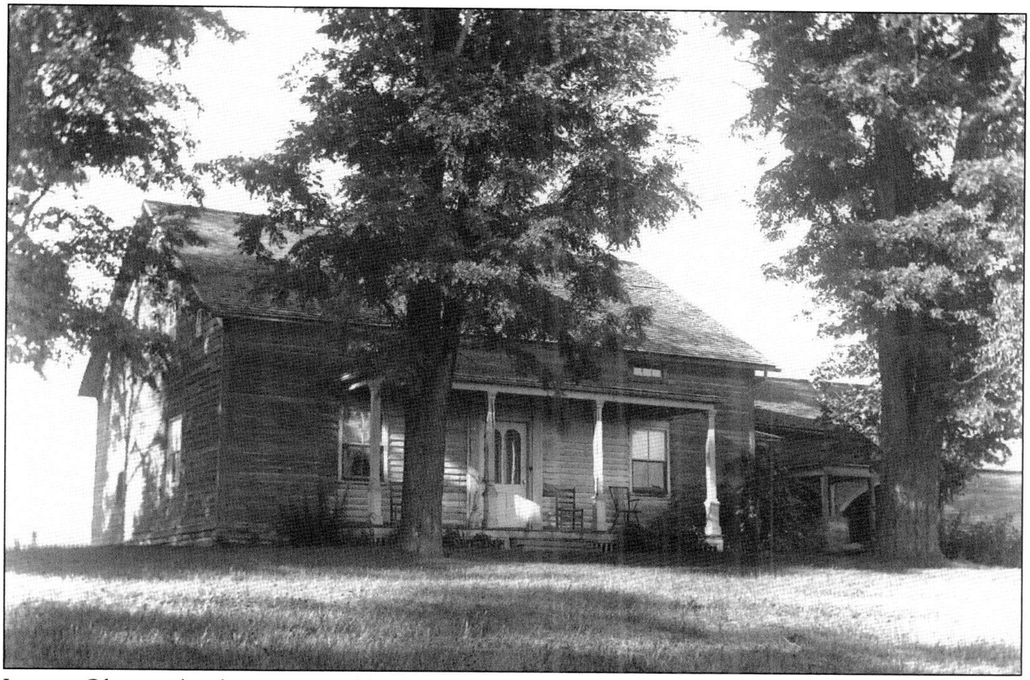

Louise Olmstead, who was a public school teacher in 1910, shared the home of her parents, James S. and Millie Olmstead, which was picturesquely named the Grove. Fields of produce can be seen behind Louise in the Olmstead's horse and carriage.

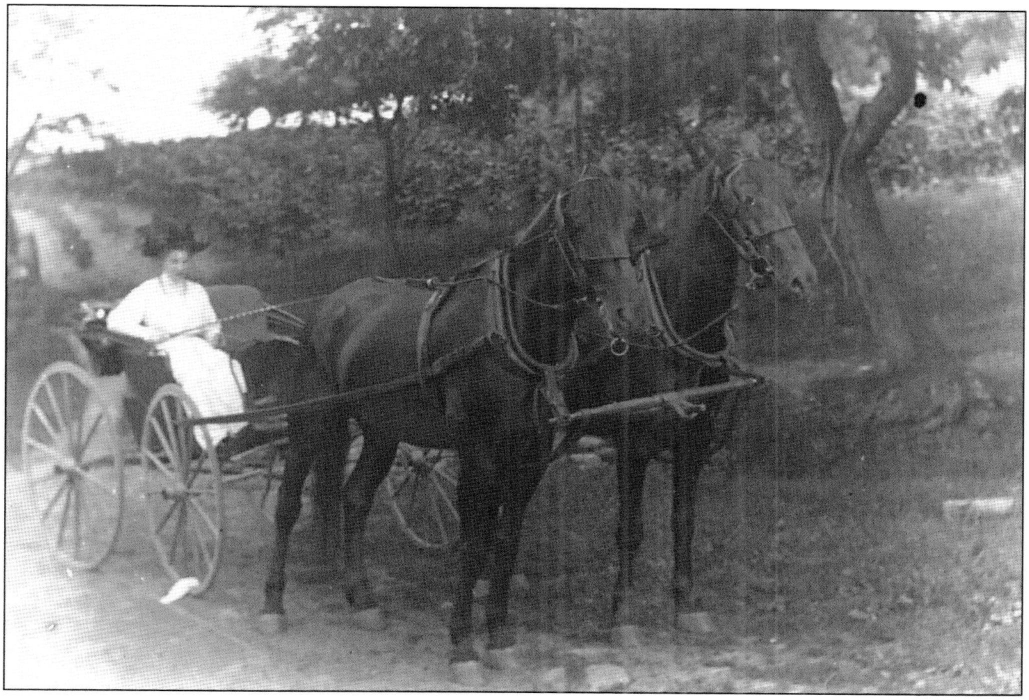

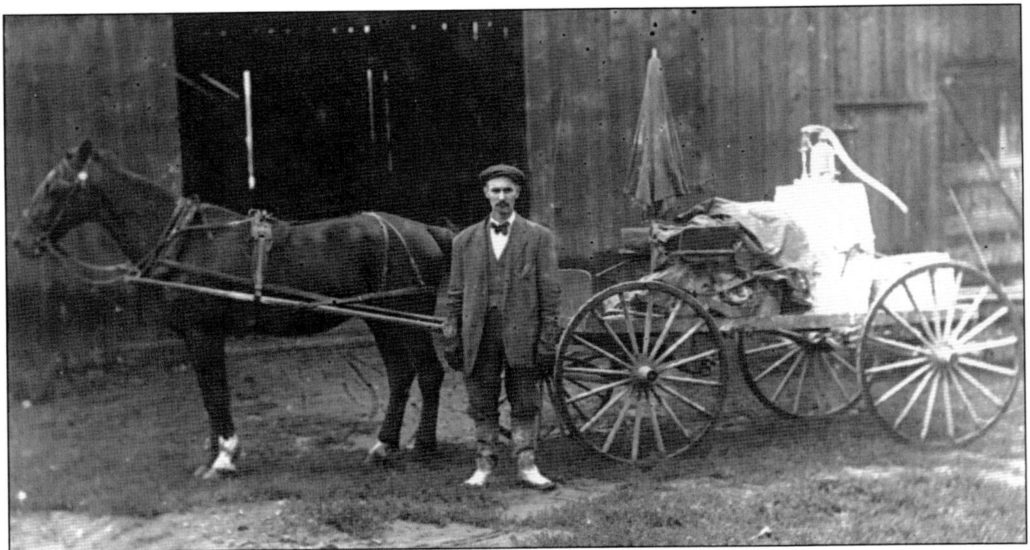

The farms of Arthur and Luman Thompson shared a common property line, but it is not known which of them was the milk inspector standing next to his wagon in this photograph.

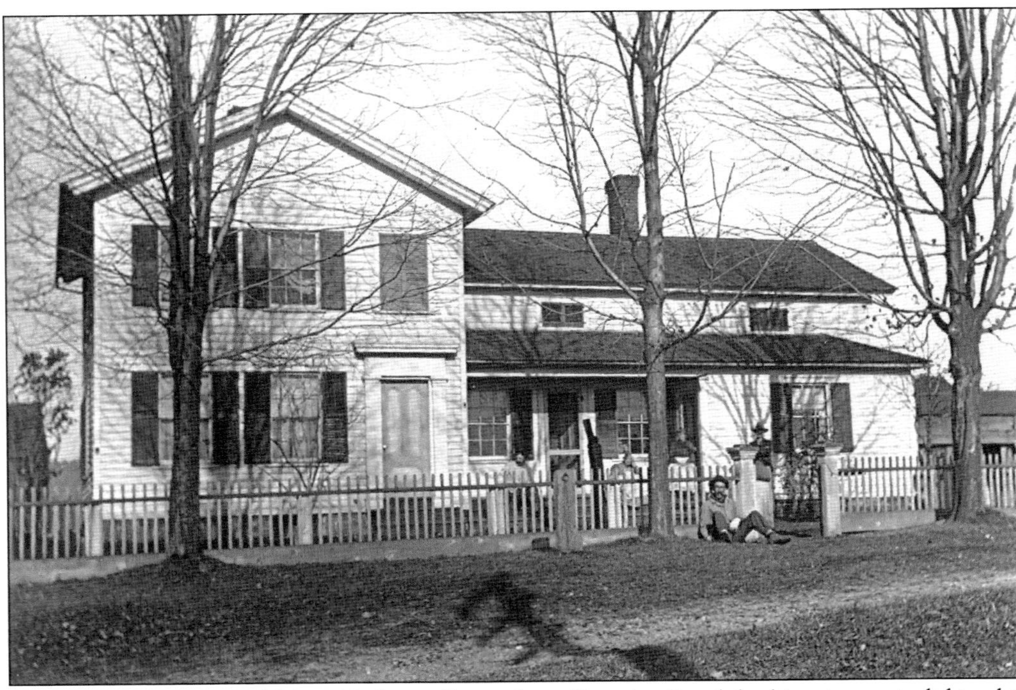

The home of Edwin and Mary Tucker still stands on Prentice Road, looking just as it did in this November 1906 photograph. The fence is now gone and the large trees obscure the house in summer, but it is easy to imagine the family on the porch and Ed reclining against the fence.

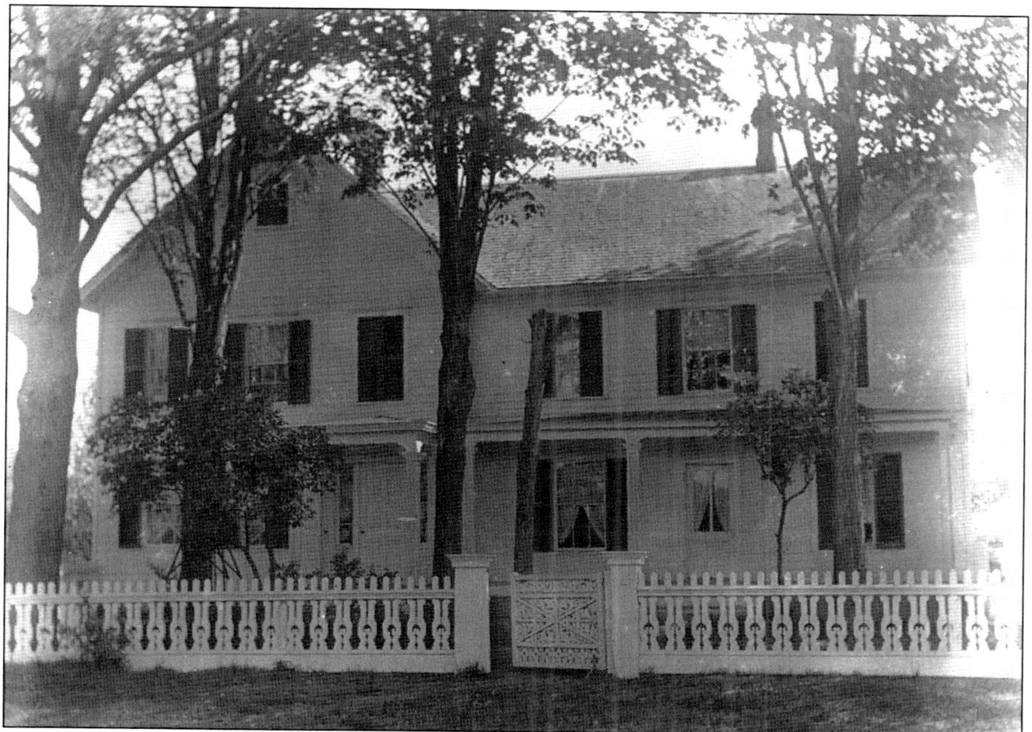

This intricately patterned fence and gate surround the Wescott home. Perhaps they are the work of the one of the two master carpenters who lived in Willow Point at the time.

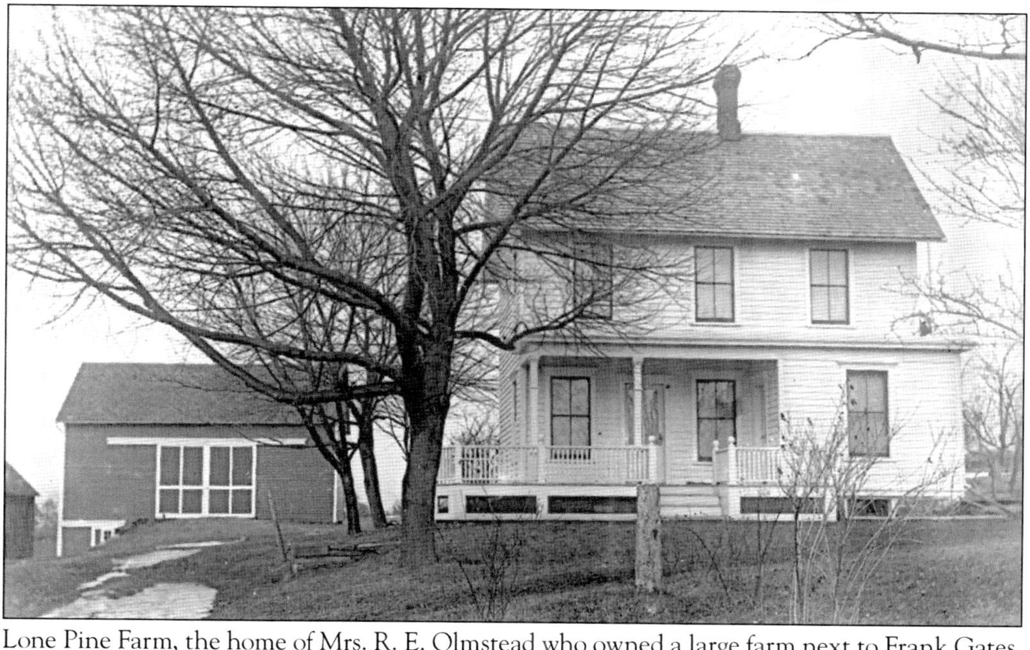

Lone Pine Farm, the home of Mrs. R. E. Olmstead who owned a large farm next to Frank Gates, was located on the Binghamton-Vestal Highway just east of Jensen Road. The property was bisected by the DL&W tracks.

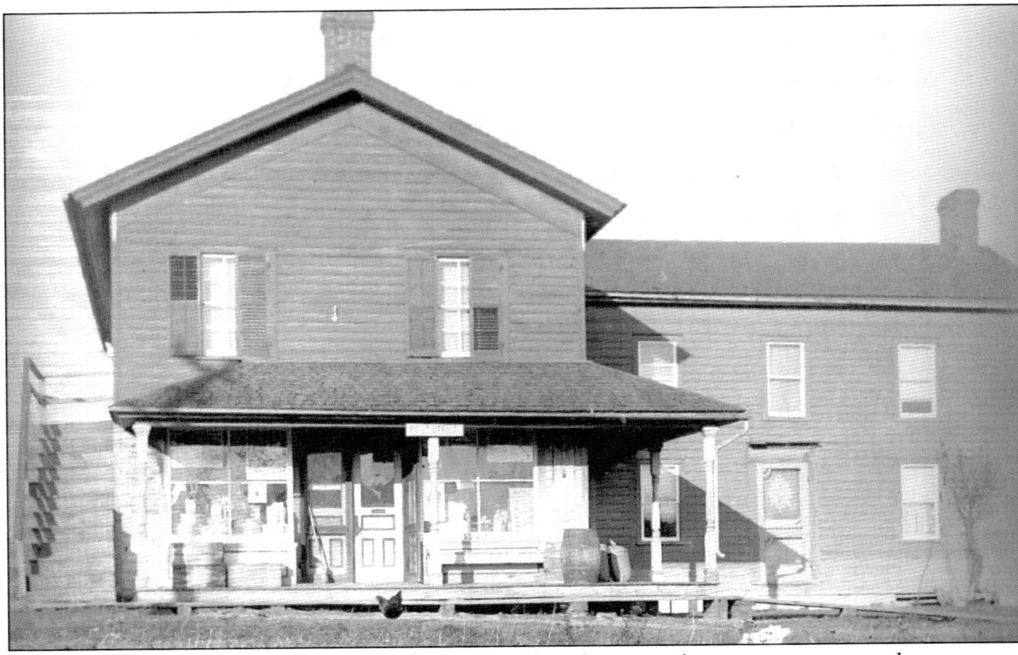

Stephen Noosbickle and his wife, Jerusha, owned and operated a grocery store at the corner of Clark Road, later renamed Prentice Road, and the Binghamton-Vestal Highway. The Willow Point Post Office was located in the store. Their home, which was a mere block away, and the store no longer exist.

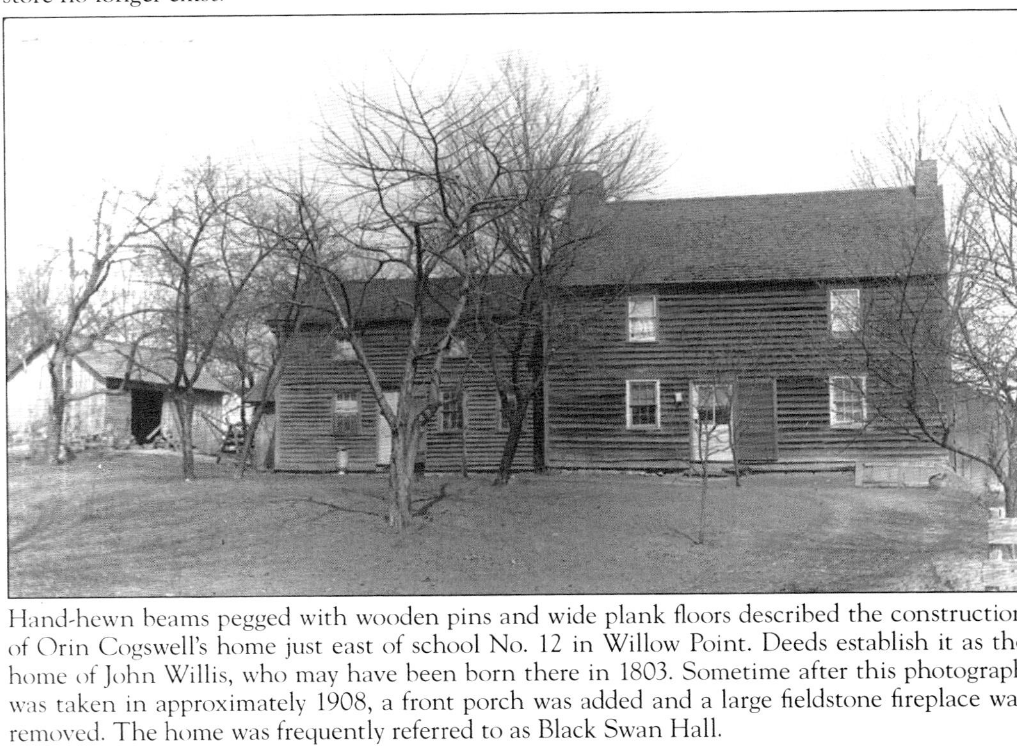

Hand-hewn beams pegged with wooden pins and wide plank floors described the construction of Orin Cogswell's home just east of school No. 12 in Willow Point. Deeds establish it as the home of John Willis, who may have been born there in 1803. Sometime after this photograph was taken in approximately 1908, a front porch was added and a large fieldstone fireplace was removed. The home was frequently referred to as Black Swan Hall.

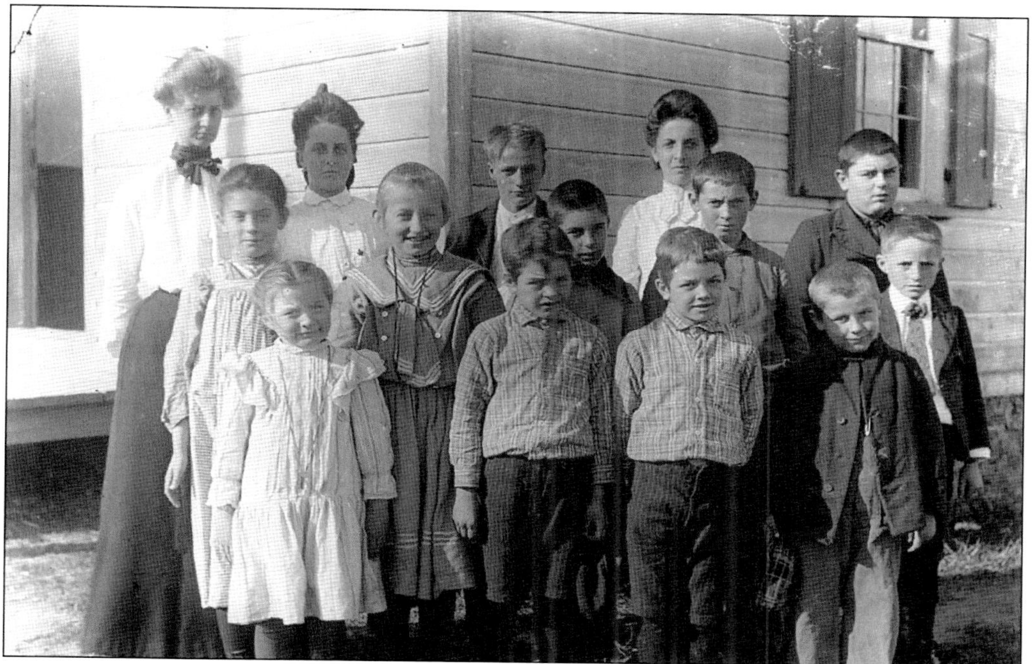

The austere facade of Upper Willow Point School No. 4 was no match for the stern-looking Miss Duel, who stands at the left with her class during the fall of 1904. The young man at the center in the back row is the same Earl Stanley seen in a previous picture.

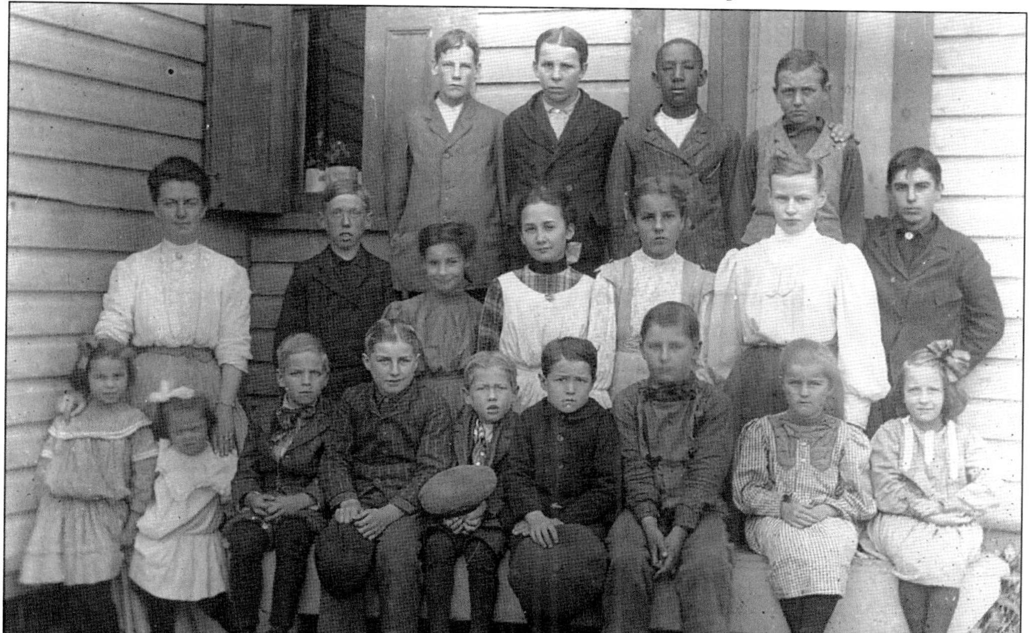

The one-room Lower Willow Point School No. 12 was slightly larger than No. 4 and could accommodate more students. The younger boys' faces seem to question the photographer's actions on this October day in 1907.

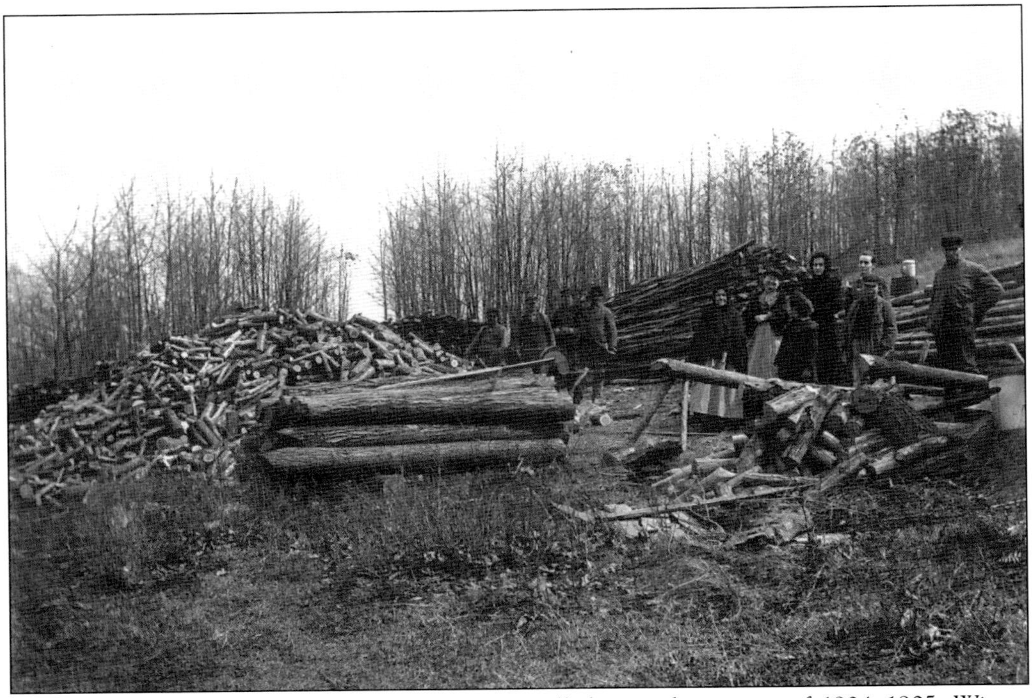

Members of the Gates family log Round Top Hill during the winter of 1904–1905. Winter logging was cold work, but it may have been easier and faster without the canopy of leaves. Frank, George, Elmer, Fred, and Allen Gates all logged the hillside. The picture below was taken in April 1905 as the Gates men cut the felled trees into logs. Notice the heavy chain on the ground at the right and the open, unprotected saw blade in the picture below.

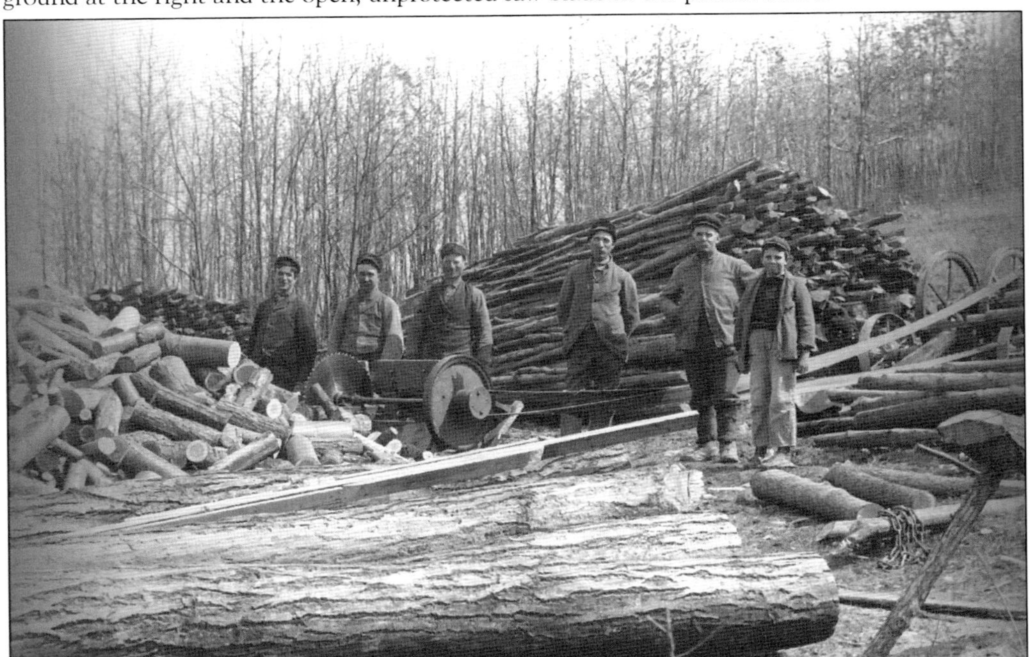

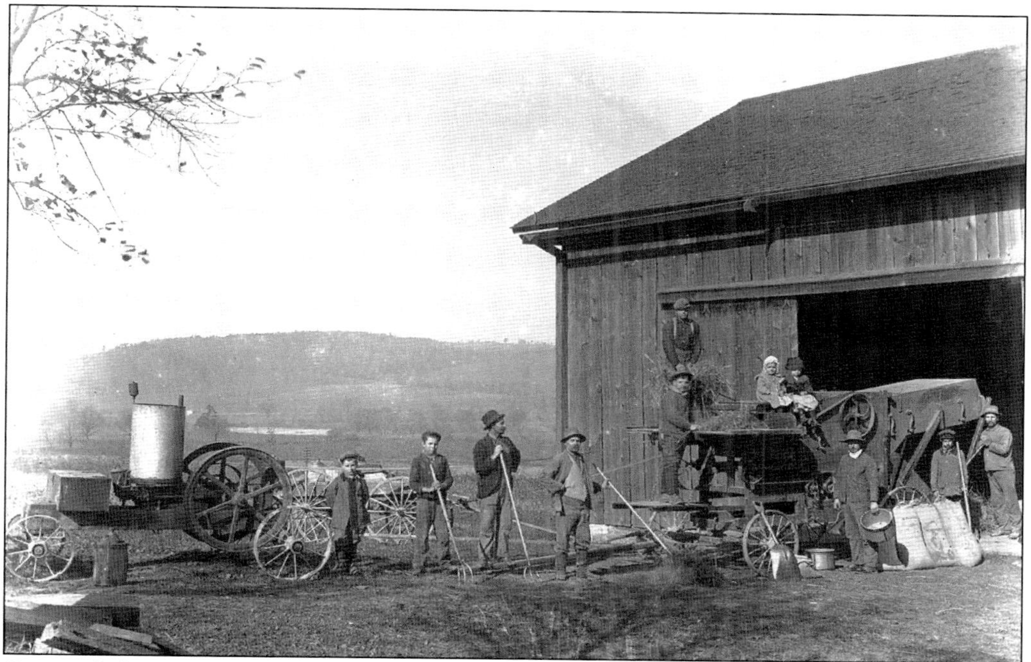

On small farms, harvested grain was beaten with flails to remove the outer husk, but large farms required the help of a crew of threshers with a threshing machine. In high demand, this threshing crew readies its steam threshing machine at the Gates farm.

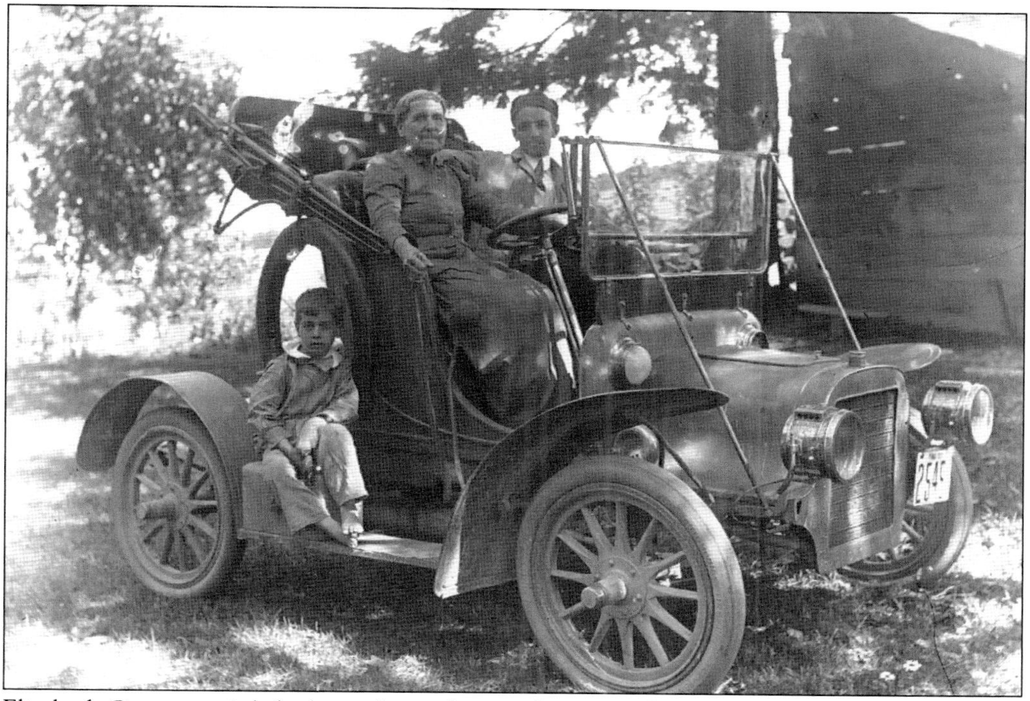

Elizabeth Gates certainly looks ready to take grandson Peter for a drive in the family automobile, but did she really drive the right-hand-drive two-seater?

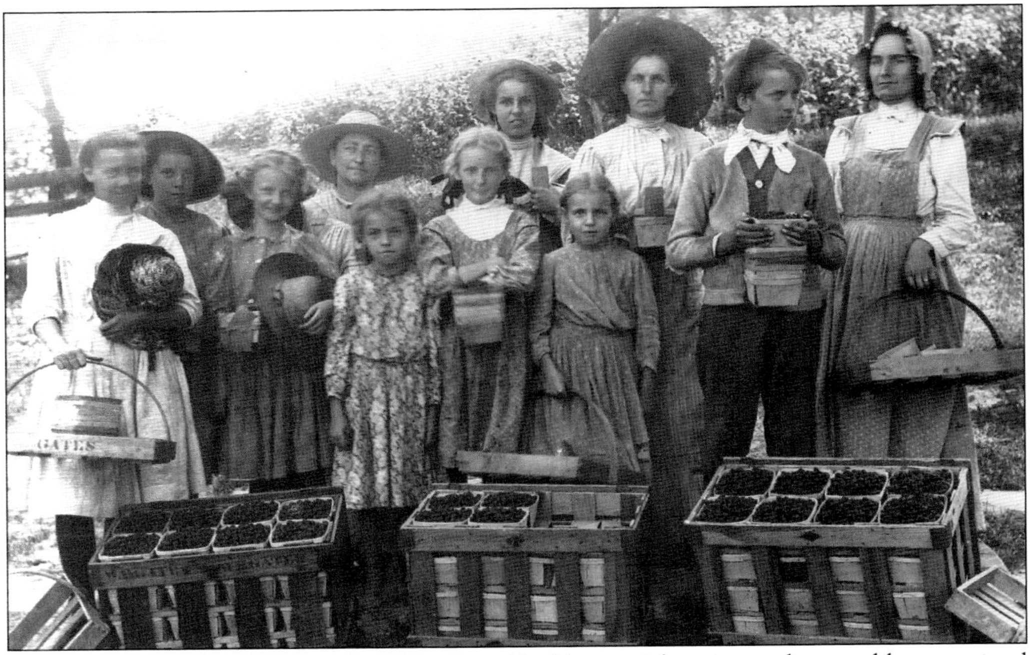

The pay was small and the sun hot, but these blackberry pickers in sun hats and berry-stained dresses proudly display the fruits of their labor in crates designed to transport the delicate berries to market. A comparison with the Gates family photograph reveals that several of the ladies in this picture are Gates family members.

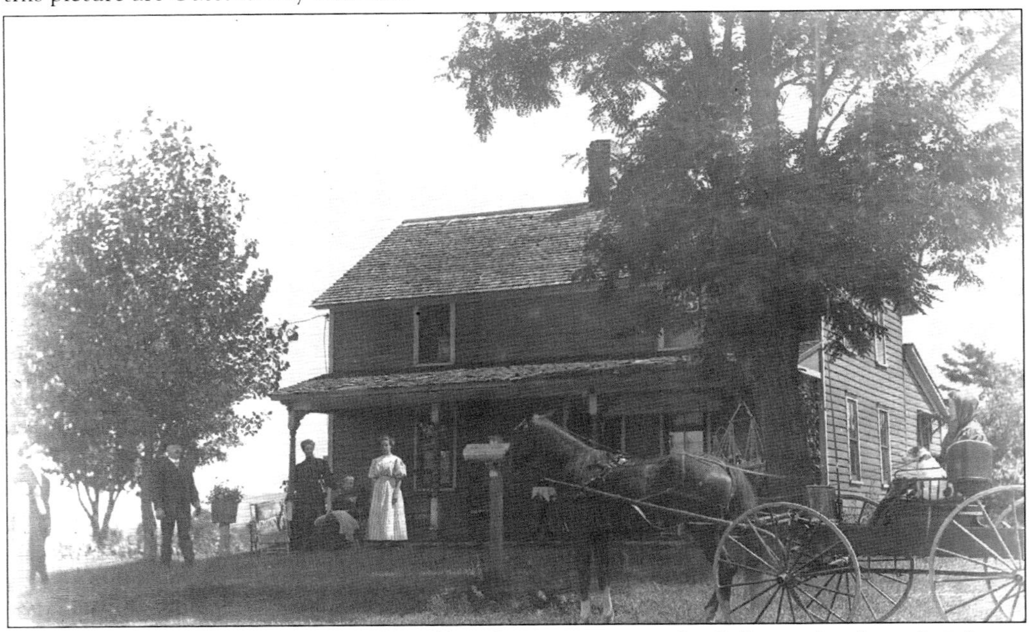

On a warm summer day Mrs. Howell and her dog pay a visit to the Gillespie family at their home in Willow Point. It is hard to imagine that the photographer of this picture, Walter Gates, just happened to be there at the time Mrs. Howell arrived. The home was on the property of Edward Forker, bordering the Willow Point Stock farm.

Eight

Mile Wide

In 1868, one year after the incorporated village of Binghamton became the city of Binghamton, the Broome County board of supervisors, which was composed of a supervisor from each town and city ward, voted to increase the area of the town of Binghamton by annexing land from the town of Vestal. A mile-wide strip in the Second Tract in Sidney from the southern Binghamton city line to the Pennsylvania border became Town of Binghamton property in 1873.

Within this area were two one-room schools, a cemetery, two sawmills, and a tannery, in addition to a number of large farms. The Binghamton Railway Company initiated but did not complete the construction of a railroad line intended to transport logs from the heavily forested French Tract to Scranton, Pennsylvania.

Farmlands are being replaced by residential development, but Table Rock Ridge and Aqua Terra Park, with its 466 acres of wildlife and trails, still provide undeveloped natural beauty. The Vestal Hills Country Club moved to this area from its original location along the Vestal Parkway.

Although photographs of the mills in the mile-wide area have not been located, several photographs representing the places that once were a part of Vestal have been included.

The 1866 map of Vestal identified the names of those affected by the annexation; they were Ingraham, Addison, Davis, Pierson, Harris, Whipple, Hance, Gage, Jaycox, Coon, Braman Von Vorst, Hoag, Hanson, Smith, and Gahagan.

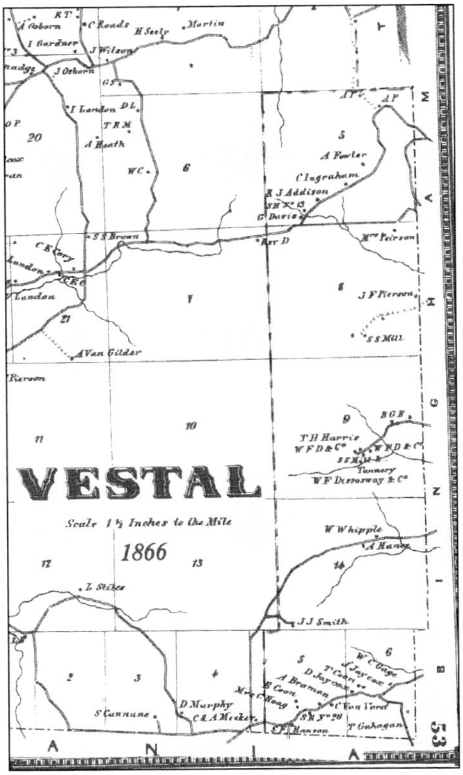

The two dashed lines on this 1866 map show the original Vestal town line on the east and the new town line created when a mile-wide strip was annexed to the town of Binghamton.

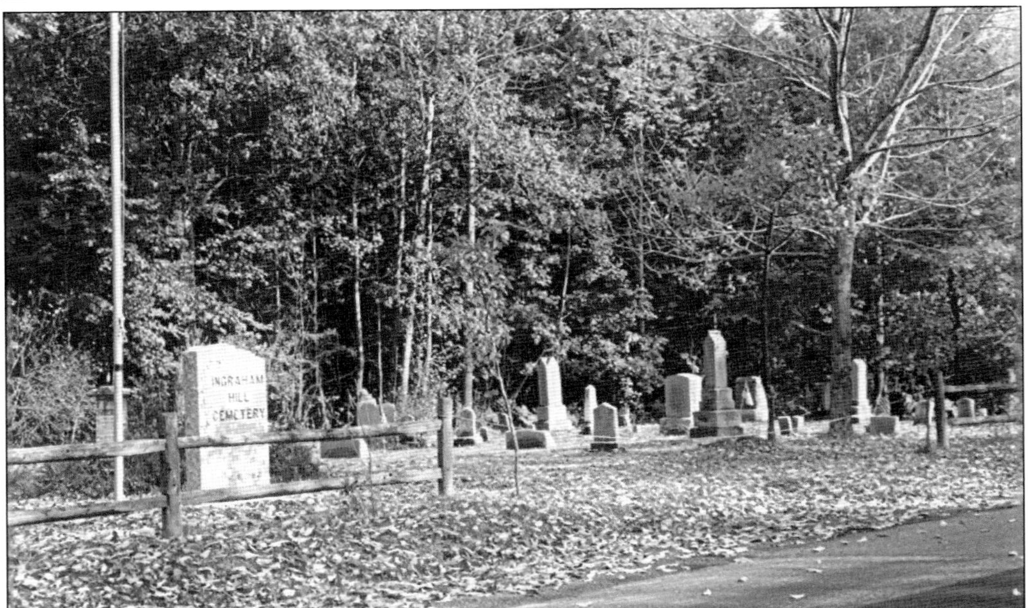

Ingraham Hill Cemetery, established in October 1862, is located along the northern edge of Ingraham Hill Road. The plots of this small, private cemetery are filled with the family names of early pioneers from the immediate area.

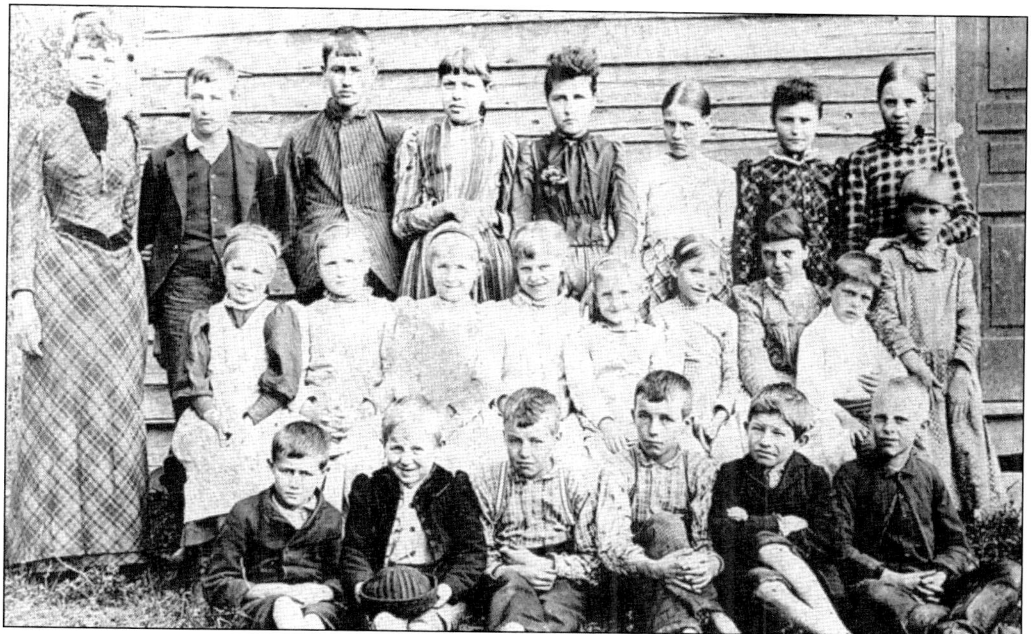

Just down the road from the cemetery is the one-room Ingraham Hill School. Built prior to 1866 as Vestal School House No. 13, it became part of the town of Binghamton school district after 1873. Students at the Ingraham Hill School, in about 1890, pose for the annual school picture. The last boy on the right in the front row is Frank Wright. The three girls on the right in the third row are, from left to right, Mary, Sarah, and Minnie Wright. Mary is the grandmother of Eleanor Maxian Haines, who attended the school for a short time before it was closed. (Courtesy of the Town of Binghamton Historical Society.)

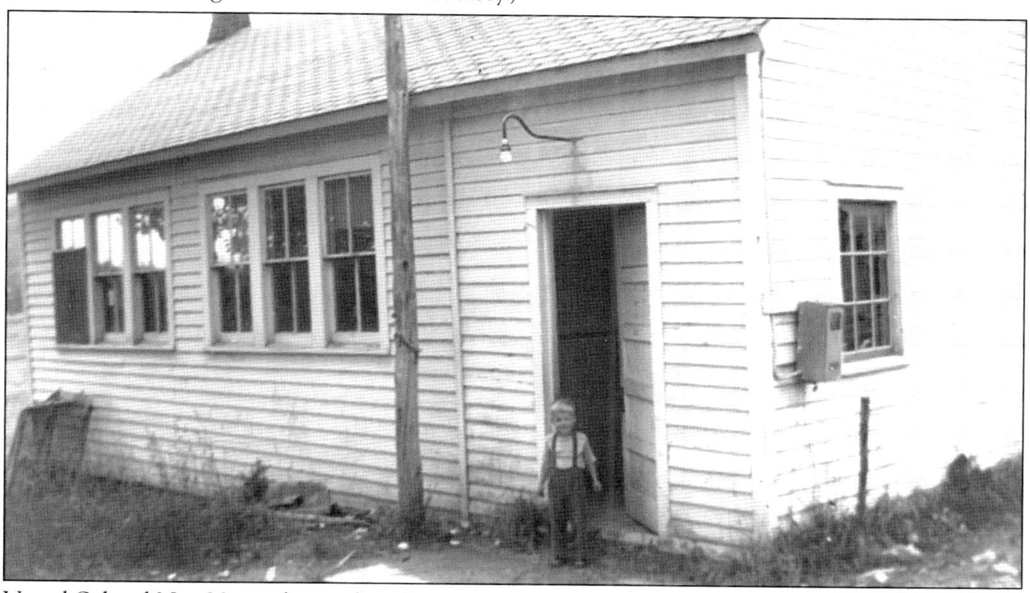

Vestal School No. 20 was located within the mile-wide strip along State Line Road close to the Pennsylvania border. The school was known as Turkey Lane School when part of the town of Binghamton school district. (Courtesy of the Town of Binghamton Historical Society.)

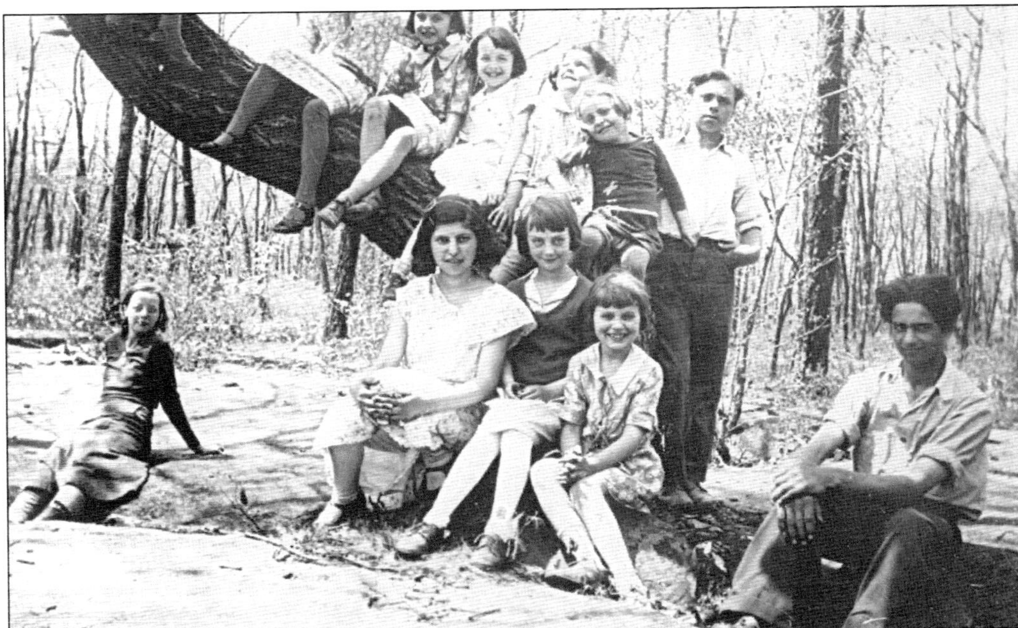

Schoolchildren from Ingraham Hill School end the school year with a picnic at the geologic formation called Table Rock Ridge in this 1933 photograph. The students sitting in the first row are, from left to right, Peter Publisi, Beverly Maxian, Jean Ingraham, Violet Publisi, and Doris Foland; (second row) Marge Himkos (body and legs only), Eleanor Maxian, Marie Hogan, Sarah LaCroix, Irene Himko, and Steve Himko.

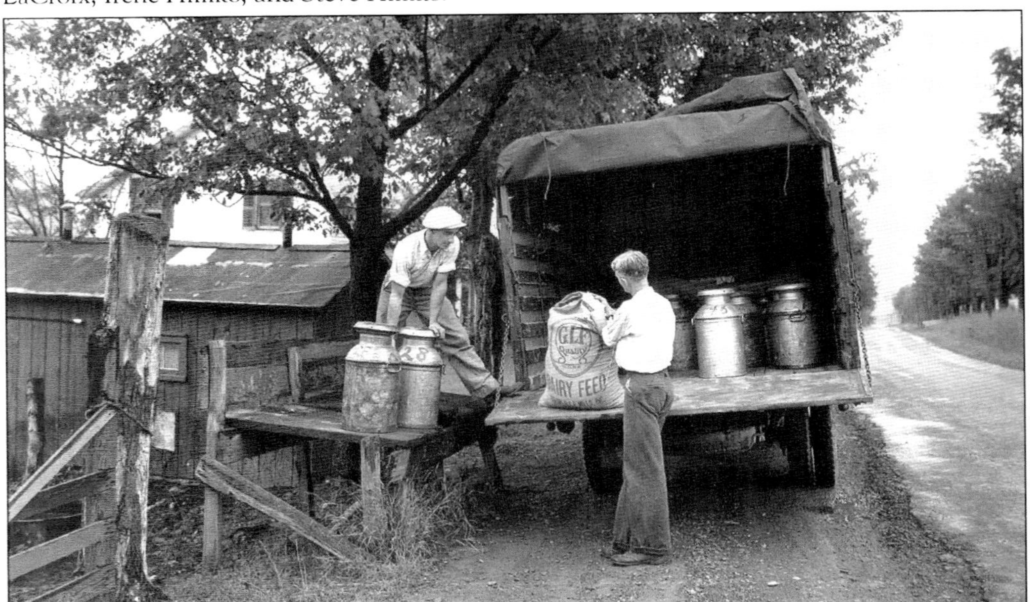

The Olin Jaycox Dairy Farm was located close the to Pennsylvania border on State Line Road. This 1937 photograph shows milkman Howard Chamberlin on the left loading milk cans, while farmer Olin Jaycox checks the tag on a feed bag. (Courtesy of the Town of Binghamton Historical Society.)

BIBLIOGRAPHY

Andrews, Winnie. *I Remember Tracy Creek in the 1930s*. June 2006.

Avery, Grace F. comp. *Vestal 1823–1973*, 1973.

Combination Atlas Map of Broome County New York. Philadelphia: Everts, Ensign and Everts, 1876.

Dickinson, Rachel. "Confronting a Conundrum." *American Archaeology Magazine*, Fall 2005.

Lawyer, W. S., ed. *Binghamton 1800-1900*. Century Memorial Publishing, 1900.

Leamer, Laurence E. *Four Corners, Vestal, New York's History*. Self-published, 1989.

Smith, Gerald R. *Partners All: A History of Broome County, New York*. Virginia Beach: Donning Company, 2006.

Smith, H. P., ed. *History of Broome County*. Syracuse: D. Mason and Company, 1885.

Versaggi, Nina. *Hunter to Farmer: 10,000 Years of Susquehanna Valley Prehistory*. Binghamton: Roberson Center for the Arts and Sciences, 1986.

Versaggi, Nina et al. *Public Archaeology Facility Information Guide*, 2004.